W9-CPE-386

Thinking Kids®
Carson-Dellosa Publishing LLC
Greensboro, North Carolina

Thinking Kids®
Carson-Dellosa Publishing LLC
P.O. Box 35665
Greensboro, NC 27425 USA

01-335167784

ISBN 978-1-4838-3493-1

Contents

Awesome Activities for Practicing Math Skills

Awesome Activities for Practicing Language Arts Skills

MATH

Oh, no! You're in a traffic jam! Starting with car 2, move through the jam counting by twos. Did you move through an odd or an even number of cars? Circle the answer.

Math path

PATTERN POWER

Skill: Telling Time

What time is it? It's time for patterns! The times shown on the clocks in each row follow a pattern. Draw hands on the last clock in each row to complete the pattern.

DARE TO DECODE

Skills: Addition, Subtraction

The equations below are written in code. Each shape stands for a digit 1 to 9. Crack the code by using what you know about doubles.

A Show of Hands

Skill: Counting Money

Cut out the coins. Beside each item, glue or tape the coins needed to buy it.

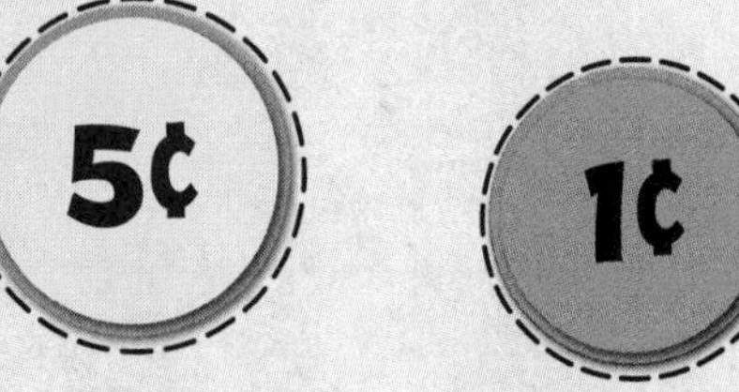

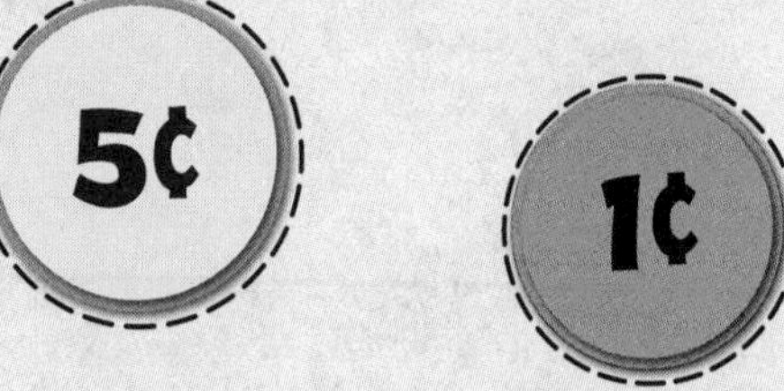

Draw a square and a triangle. The sides of each shape should be 3 inches long. Then, decorate each shape with a colorful pattern.

Skills: Drawing Shapes, Measuring Length

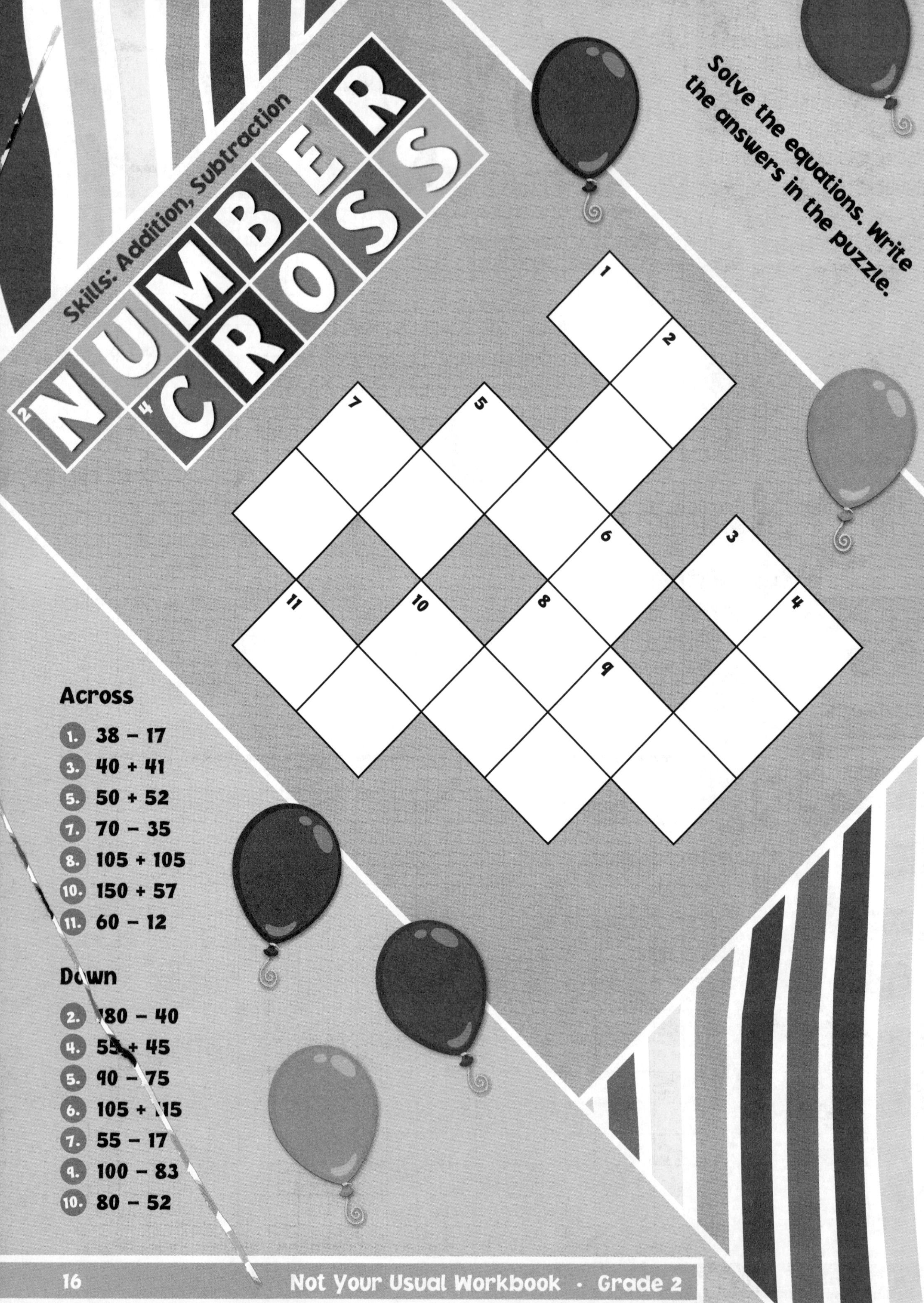

Skills: Addition, Subtraction

NUMBER CROSS

Solve the equations. Write the answers in the puzzle.

Across

1. 38 − 17
3. 40 + 41
5. 50 + 52
7. 70 − 35
8. 105 + 105
10. 150 + 57
11. 60 − 12

Down

2. 180 − 40
4. 55 + 45
5. 90 − 75
6. 105 + 115
7. 55 − 17
9. 100 − 83
10. 80 − 52

GUESS AGAIN

Read each set of clues carefully.
Use math and logic to figure out the mystery numbers.

All 3 digits are even numbers.

The digit in the tens place is double the digit in the hundreds place.

The digit in the ones place is double the digit in the tens place.

What is the mystery number?

The mystery number is ___ ___ ___ .

Hundreds Tens Ones

Skill: Place Value

The digit in the hundreds place is 8 more than the digit in the ones place.

The digit in the tens place is one less than the digit in the ones place.

What is the mystery number?

The mystery number is ___ ___ ___ .

Hundreds Tens Ones

Magic Square

The numbers shown by the dice in each row and column add up to the same number.
Can you draw the missing dice?

Skills: Addition, Subtraction

Skill: Counting Squares

SHAPE MASTER

How many different squares can you find in the picture? Count each one. Write the total on the line. Hint: The total is more than 50.

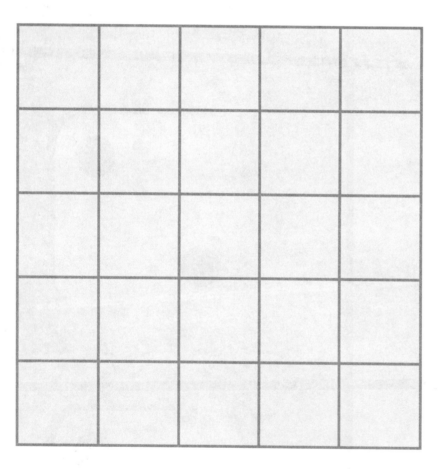

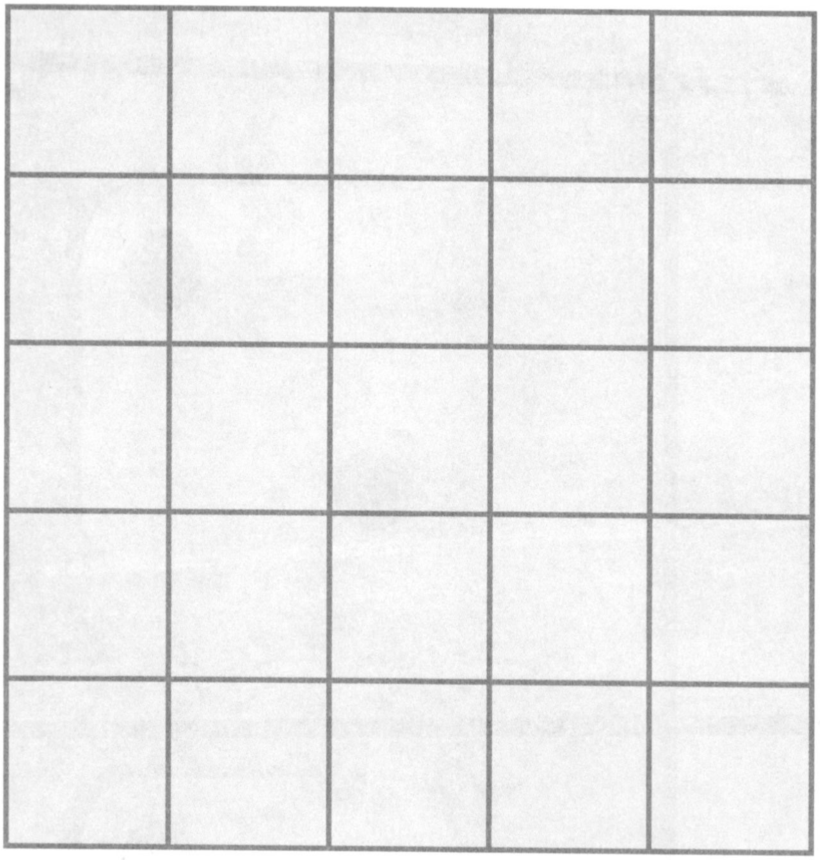

Total number of squares:

On the Lookout!

Skills: Addition, Subtraction

Hidden in the puzzle are 10 addition and subtraction equations. The operation signs are not included. For example, 6 + 8 = 14 would appear in the puzzle as 6, 8, and 14 in a row. Can you find and circle all the equations?

2	7	3	8	4	4	10	2
1	9	10	20	7	19	17	6
5	7	8	3	1	6	5	7
18	16	1	5	10	15	10	13
12	11	6	8	16	11	18	3
1	9	13	18	2	2	4	15
19	6	6	12	17	3	5	1
4	15	2	8	11	13	9	20

STORY STUMPERS

Skill: Using Arrays

Draw pictures in the arrays to match each story. Then, write an equation that helps you find the total number of items in the array.

Mom went to the grocery store 3 times in May. Each time, she bought 4 boxes of cereal.

☐ + ☐ + ☐ = ☐

Grandpa went fishing on 4 Saturdays. Each Saturday, he caught 5 fish.

☐ + ☐ + ☐ + ☐ = ☐

IT FITS!

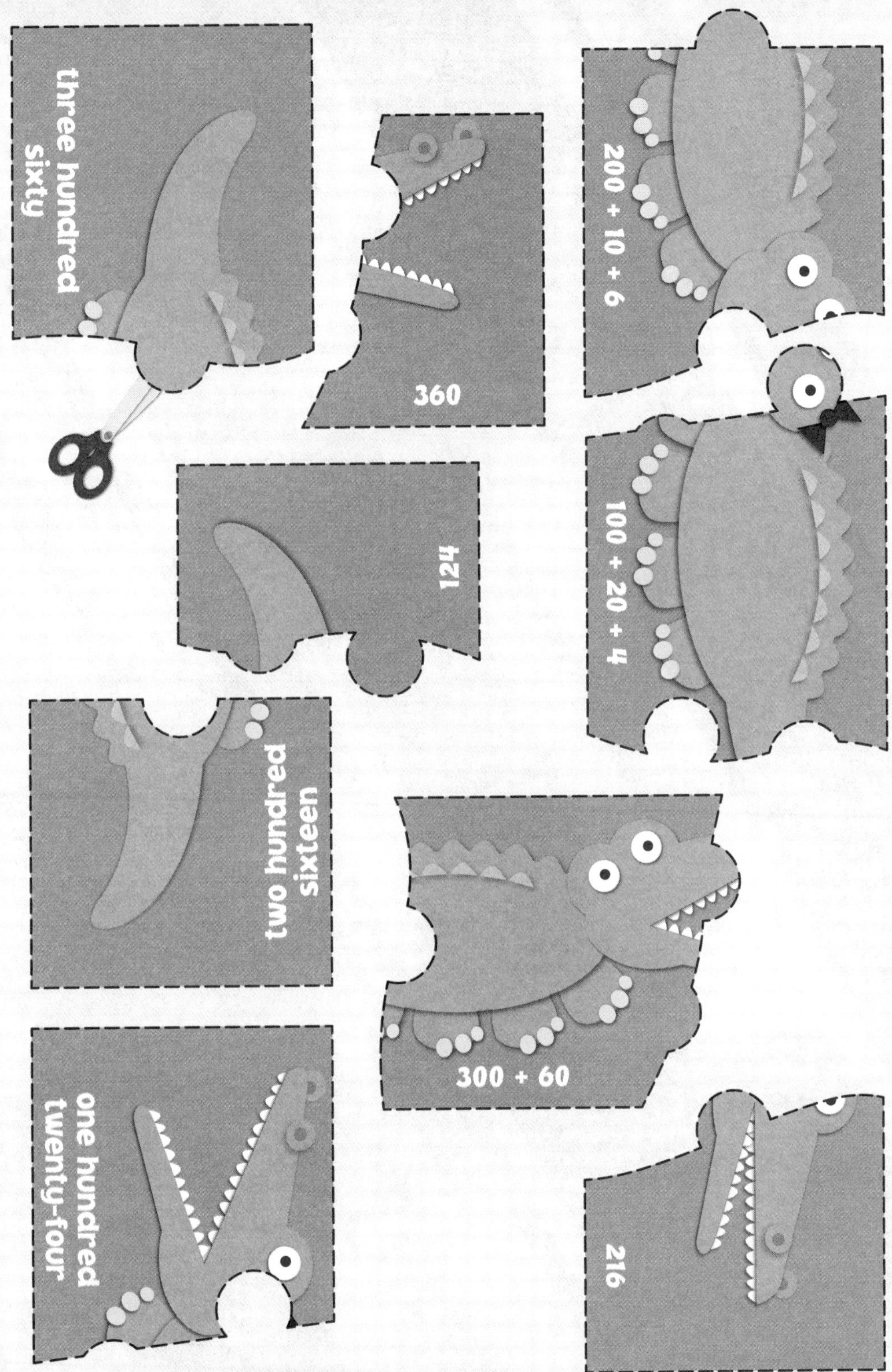

Skills: Numerals, Number Names, Expanded Form

Cut out the pieces. Put them together to make three different alligators. Each alligator's pieces will show the same number written three different ways.

Skills: Addition, Subtraction, Odd and Even, Bar Graphs

First, solve the equations. Next, color the balloons according to the key. Last, fill in the bar graph to show how many balloons of each color.

= even numbers less than 10

= odd numbers less than 10

= even numbers 10 or greater

= odd numbers 10 or greater

12 − 1 = ☐

2 + 3 = ☐

6 + 7 = ☐

10 + 8 = ☐

12 − 5 = ☐

15 − 9 = ☐

18 − 10 = ☐

5 + 3 = ☐

5 + 11 = ☐

19 − 12 = ☐

16 − 13 = ☐

9 + 8 = ☐

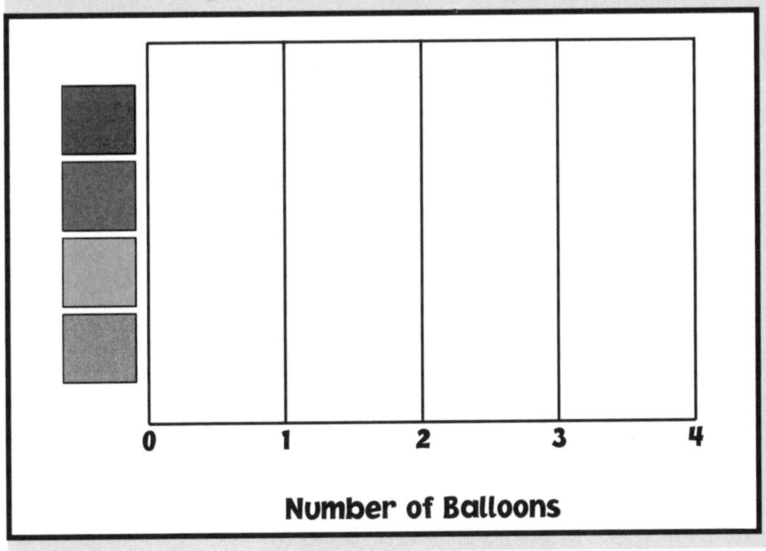

0 1 2 3 4

Number of Balloons

Picture Perfect!

PATTERN POWER

Skills: Addition, Subtraction

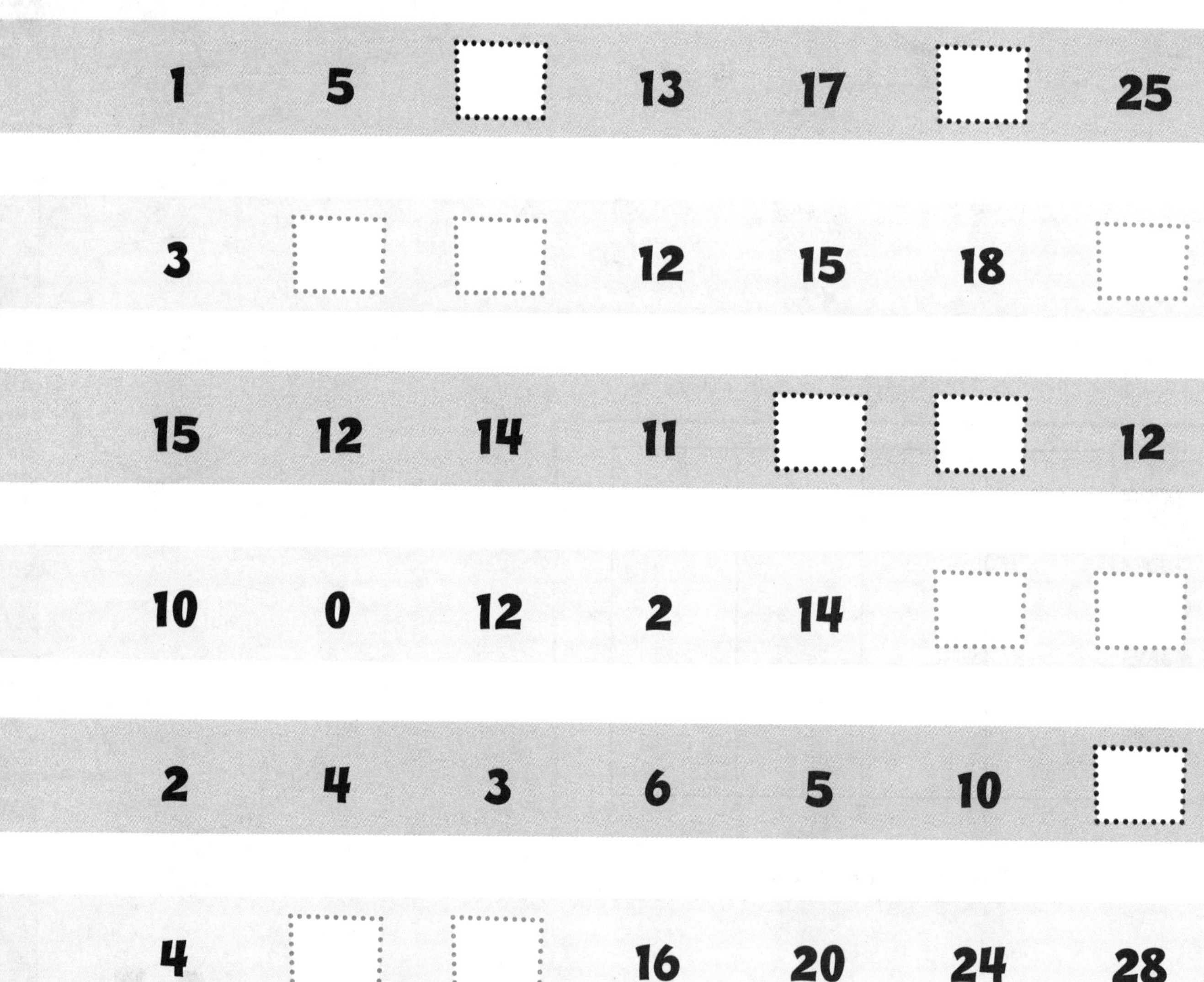

1	5		13	17		25
3			12	15	18	
15	12	14	11			12
10	0	12	2	14		
2	4	3	6	5	10	
4			16	20	24	28

Each row of numbers follows a pattern. Use logic and math to find the pattern. Then, fill in the missing numbers.

START	25	30	40	100
10	100	35	50	200
20	200	40	60	300
30	50	45	75	85
60	55	60	65	END

START	100	50	60	100
50	200	300	400	500
60	70	80	700	600
90	110	200	800	900
70	75	80	90	END

START	20	25	30	40
40	30	100	45	60
50	60	70	80	90
90	95	75	85	100
70	75	80	90	END

START	100	105	200	300
90	120	110	210	400
80	70	115	450	500
130	125	120	500	600
135	140	145	150	END

Find a path through each puzzle from START to END. Decide whether to count by fives, tens, or hundreds to find the path.

Math path

DARE TO DECODE

Skill: Number Names

The number names "one" through "ten" are written in code. Each numeral stands for the same letter in all the codes. Crack the code. Fill in the key and write the number names.

Code Key	1	2	3	4	5	6	7	8	9	10	11	12	13	14

1 5 3 4 10

7 6 1

10 13 7

10 4 8 1 1

2 7 11 8

10 1 6

9 5 14

9 1 12 1 6

2 5 12 1

6 5 6 1

QUICK DRAW

Follow the directions to draw four different shapes.

Skill: Drawing Shapes

Draw the shape you find at each end of a cylinder.

Draw a shape that has three sides and three angles.

Draw a shape that has five sides.

Draw a quadrilateral that has four equal sides.

PATTERN POWER

Skill: Telling Time

Find the pattern formed by the times shown on the clocks in each row. Draw the missing hands on the clock faces to complete the patterns.

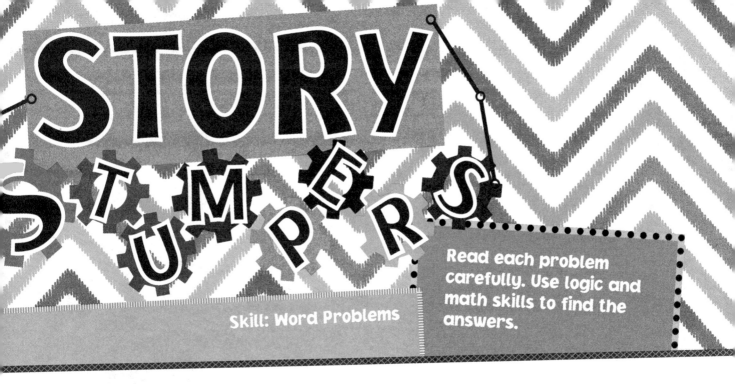

STORY STUMPERS

Skill: Word Problems

Read each problem carefully. Use logic and math skills to find the answers.

1. Mathew, Nick, Nola, and Emma blew up 84 balloons for a party. Mathew blew up 22 balloons. Nick blew up half as many balloons as Mathew. Nola blew up as many as Mathew and Nick combined. How many balloons did Emma blow up?

balloons

2. Daniel cut four ribbons. The blue ribbon is 1 foot long. The yellow ribbon is 3 inches shorter than the blue ribbon. The green ribbon is twice as long as the yellow ribbon. The red ribbon is 5 inches shorter than the green ribbon. How long is each ribbon in inches?

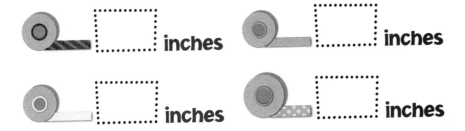

inches inches

inches inches

ON THE DOT

Skills: Addition, Subtraction

1. 54 − 27 =
2. 18 + 62 =
3. 66 − 23 =
4. 90 − 15 =
5. 49 − 26 =
6. 38 + 28 =
7. 55 − 19 =
8. 34 + 62 =
9. 29 − 27 =
10. 37 + 24 =

Solve the equations. Connect the dots in the order of your answers. Color the picture.

IT FITS!

Skill: Comparing Three-Digit Numbers

Cut out the pieces. Put them together to form butterflies that show true inequalities.

Skills: Numerals, Number Names, Expanded Form

NUMBER CROSS

Across

1. 300 + 70 + 9
4. one hundred forty-nine
5. four hundred eighty-eight
7. 200 + 60 + 3
9. 200 + 10 + 2
11. five hundred ninety-seven

Down

1. three hundred fifty-four
2. 900 + 10 + 8
3. forty-nine
6. eight hundred sixty-one
8. 600 + 40 + 7
10. 20 + 5

The clues show number names and expanded forms. Write the matching numerals in the puzzle.

SHAPE MASTER

Measure the sides of each shape to the nearest inch. Add to find the total length of each shape's sides. Then, follow the directions to color the shapes.

Color the shape with a total of 3 inches yellow.

Color the shape with a total of 5 inches red.

Color the shape with a total of 6 inches green.

Color the shape with a total of 8 inches blue.

☐ inches total

☐ inches total

☐ inches total

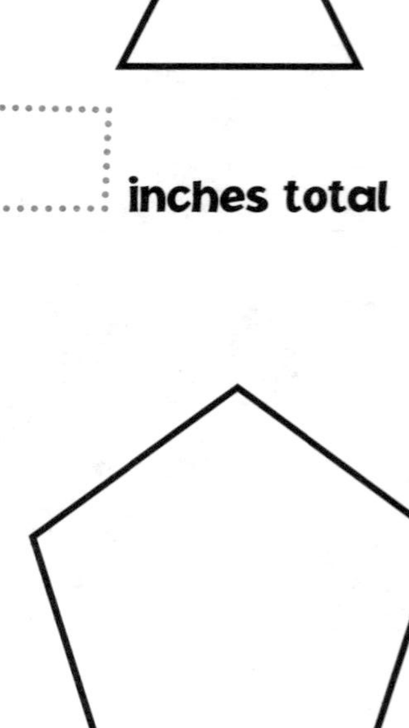

☐ inches total

Skill: Measuring Length

Draw a line to connect each pizza with the cup that describes it.

three-thirds

one-third

one-half

one-fourth

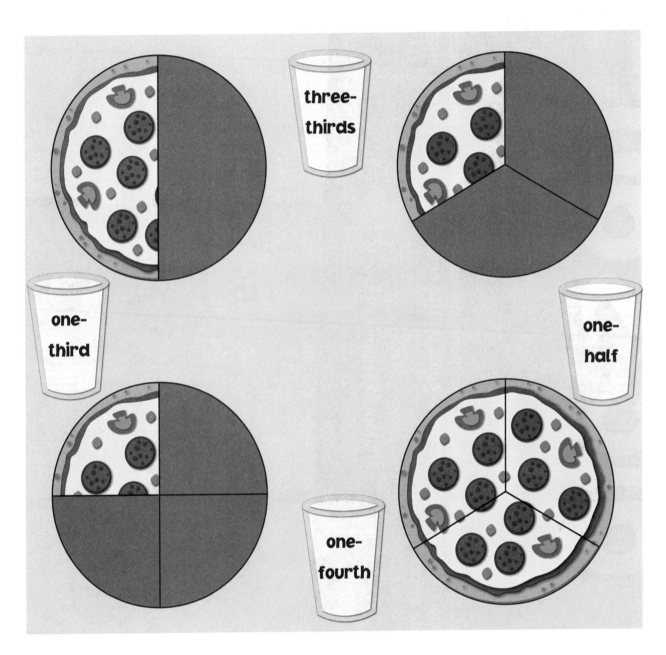

Picture Perfect!

Magic Square

When the puzzle is solved correctly, the money in each row, column, and diagonal will add up to the same amount. Place coins or draw coins on the empty squares to finish the puzzle. Write the amount in the space below.

Magic Square Amount: ____ ¢

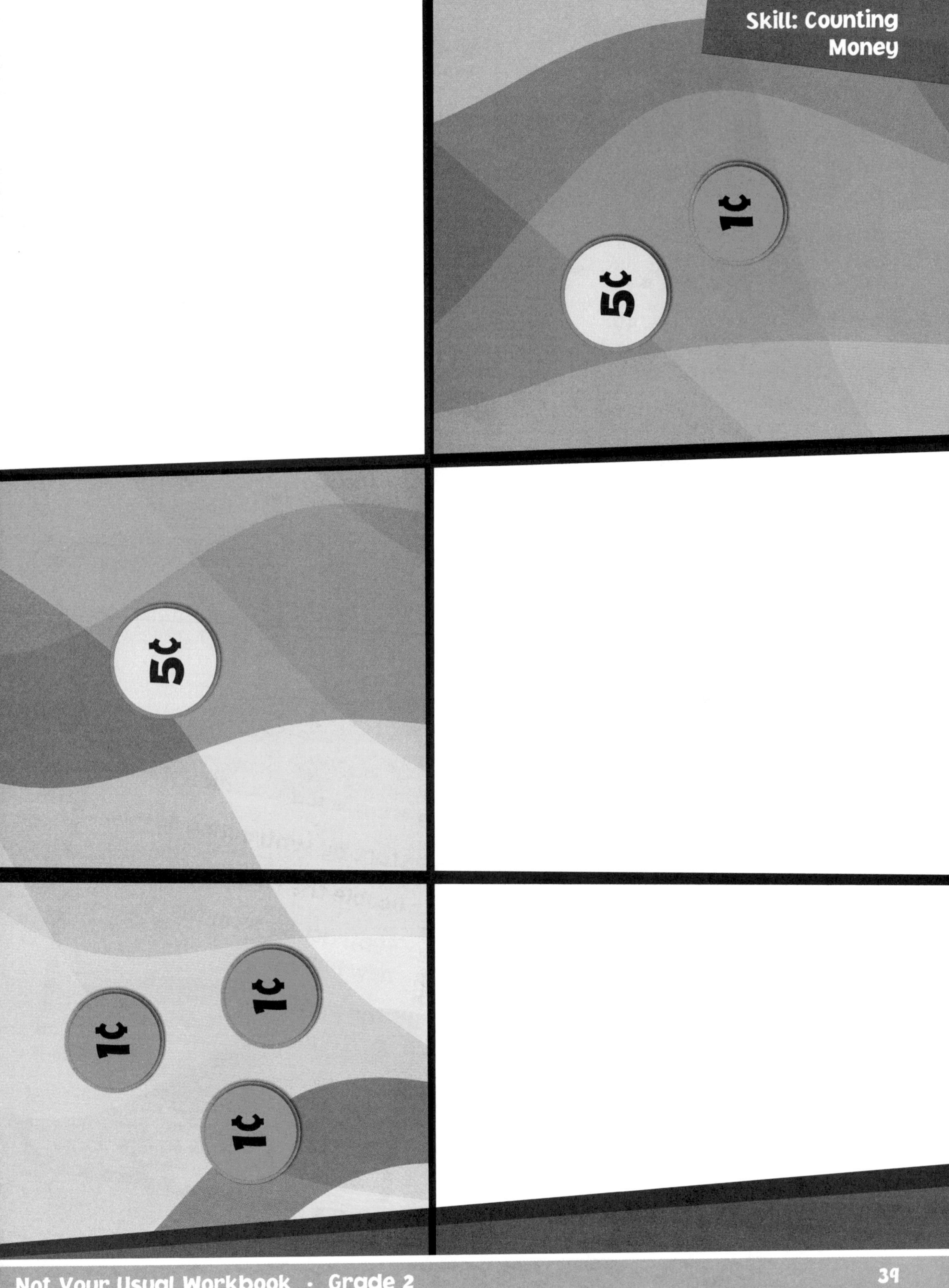
1¢
5¢
5¢
1¢
1¢
1¢

GUESS AGAIN

Use each set of clues to find the mystery number.

It is greater than 90 − 45.

It is less than 32 + 22.

The sum of its two digits is 7.

The mystery number is ☐.

It is greater than 39 + 49.

It is less than 150 − 53.

The difference between its two digits is 3.

The mystery number is ☐.

Skills: Addition, Subtraction

Start with the sum of 15 + 72.

Switch the digits' places.

Subtract 32 from the new number.

The mystery number is ☐.

Start by subtracting 56 − 16.

Double the number.

Subtract 55 from the new number.

The mystery number is ☐.

e(quation) sen+sation

Skills: Place Value, Addition, Subtraction

Some numbers are missing from the math problems. Use the blocks to help you complete the equations.

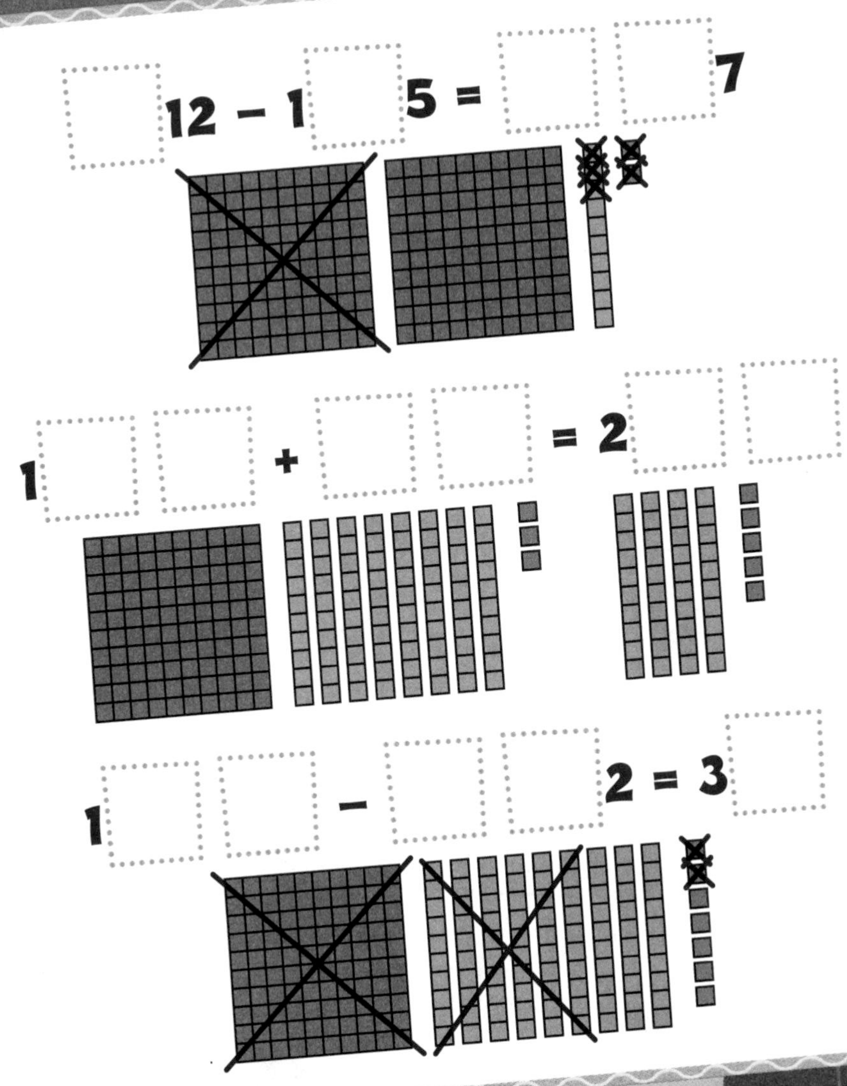

On the Lookout!

Skills: Addition, Subtraction

The combination to the safe is hidden in the puzzle. Solve each equation. Find and circle the answers in the puzzle. The four unused numbers, arranged from least to greatest, will open the safe.

1. 250 + 122 = ____
2. 630 − 218 = ____
3. 432 + 525 = ____
4. 700 − 75 = ____
5. 55 + 61 = ____
6. 310 − 71 = ____
7. 758 − 228 = ____
8. 356 + 372 = ____
9. 215 + 130 = ____
10. 652 − 81 = ____

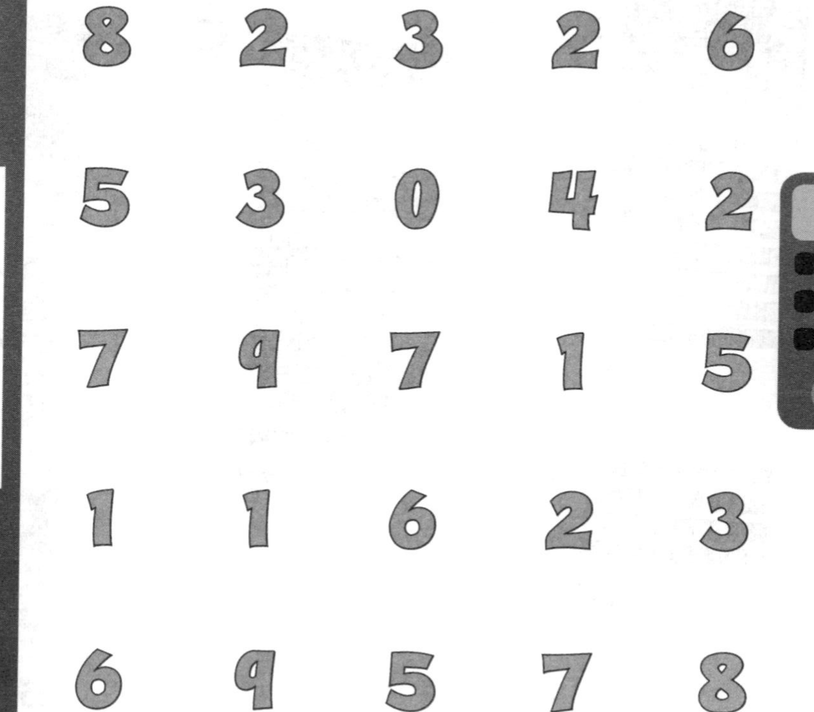

8	2	3	2	6
5	3	0	4	2
7	9	7	1	5
1	1	6	2	3
6	9	5	7	8

Combination = ____ ____ ____ ____

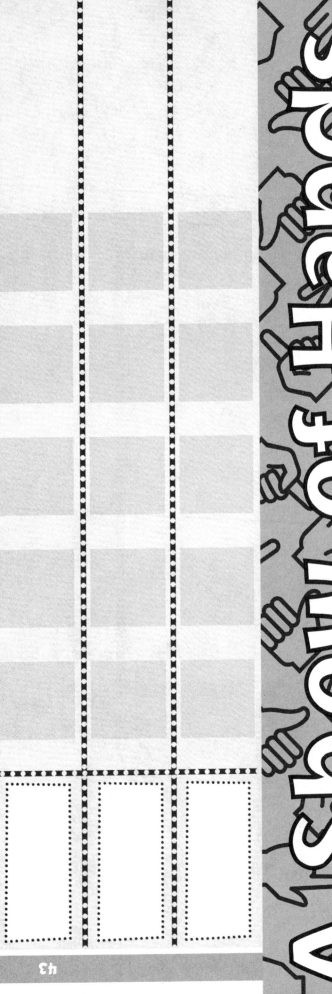

Skill: Picture Graphs

Cut out the pictures of animals Ella saw at the zoo. Glue or tape them in the columns to show how many of each animal she saw. Write a label at the top of each column.

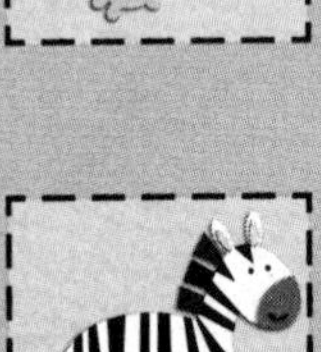

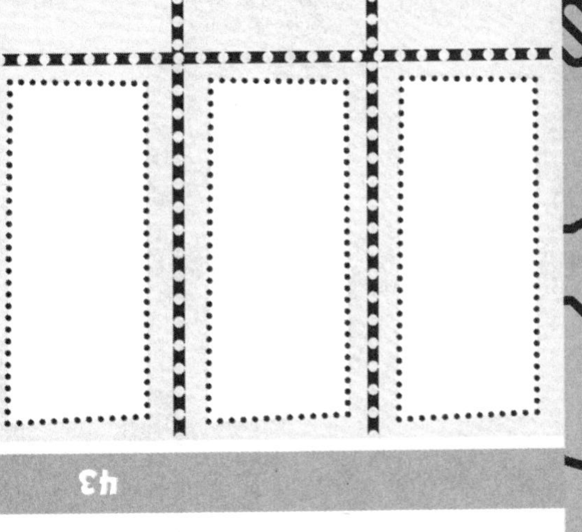

How much money is in the bag? It depends on how you arrange the numbers! Make the four highest numbers you can using digits shown on the bag. Use each digit only once.

3 9 1 1 5 4 7 8 5 9 4 2

$ ☐☐☐ $ ☐☐☐

$ ☐☐☐ $ ☐☐☐

Picture Perfect!

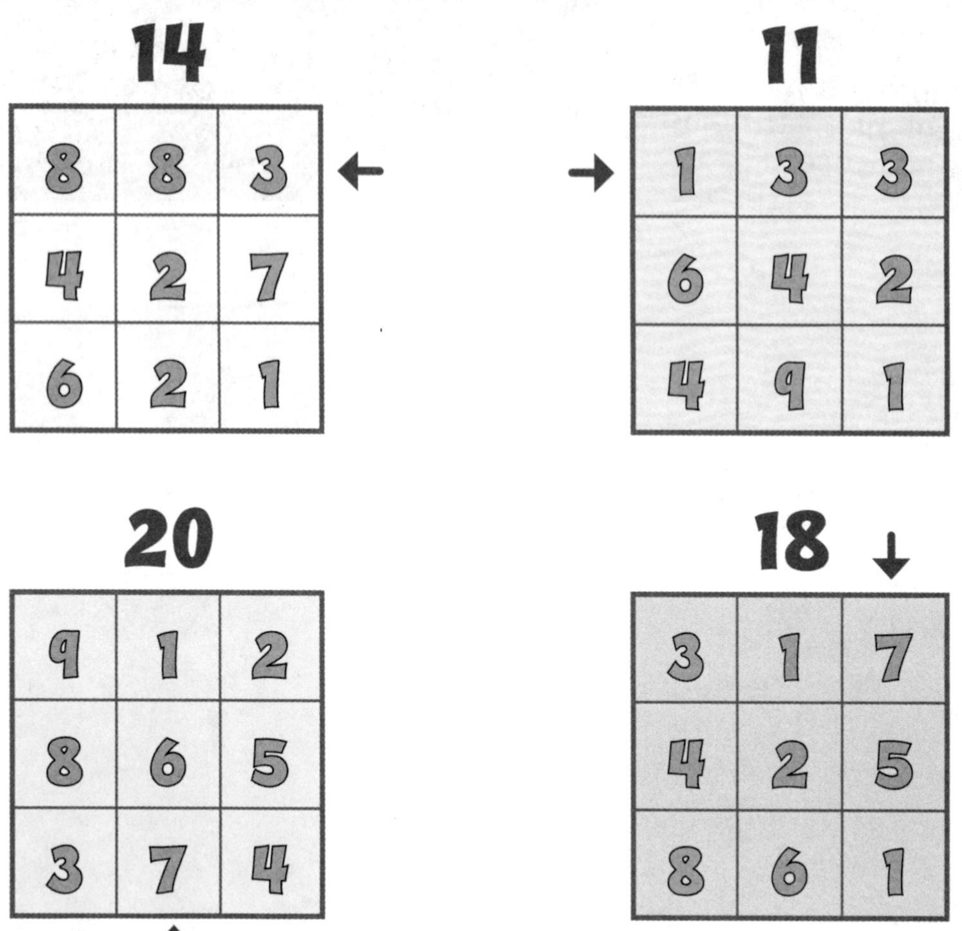

14
8 8 3
4 2 7
6 2 1
11
1 3 3
6 4 2
4 9 1
20
9 1 2
8 6 5
3 7 4
18
3 1 7
4 2 5
8 6 1

Begin each puzzle at the arrow. Find a path by adding numbers until you reach the sum shown above the puzzle. The path for each puzzle should include at least four squares.

QUICK DRAW

Grab some crayons, read the directions, and color your way to some fraction fun!

Skills: Drawing Shapes, Understanding Halves, Thirds, and Fourths

Draw a square. Color one half red. Color the other half blue.

Draw a rectangle. Color one third purple, one third yellow, and one third green.

Draw a triangle. Color one half red. Color the other half green.

Draw a circle. Divide the circle into fourths. Color each fourth a different color.

STORY STUMPERS

Read each problem carefully. Use logic and math skills to find the answers.

Skills: Word Problems, Counting Money

1. Hailey has 57¢. None of the coins are quarters. The number of nickels equals the number of dimes and pennies combined. How many of each coin does she have?

1¢ ☐ pennies 5¢ ☐ nickels 10¢ ☐ dimes

2. Robbie bought a toy car for 69¢. He paid with one dollar. He received three different coins as change. Circle the coins that made up his change. Write the amount.

69¢

1¢ 5¢ 10¢ 25¢ ☐ ¢

3. A yo-yo costs 45¢. Lexi paid using two different types of coins. She used an equal number of each coin. How many of which coins did she use?

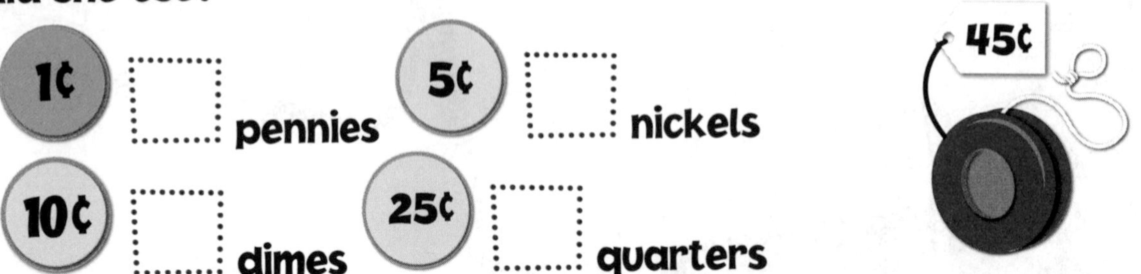

1¢ ☐ pennies 5¢ ☐ nickels

10¢ ☐ dimes 25¢ ☐ quarters

45¢

PATTERN POWER

Skill: Adding 10 or 100

1. 156 256 3___6 45___ ___56 ___56

2. ___00 5___0 60___ ___00 8___0 90___

3. 2___ ___6 46 56 ___6 7___

4. ___28 1___8 14___ 15___ 1___8 ___78

Find the pattern shown by the numbers in each row.
Then, fill in the missing digits.

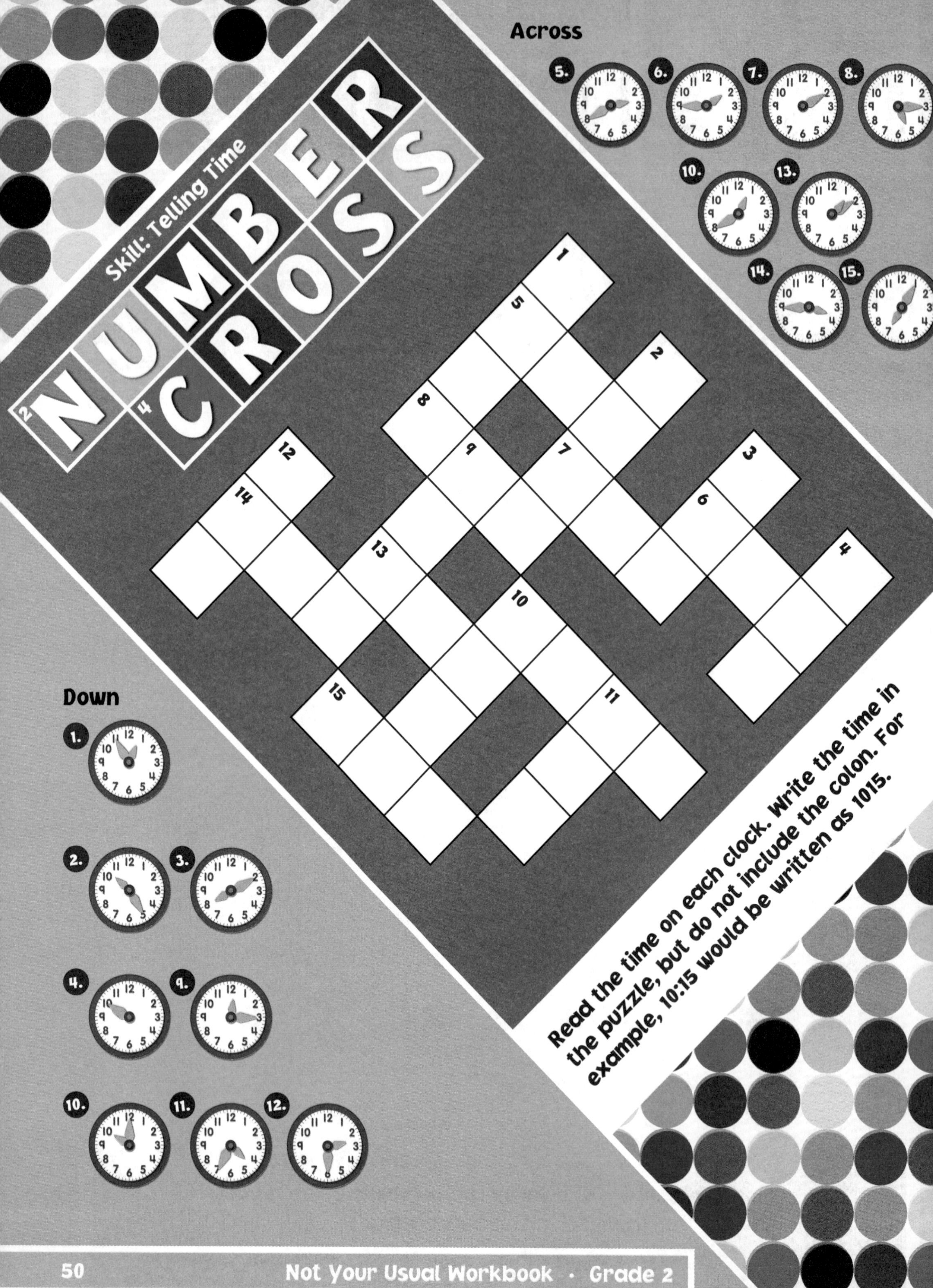
Skill: Telling Time
NUMBER CROSS
Across
5. 6. 7. 8. 10. 13. 14. 15.
Down
1. 2. 3. 4. 9. 10. 11. 12.
Read the time on each clock. Write the time in the puzzle, but do not include the colon. For example, 10:15 would be written as 1015.

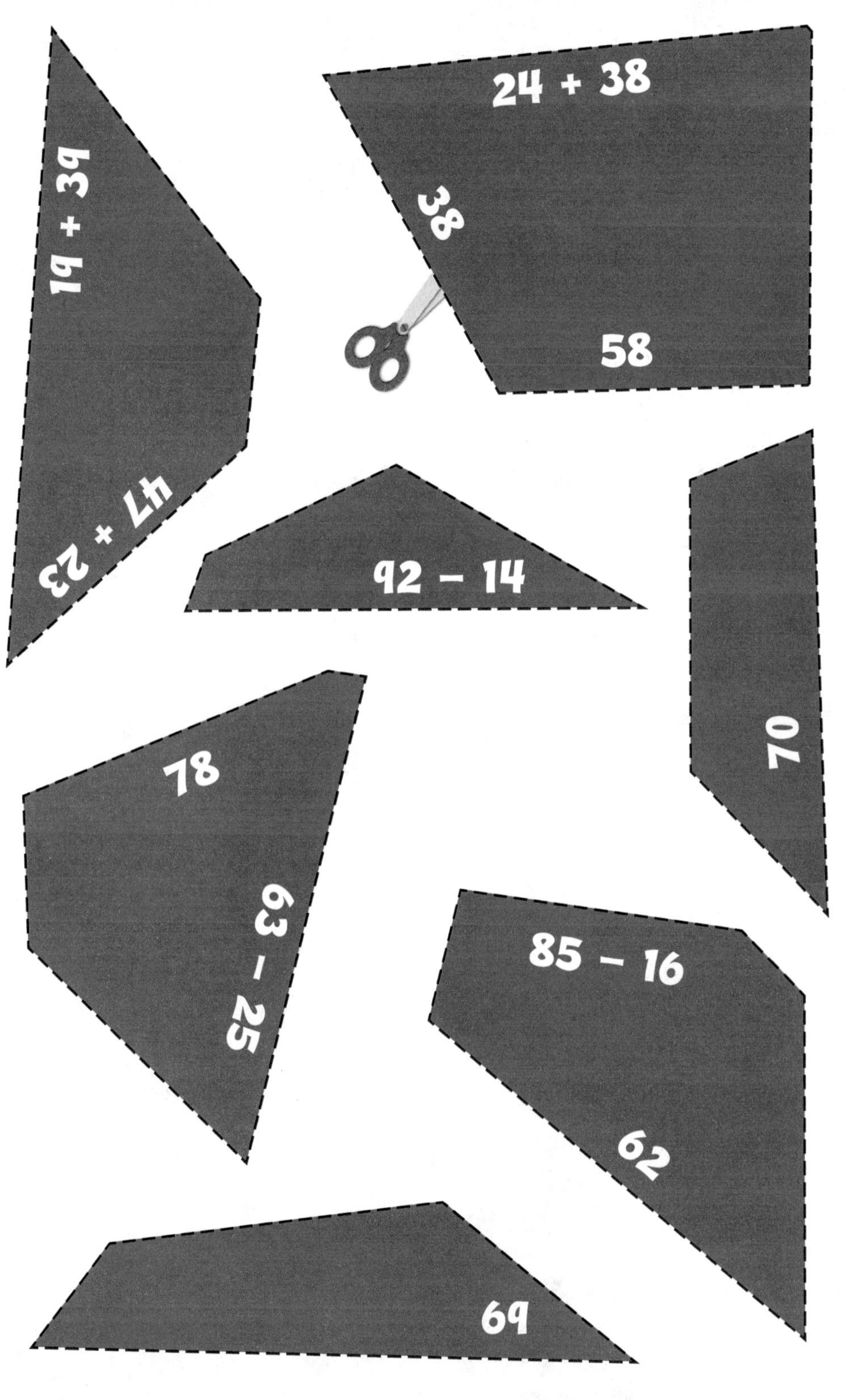

IT FITS!

Skills: Addition, Subtraction

Cut out the puzzle pieces. Put them together to make a shape. When the puzzle is solved, each equation and its solution will be next to each other.

A secret letter is hidden in the dots. Start at the number 3. Connect the odd-numbered dots in order. When you reach the last possible number, draw a line back to where you began. Color the secret letter. Write it below.

Secret Letter:

ON THE DOT

Skill: Odd and Even

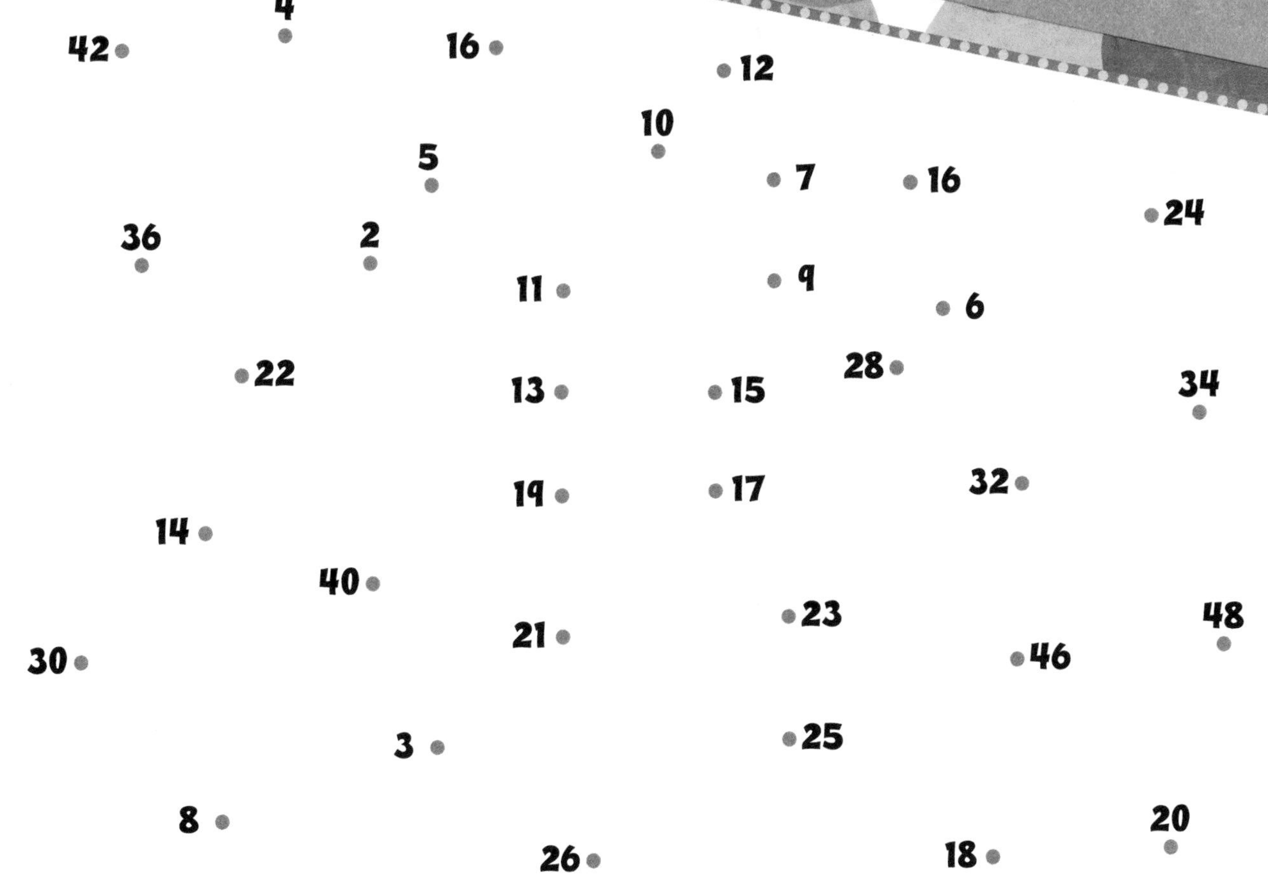

Magic Square

Arrrgh, matey! Find the sums of the rows and columns using the code. Use number names to write your answers in the blanks.

GUESS AGAIN

Read each set of clues carefully. Use math and logic to figure out the mystery numbers.

It is greater than 200.

The number in the hundreds place is half the number in the tens place.

The number in the hundreds place is 6 less than the number in the ones place.

One of the digits is an even number. The other two are odd.

The mystery number is

Hundreds	Tens	Ones

Skill: Place Value

The sum of the three digits is 5.

Two of the digits are the same number.

The smallest digit is in the hundreds place.

The number in the tens place is an even number.

The mystery number is

Hundreds	Tens	Ones

MASTER SHAPE

Skill: Counting Squares

Use a ruler and a pencil to connect the dots side-to-side and top-to-bottom. This will divide the shape into equal squares. One line has been drawn for you. When you are finished connecting lines, count the squares. Write the total.

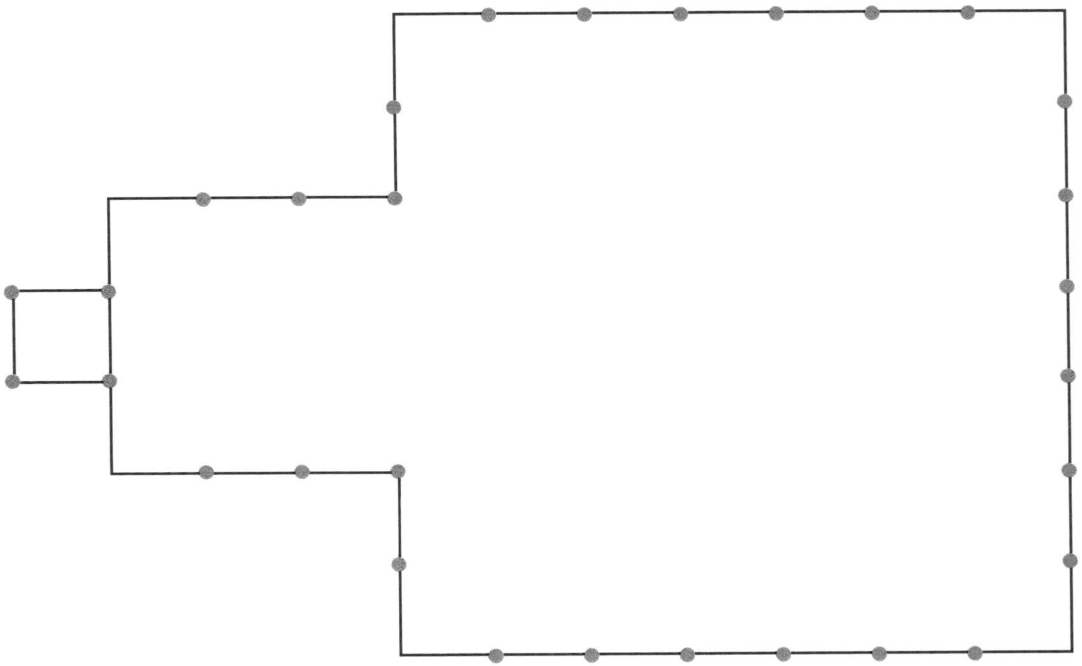

Total Number of Squares: ______

e(quation) / sen+sation

Skills: Addition, Subtraction

Write + or – on each balloon to make the equation true.

1. 16 ◯ 5 ◯ 2 = 13

2. 8 ◯ 9 ◯ 11 = 6

3. 5 ◯ 10 ◯ 3 = 18

4. 2 ◯ 19 ◯ 5 = 16

5. 7 ◯ 12 ◯ 1 = 18

6. 18 ◯ 1 ◯ 5 = 12

DARE TO DECODE

Skill: Counting Money

The coins of Animalonia are worth the same amounts as American coins. Draw a line to match the coins with the same values. Use the amounts shown below as clues.

   = 51¢

   = 40¢

   = 21¢

   = 35¢

QUICK DRAW

Make a drawing to illustrate each story problem. In the blanks, use doubles to write an equation that shows the solution.

Skills: Using Arrays, Word Problems

Aunt Minnie planted 4 rows of bean plants. She planted 4 bean plants in each row. How many bean plants are in Minnie's garden? Use doubles in your equation.

☐ + ☐ = ☐

In a parking lot, cars were parked in 4 rows. There were 5 cars in each row. How many cars were parked in the lot? Use doubles in your equation.

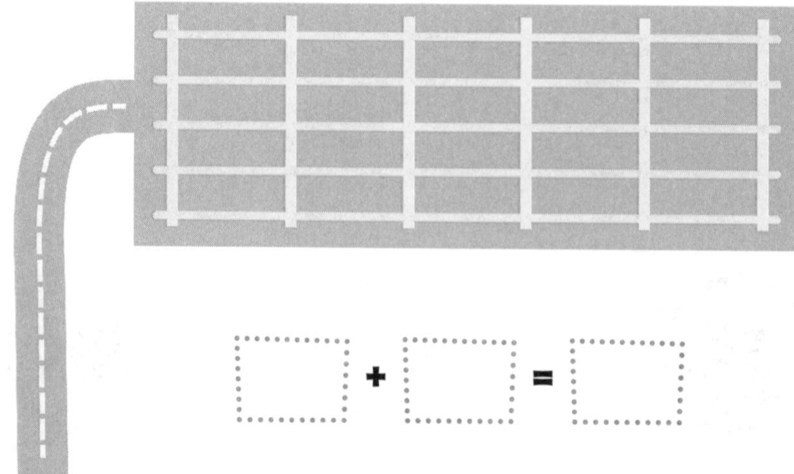

☐ + ☐ = ☐

A Show of Hands

Skill: Measuring Length

Cut out each ruler. Then, go on a measuring scavenger hunt. What can you find that is about the same length as each ruler? Draw or write the name of each item you find.

1 2

1 2 3

1 2 3 4 5

1 2 3 4

Length = 2 inches

Length = 3 inches

Length = 4 inches

Length = 5 inches

On the Lookout!

Skills: Numerals, Expanded Form

Read the expanded forms. Find the matching numerals in the puzzle.

1. 100 + 50 + 6 = ______
2. 400 + 30 + 5 = ______
3. 300 + 70 + 5 = ______
4. 500 + 40 + 3 = ______
5. 400 + 80 + 2 = ______
6. 200 + 20 + 9 = ______
7. 100 + 90 + 6 = ______
8. 700 + 10 + 5 = ______
9. 800 + 50 + 3 = ______
10. 300 + 60 + 4 = ______

5	7	6	2	4	1	3
7	4	9	6	3	3	7
1	8	3	2	2	8	5
6	2	8	7	1	5	7
4	5	1	4	9	3	6
2	2	9	3	1	5	6
3	1	6	2	7	6	4

Write numbers in the circles that describe them. If a number can be described by more than one circle, write it where the circles overlap. Not all numbers will be used. Hint: A multiple of 5 is a number you would say if you counted by fives (60, 65, 70, 75, 80, 85, and so on).

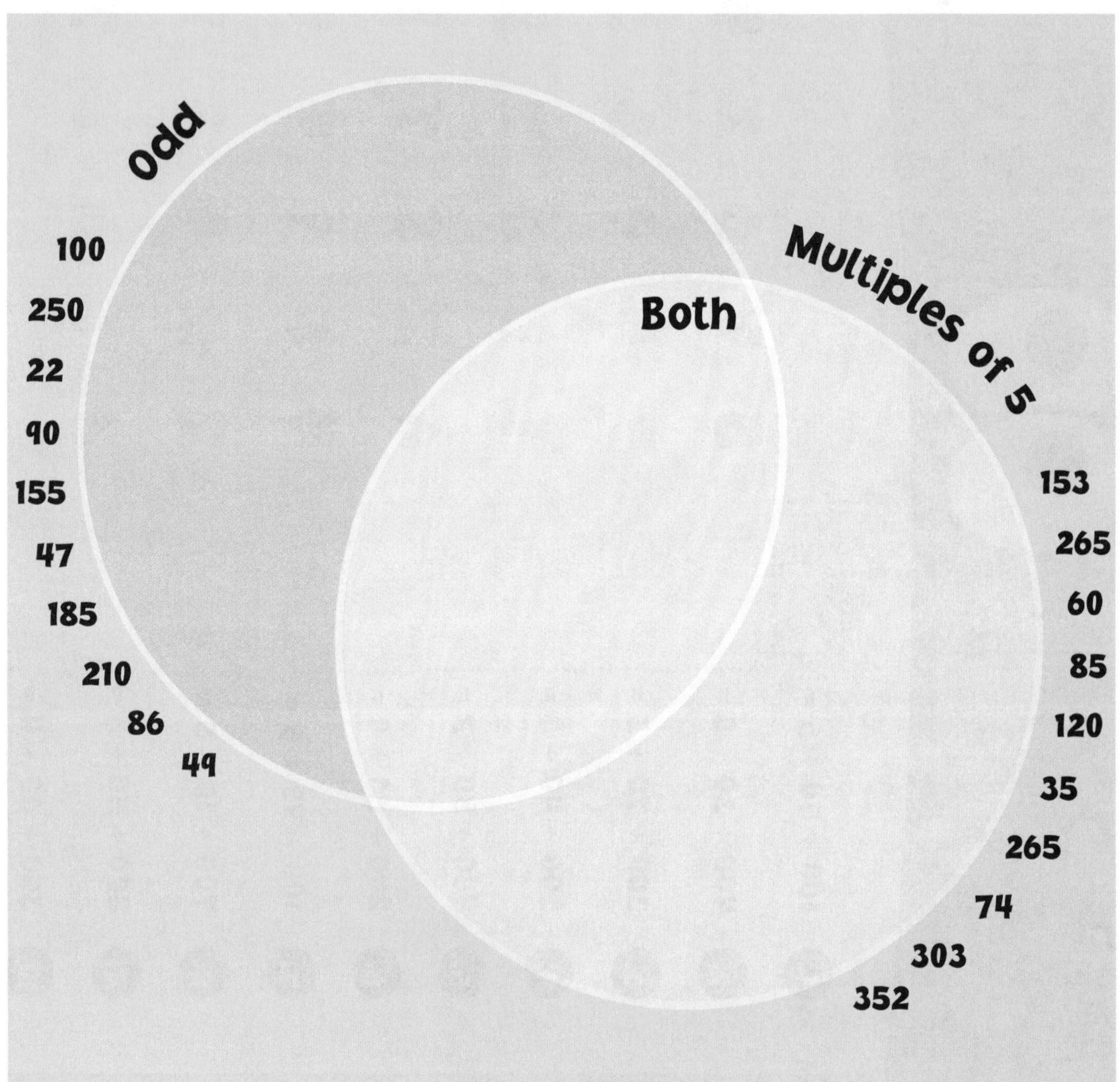

Picture Perfect!

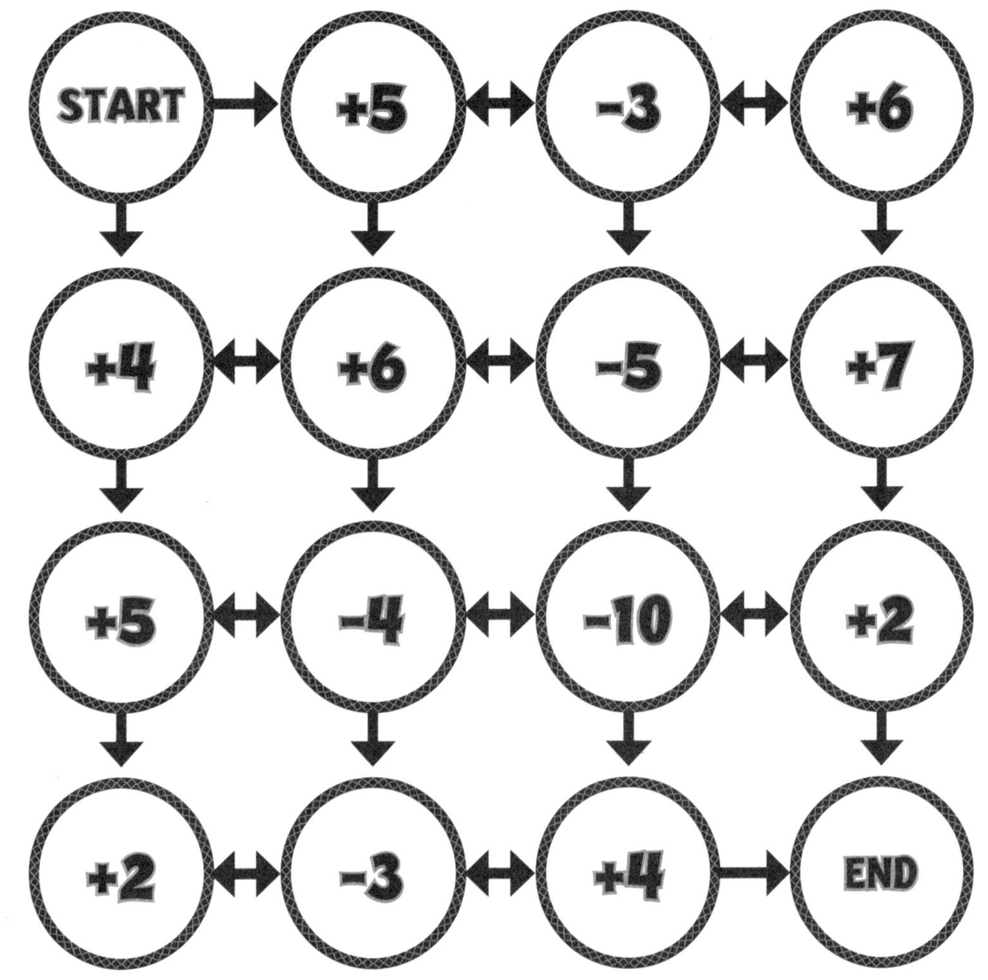

Start with 0. Follow the arrows and perform each operation. Keep a running total. Can you end with 11? There is only one correct path.

Math path

STORY STUMPERS

Skills: Telling Time, Word Problems

Do you have perfect timing? Read each problem. Draw hands on the clock to show what time it is at the end of the story.

1. Marco woke up at 7:30. He spent 20 minutes getting ready for school. He spent 10 minutes eating breakfast. It took him 15 minutes to get to school. What time did Marco arrive at school?

2. Nina got to the library at 2:45. Her sister Lily had arrived 10 minutes earlier. As soon as Lily got to the library, she began to read. She read for 1 hour. Then, Lily and Nina left together. What time did the sisters leave the library?

3. At 11:30, the Number 4 bus left the main downtown station. It made 7 stops before reaching its last stop at Shoptown Mall. It took 5 minutes to travel between stops. What time did the Number 4 bus reach Shoptown Mall?

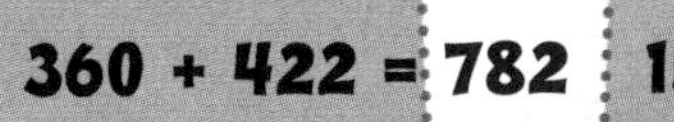

Skills: Addition, Subtraction

NUMBER CROSS 4

360 + 422 = 782

150 + 107 =

254 + 478 =

198 − 150 =

205 + 210 =

963 − 652 =

485 − 430 =

250 + 599 =

200 + 344 =

990 − 39 =

80 + 86 =

200 − 135 =

144 + 112 =

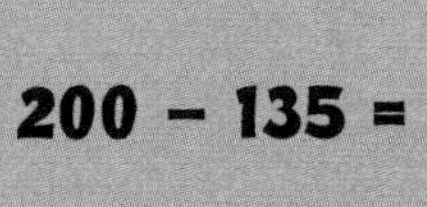

Solve the equations. Find where each answer fits in the puzzle. One has been done for you.

Magic Square

Write the nine numbers shown in the magic square. One three-digit number goes in each space. Follow this rule: From top to bottom, and from left to right, the numbers in each row or column must go from greatest to least.

810 705 847 983 512 670 855 962 736

Hundreds	Tens	Ones	Hundreds	Tens	Ones	Hundreds	Tens	Ones

Ones

Tens

Hundreds

Ones

Tens

Hundreds

Ones

Tens

Hundreds

Ones

Tens

Hundreds

Ones

Tens

Hundreds

Ones

Tens

Hundreds

On the Lookout!

Skill: Subtracting 10 or 100

Ten subtraction problems are hidden in the puzzle. The minus and equal signs are not included. For example, 150 – 10 = 140 would appear as 150, 10, and 140 in a row in the puzzle. Find and circle all 10 problems.

375	100	475	100	247	323	100	99
10	90	10	201	195	10	185	100
365	125	257	578	785	293	10	299
244	674	10	664	322	10	360	530
168	100	247	200	455	393	100	144
199	10	189	253	100	602	260	620
100	210	319	203	555	100	460	100
911	100	329	10	319	687	10	720

PATTERN POWER

Skill: Understanding Halves, Thirds, and Fourths

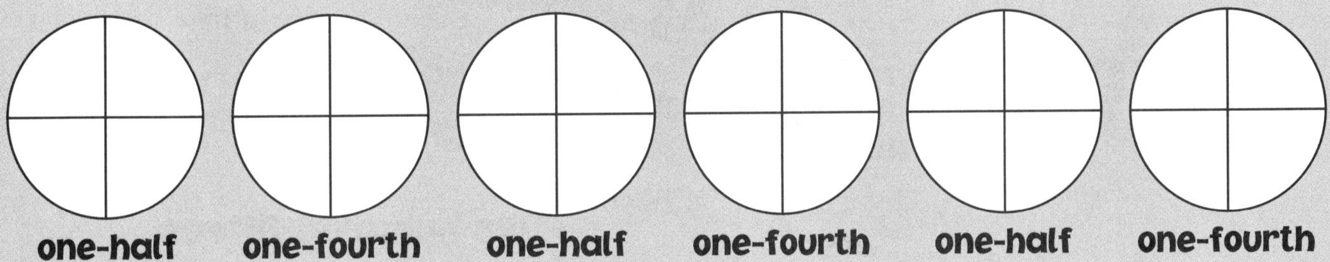

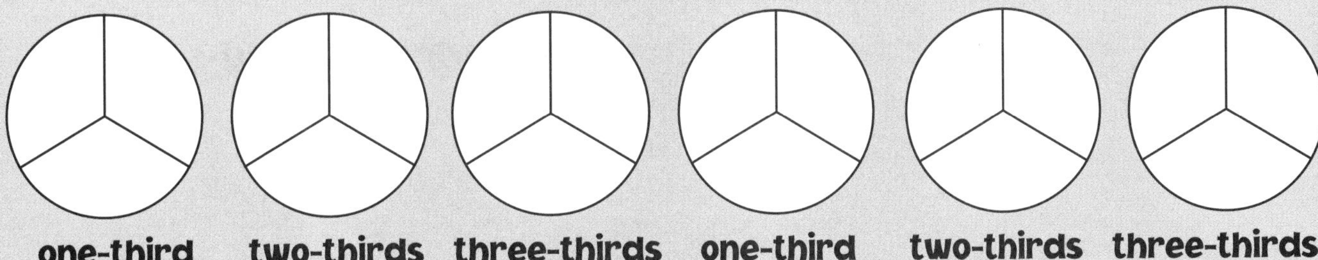

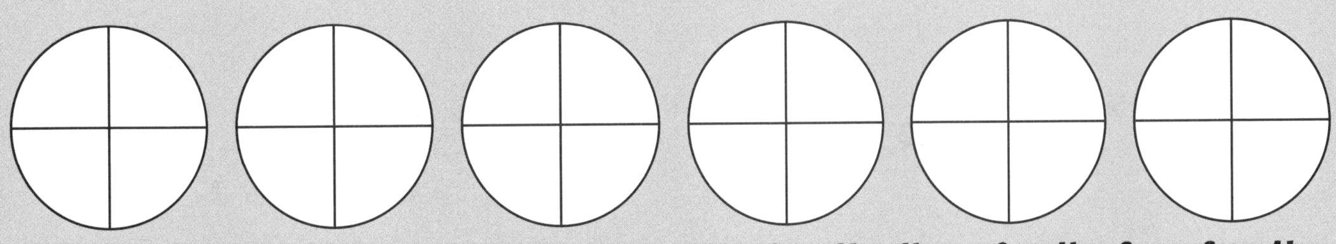

Color the shapes to show each pattern. If you use different colors, make them a part of the pattern, too.

To solve the puzzle, draw a line to connect each set of three dots that show the same number in three different ways (numeral, number names, and expanded form). When you are done, you will have four triangles. Color the triangles to reveal the finished picture.

• two hundred fifteen

• one hundred twenty-seven

215 •

100 + 50 + 3
•

• 200 + 10 + 5

462 •

• 400 + 60 + 2

• 153

127 •

• 100 + 20 + 7

one hundred fifty-three •

• four hundred sixty-two

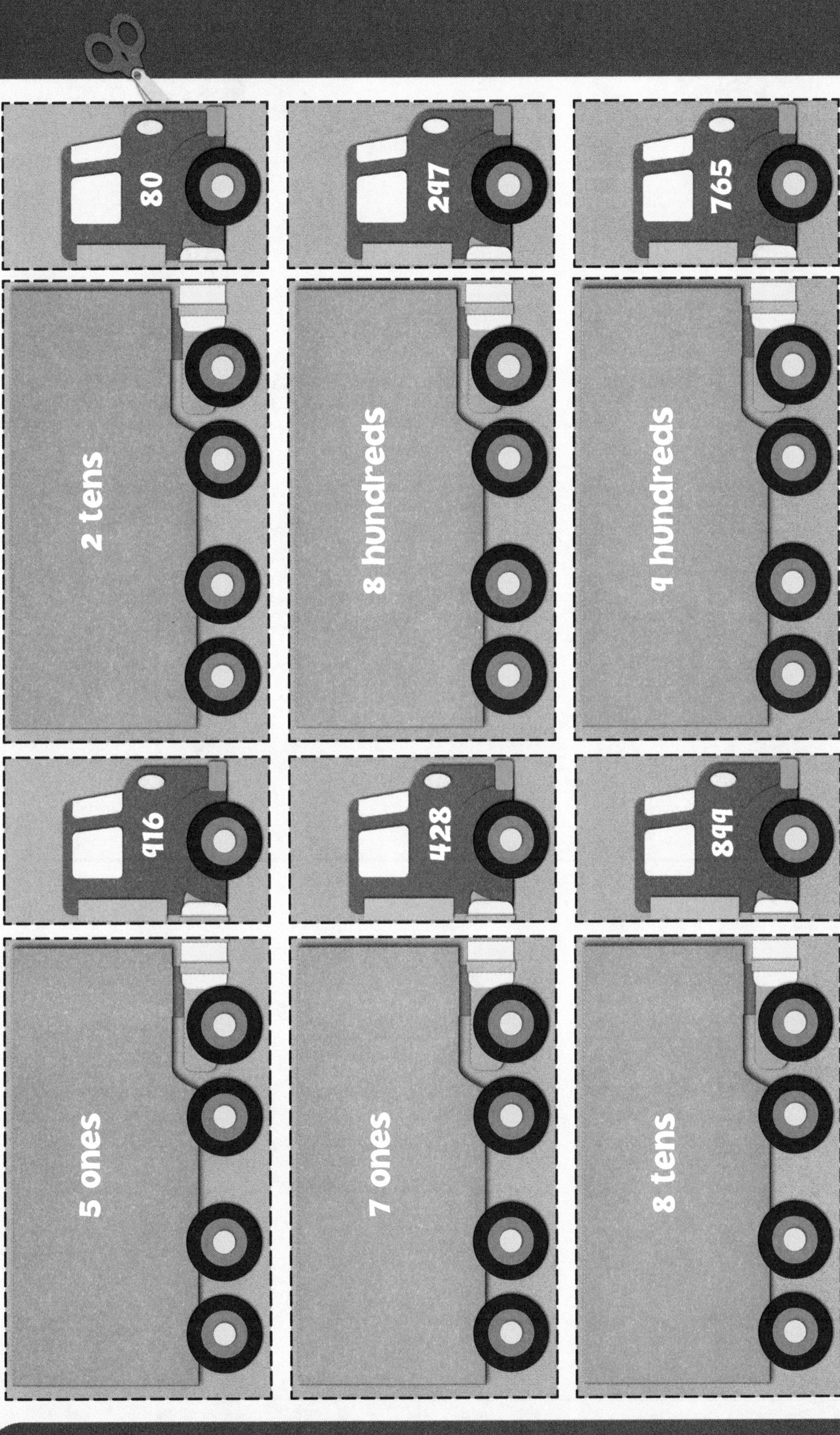

IT FITS!

Skill: Place Value

Cut out the puzzle pieces. Put them together by matching each number to its description.

GUESS AGAIN

Use each set of clues to discover the mystery number.

It is greater than 100 – 35.

It is less than 43 + 37.

The sum of its two digits is 9.

The mystery number is ____.

It is less than 52 + 39.

It is more than 25 + 59.

The sum of its two digits is 16.

The mystery number is ____.

Skills: Addition, Subtraction

Start by subtracting 92 – 55.

Add the digits of the answer together.

Add 56 to the new number.

The mystery number is ____.

Start with the sum of 29 + 49.

Subtract 32.

Add the digits of the answer together.

The mystery number is ____.

e(quation) sen+sation

Skill: Using Arrays

Look at each group of dots. Solve the equations beside it. Then, circle all the equations that describe the dots.

4 + 4 + 4 = ☐

3 + 3 + 3 + 3 = ☐

4 + 3 + 4 = ☐

6 + 6 = ☐

12 + 12 = ☐

5 + 5 + 5 + 5 + 5 = ☐

10 + 10 + 5 = ☐

12 + 12 + 1 = ☐

5 + 5 + 5 + 5 = ☐

4 + 4 + 4 + 4 + 4 = ☐

8 + 10 = ☐

10 + 10 = ☐

5 + 5 + 5 = ☐

7 + 7 = ☐

7 + 7 + 1 = ☐

3 + 3 + 3 + 3 + 3 = ☐

SHAPE MASTER

Skill: Counting Shapes

How many different triangles can you find in the shape?
Write the total in the box.
Hint: The total is more than 16.

Total Number of Triangles:

DARE TO DECODE

Skill: Counting by Fives, Tens, and Hundreds

Can you crack the code? Each shape stands for a number. The groups of shapes in each row form a number pattern. The patterns count by fives, tens, or hundreds. Decode the patterns by writing a number below each group of shapes. Write a number below each shape to complete the code. Two are given for you.

CODE KEY

			0			5			

Draw a picture that includes a tree that is 18 feet tall, an adult who is 6 feet tall, a child who is 4 feet tall, and a dog that is 2 feet tall. Use the ruler to help you.

Skill: Measuring Length

20 19 18 17 16 15 14 13 12 11 10 9 8 7 6 5 4 3 2 1 0 feet

Imagine you have only the coins shown below. Draw the coins to meet each challenge.

10¢ 1¢ 5¢ 1¢ 5¢ 10¢ 5¢ 25¢

What is the largest odd-numbered amount you can show using 3 coins?

☐¢

What is the largest even-numbered amount you can show using 4 coins?

☐¢

Draw all 8 coins in a line. The amount of the first 4 coins should be 21¢. The amount of the last 4 coins should be 41¢.

Draw all 8 coins in a line. The amount of the first 5 coins should be 26¢. The amount of the last 3 coins should be 36¢.

Picture Perfect!

A Show of Hands

Skill: Understanding Halves, Thirds, and Fourths

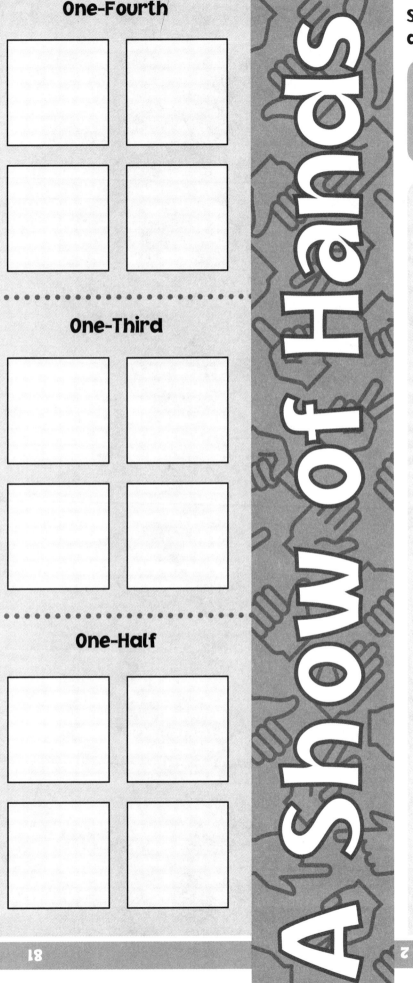

Cut out the pictures that show parts of foods. Glue or tape each one under the label that describes it.

One-Fourth

One-Third

One-Half

Skill: Counting by Fives and Tens
NUMBER CROSS 4
To fill in the puzzle, count by fives from top to bottom in each column. Count by tens from left to right in each row. Some numbers have been filled in for you. Then, follow the directions to find the secret number.
10
15
20
25
30
30
Find the three numbers you wrote in colored squares. Write them in the spaces below. Their sum is the secret number.
+
The secret number is .

Magic Square

The sum of the numbers in each row, column, and diagonal is the magic number. Fill in the missing numbers. Write the magic number below.

The magic number is ______ .

20

50

30

40

STORY STUMPERS

Read each clue carefully. Use your math skills to find the answer.

Skill: Word Problems

- Kayla has 2 red pots and 1 brown pot.
- Larkin has 2 more brown pots than Kayla and 2 white pots.
- Mike has 1 fewer brown pot than Larkin and 1 more red pot than Kayla.

How many flowers does each person have in all?

Kayla: ______ flowers Larkin: ______ flowers Mike: ______ flowers

Start at the clock showing 12:00. Find a path through the puzzle from clock to clock. Add 25 minutes each time you move to a new space. Circle the last clock in the path.

Math path

On the Lookout!

Skills: Numerals, Number Names

Read the number names. Find and circle the matching numerals in the puzzle.

seven hundred ninety-five
five hundred seventy-one
three hundred fifty-three
four hundred thirty-six
two hundred twelve
eight hundred eighty-three
three hundred ninety-seven
six hundred twenty-five
nine hundred seventy-nine
seven hundred sixty-four

2	6	5	9	2	3	6
7	4	7	1	8	1	4
1	3	9	7	8	6	2
4	1	5	6	3	0	8
3	9	8	4	2	5	6
6	5	7	1	0	9	3
5	2	3	9	6	2	5

IT FITS!

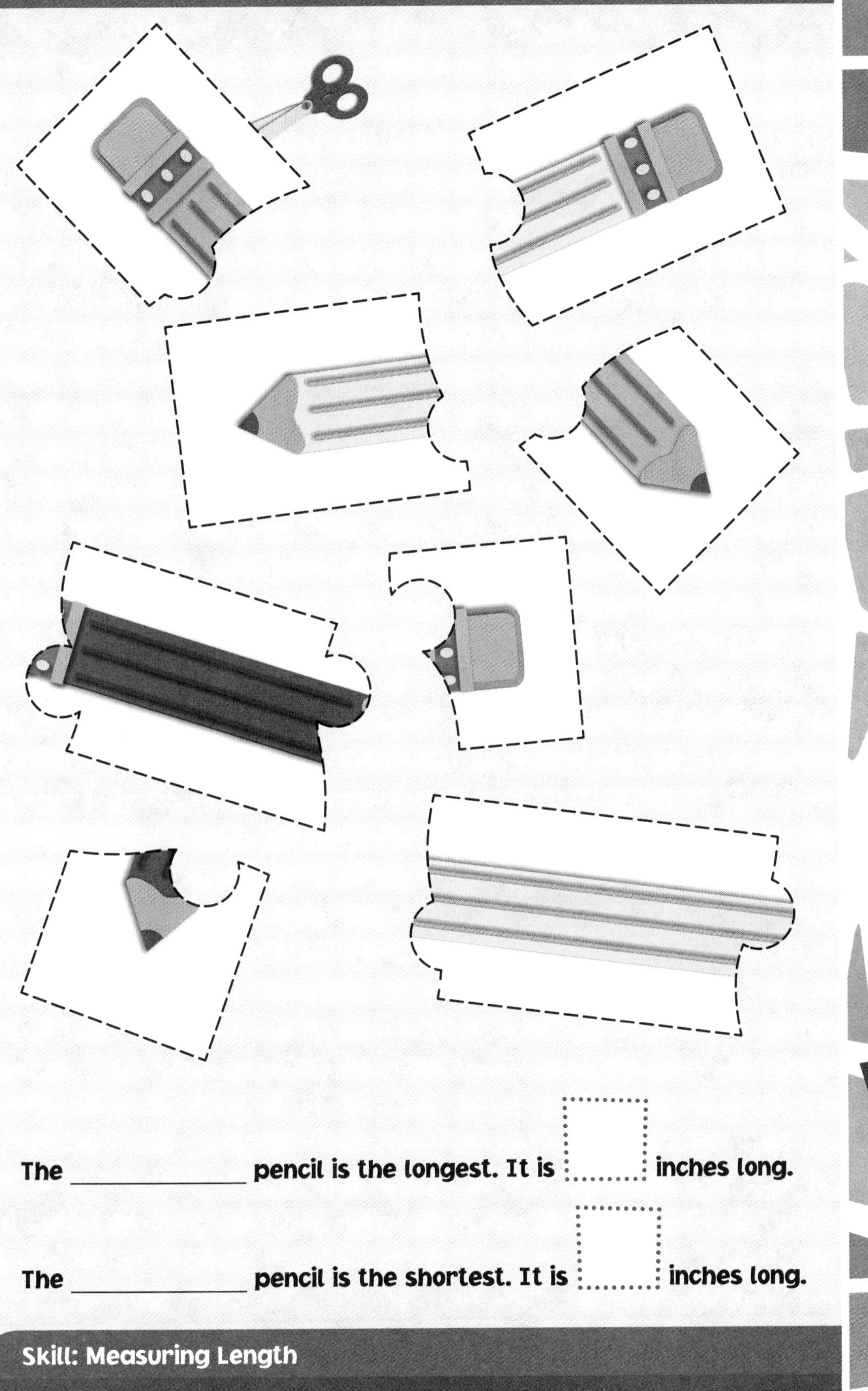

The ______________ pencil is the longest. It is ☐ inches long.

The ______________ pencil is the shortest. It is ☐ inches long.

Skill: Measuring Length

Cut out the puzzle pieces. Put them together to make three pencils. Then, use a ruler to help you complete the sentences.

PATTERN POWER

Skills: Addition, Subtraction

12	☐	36	48	60	☐	84
75	65	☐	45	35	☐	15
9	☐	27	☐	45	54	63
2	4	8	☐	32	☐	128
84	☐	64	54	☐	34	24

Find the pattern in each row of numbers.
Fill in the missing numbers.

GUESS AGAIN!

**Read each set of clues.
Circle the correct number.**

The sum of the three digits is 8.

The first digit is the same as the last digit.

The correct number is twice as much as one of the incorrect numbers shown.

350 323
121 242
251 130

Skill: Comparing Three-Digit Numbers

The digits are three numbers in a row.

The sum of the three digits is 9.

The digit in the hundreds place is half the digit in the ones place.

254 234
123 456
432 356

Start at 199. Count backward by tens to connect the dots. When you reach 129, draw a line back to 199.

What shape did you draw?

Use a ruler to measure each side of the shape to the closest inch. Add the lengths and write the total below.

Total length of the sides:

inches

ON THE DOT

Skills: Subtracting 10, Measuring Length

55
40
169
210
95
85
179
159
155
90
114
165
189
100
225
149
191
125
195
115
156
135
199
129
139
145
175
185
183
55
70

e(quation) / sen+sation

Skills: Addition, Subtraction

Someone stole numbers from these equations! Use logic and math to write in the missing digits.

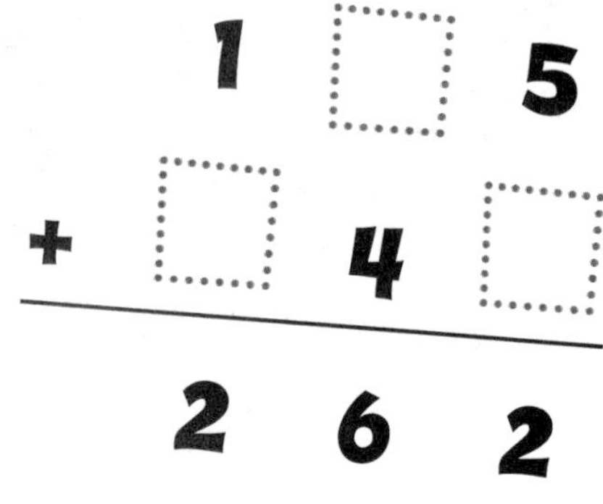


```
  □ 0 □
+ 2 □ 4
-------
  5 5 0
```

```
  □ 1 □
+ 2 □ 3
-------
  7 0 5
```

```
  2 □ 2
+ □ 1 □
-------
  8 0 1
```

Read and follow the directions.

1. Draw a large octagon.
2. Divide it in half.
3. Color the left half blue.
4. Draw a large triangle in the right half.
5. Color half the triangle red.
6. Draw a small circle in the other half of the triangle.
7. Color the circle yellow.

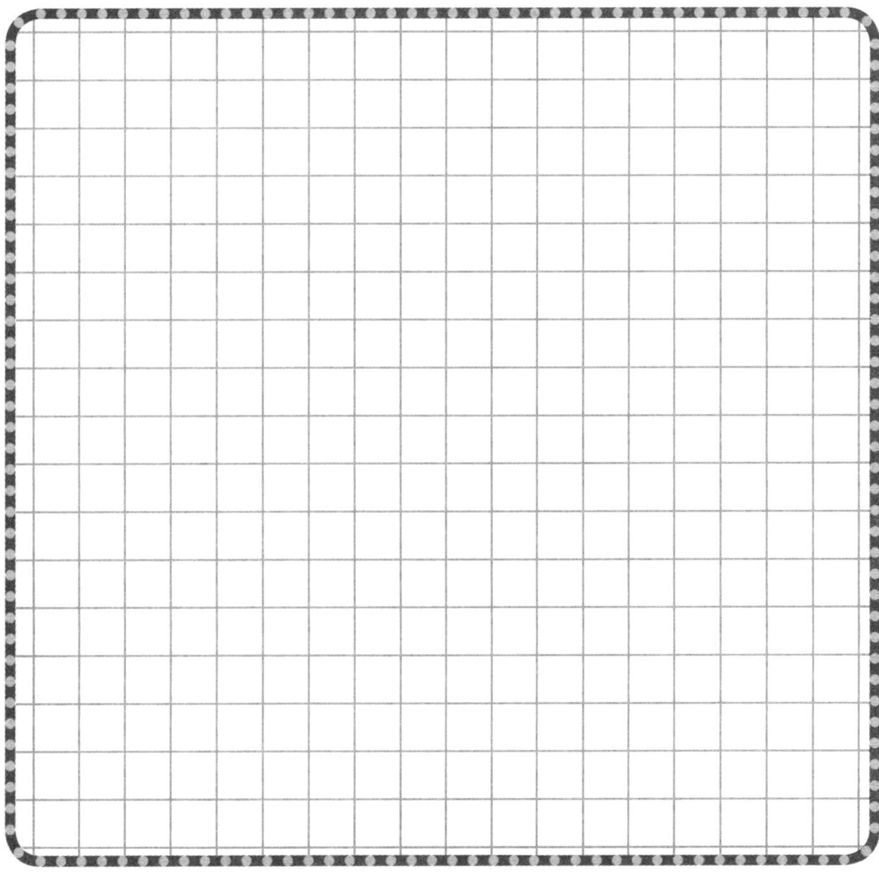

SHAPE MASTER

Skill: Drawing Shapes

Try to draw lines so that the following shapes appear inside the rectangle:

- 2 squares
- 2 triangles

Color each small shape a different color.

STORY STUMPERS

Read each problem. Use your math skills to find the answer.

Skill: Word Problems

1. Sixteen students went to the museum. 6 fewer girls went than boys. How many boys and how many girls went to the museum?

2. The zoo got 14 new animals. Half of the animals were pandas. There were 3 fewer penguins than pandas. The rest of the animals were tigers. How many of each animal did the zoo get?

3. A bag of candy contained 12 red gummy bears. It had 5 fewer yellow gummy bears than red. It had 10 more green gummy bears than yellow. How many gummy bears were in the bag?

☐ gummy bears

Magic Square

When the puzzle is solved correctly, the money in each row, column, and diagonal will add up to the same amount. Place coins or draw coins on the empty squares to finish the puzzle. Write the amount in the space below.

Magic Square Amount: ______ ¢

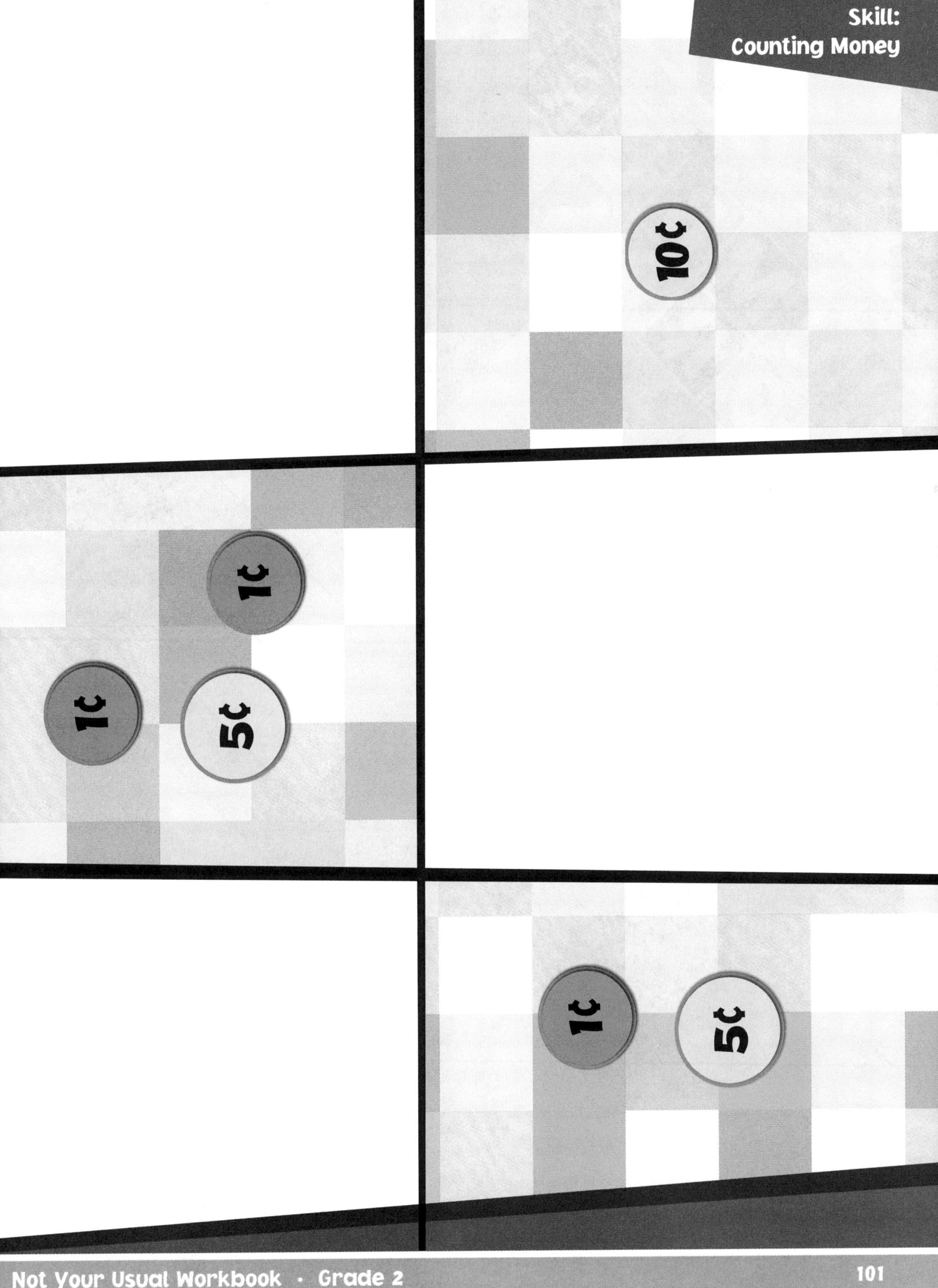
10¢
1¢
1¢
5¢
1¢
5¢

Skills: Adding 100, Subtracting 10
NUMBER CROSS
Can you find the secret number? To begin, add 100 and subtract 10 from each number shown. Write the answers in the puzzle, starting from the outer squares and working in. When you are done, write the numbers in the colored squares from least to greatest to find the secret number.
8
7
1
2
6
5
3
4
1. 356
2. 485
3. 415
4. 662
5. 482
6. 701
7. 651
8. 146
Secret Number:

DARE TO DECODE

Skill: Telling Time

The times on the digital clocks are shown in code. Use the matching times on the clock faces to crack the code. The same code is used for all the clocks.

Code Key

2	5	7	1	6	0	9	8	4	3

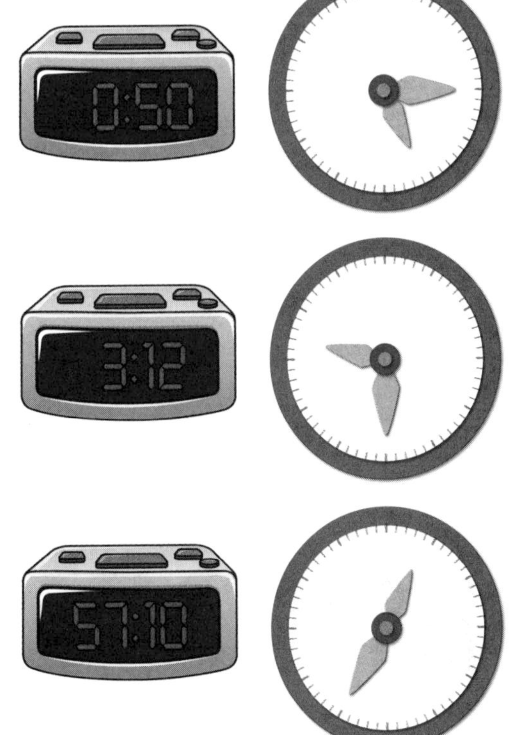

Ask 12 people which kind of movie they like best: movies about space, movies about animals, or movies about adventures. Keep track of the votes. Starting at the bottom of the graph, color in a rectangle above each picture to show each vote. Use the completed graph to answer the questions.

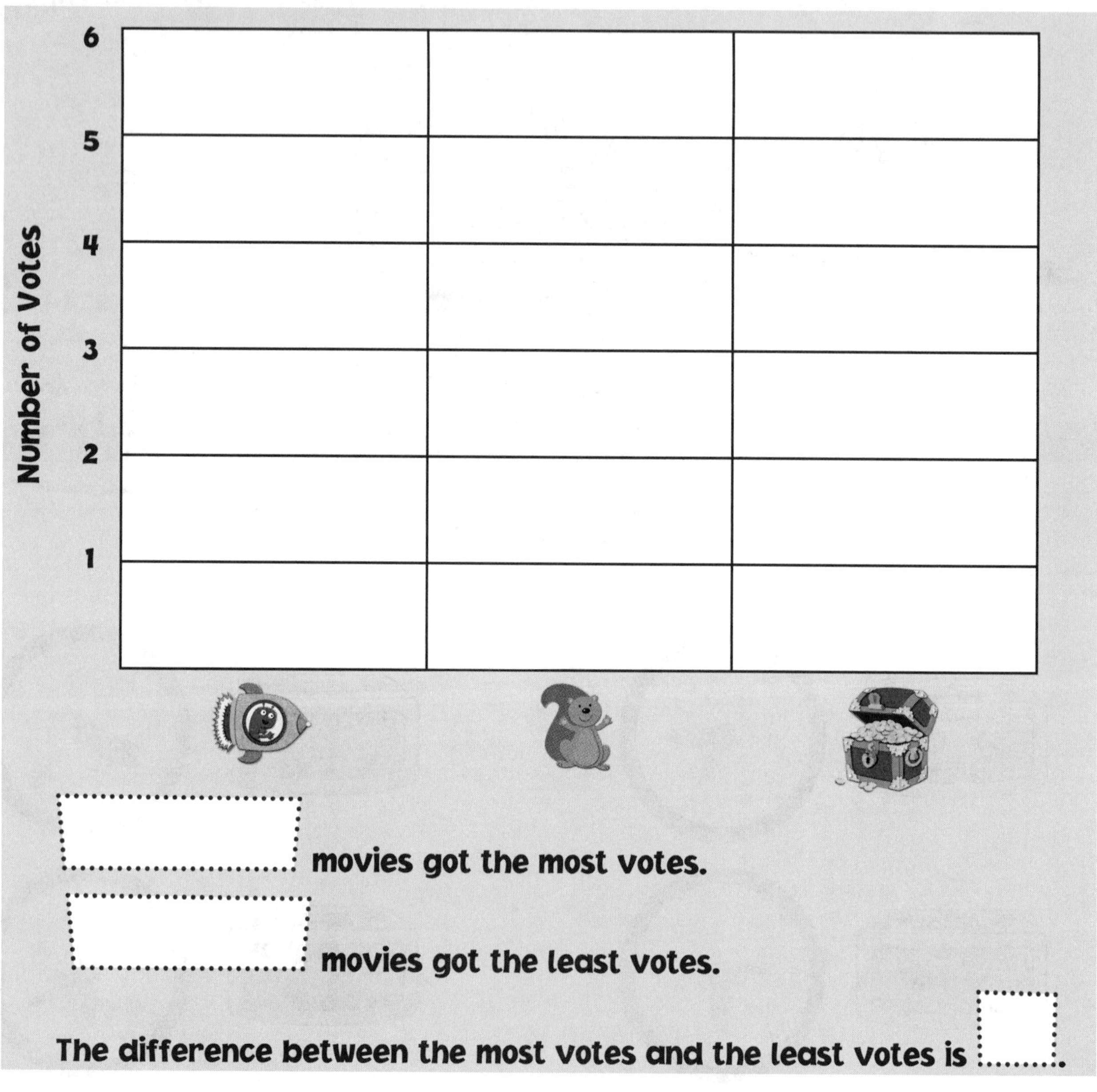

______ movies got the most votes.

______ movies got the least votes.

The difference between the most votes and the least votes is ______.

Picture Perfect!

IT FITS!

Skill: Using Arrays

Cut out the puzzle pieces and fit them together. When the puzzle is solved, each array of dots will be next to a matching equation.

LANGUAGE
ARTS

Skill: Adjectives

In Search Of

Circle the adjective in each phrase. Find it in the puzzle.

a sweet peach

the furry kitten

a sunny day

a full glass

a chilly rain

a safe place

the deep pool

a red pen

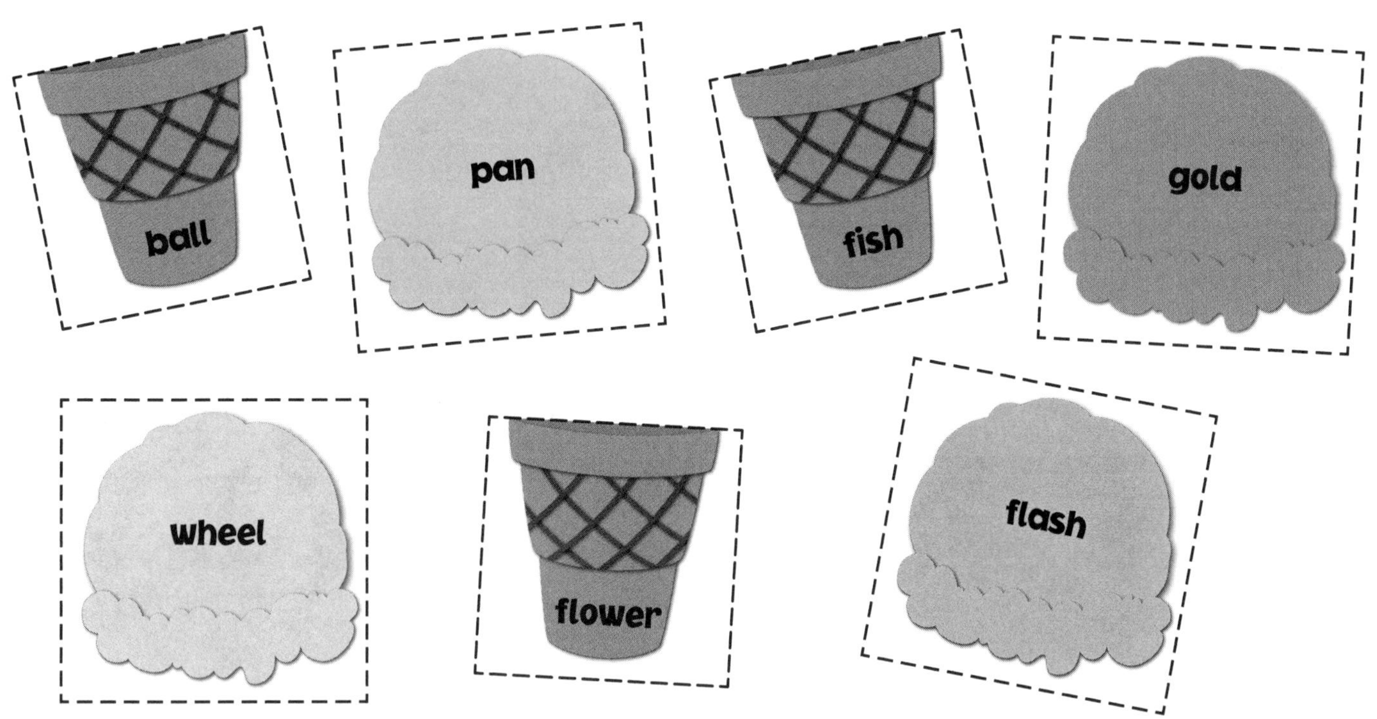

Skill: Compound Words

IN PIECES

Cut out the puzzle pieces. Match them to make ice cream cones that show compound words.

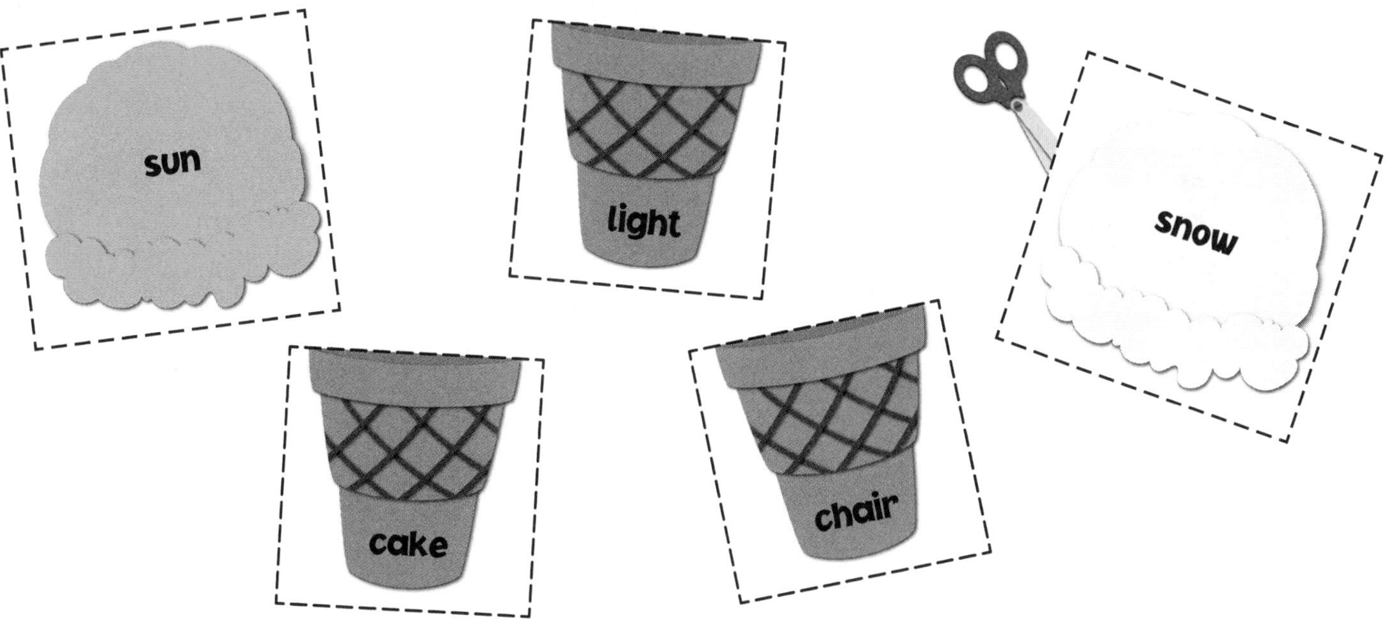

Sudoku for You

Skill: Irregular Plurals

Write letters in the boxes so that each row and column has the letters to spell the plural of "mouse." No letter should appear twice in the same row or column. Do not guess. Use logic!

	M		I
		E	
C			

MAZE CRAZE

Skill: Spelling

Each puzzle has a six-letter word hidden inside. Start at the square with the arrow. Move from letter to letter to spell the word. The clues will help you figure out what words you need to find.

I	L	S ←
C	O	P
C	E	R

T	S	P
→ H	A	E
O	R	S

D	O	M
W	E	L
B	R	F ↑

T	O ↓	R
S	A	M
E	G	N

Clues

- It can be a fruit or a color.
- These animals are used for work and racing.
- This is the most popular sport in the world.
- You might find this in a garden.

Across

3. send

5. begin

7. feel

8. buy

Down

1. make

2. mean

4. think

5. bleed

6. get

Skills: Prefixes, Suffixes, Word Roots

MIRROR

Write a word with the prefix "re-".	Write a word with the suffix "-er".	Write a word with the suffix "-ful".
Write a word with the suffix "-ing".	Write a word with the prefix "un-".	Write a word with the prefix "mis-".
Write a word with the prefix "dis-".	Write a word with the suffix "-less".	Write a word with the suffix "-est".

Hold this page up to a mirror to read the directions in each box. Write a word that fits the description.

MAZE CRAZE

Skill: Short and Long Vowel Sounds

Help the bat find the cave. Color each space that has a word with a short vowel sound. Then, write three short-vowel words and three long-vowel words on the lines. In each word, underline the letters that spell the vowel sound.

neck	fox	hang	goat	joke	cute
freeze	kite	lump	hail	read	sale
rake	clean	wink	might	crate	vote
true	moon	switch	draft	smell	stray
eight	sweep	hope	kind	flip	coop
grow	plain	gross	flew	back	lend

____

____

____

____

____

____

RIDDLE ME

Write a letter for each clue. Write the letters in order to spell a word that answers the riddle.

Skill: Spelling

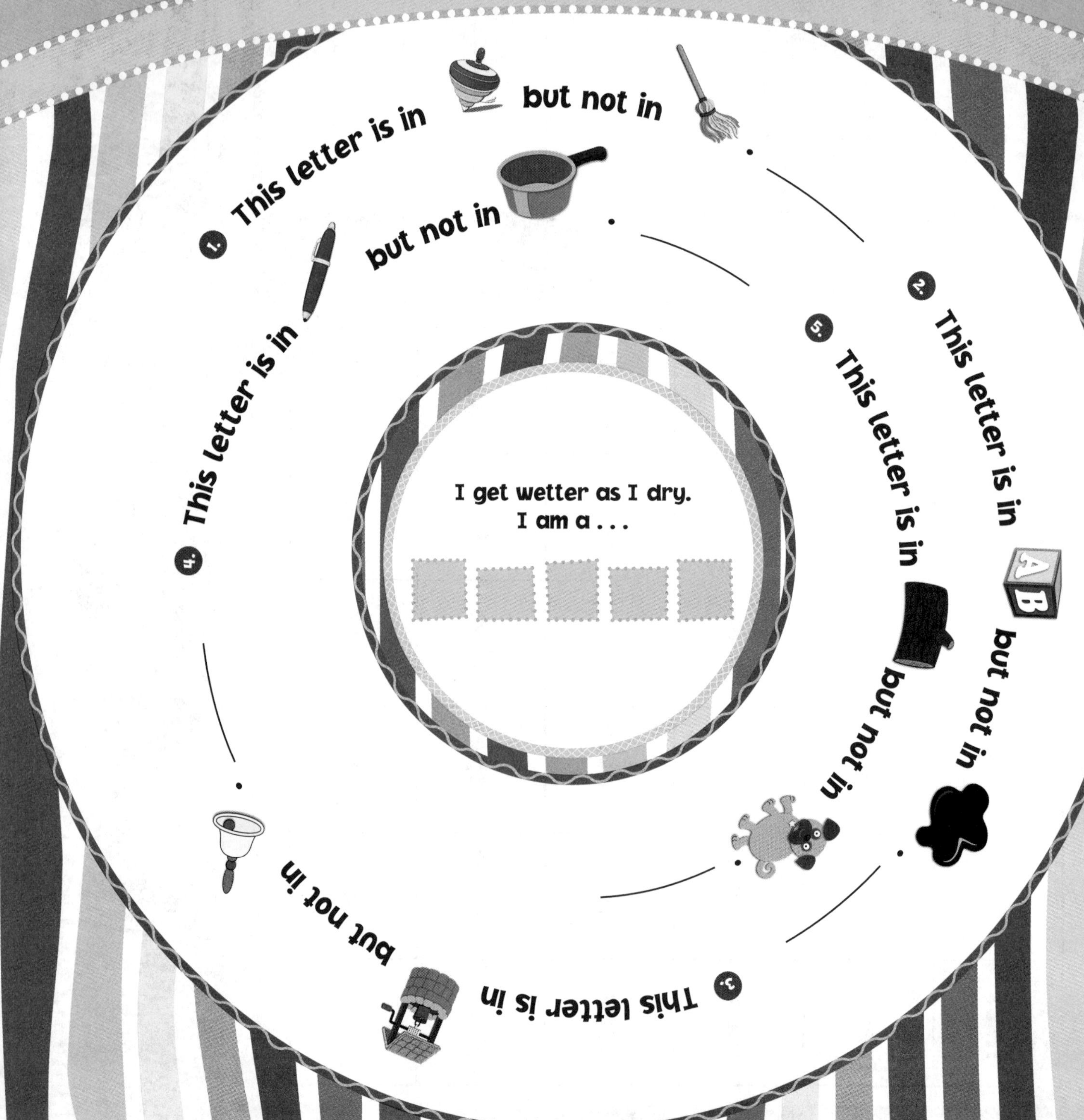

1. This letter is in but not in .
2. This letter is in but not in .
3. This letter is in but not in .
4. This letter is in but not in .
5. This letter is in but not in .
I get wetter as I dry.
I am a . . .

JUMBLED UP

Skill: Capitalization

Look at the jumbled name of each place on the map. Write the names correctly on the lines. Don't forget to capitalize the first letter of each word in the name of a specific place.

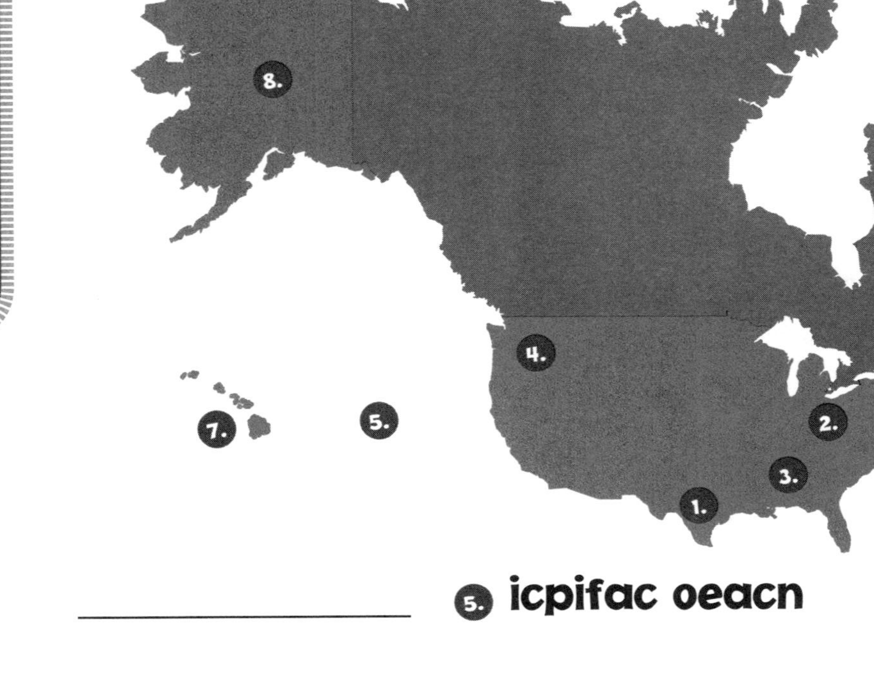

1. tsxea ______________
2. iooh ______________
3. ssippimiiss ______________
4. sawtghinon ______________
5. icpifac oeacn ______________
6. citalant econa ______________
7. wiiaha ______________
8. akalsa ______________

WORD MATH

Skill: Point of View

Use the letters and pictures to decode each sentence. Write it in the blank. Is the sentence in first-person point of view? Write "F" in the box. Is it in third-person point of view? Write "T" in the box.

1. l + − b 2 pl + − gr the + s.

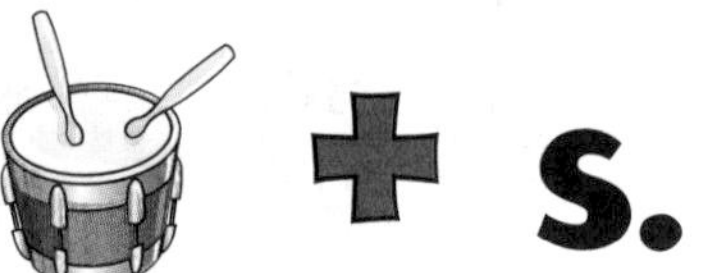

2. M + m + − f his fr + − b the p+ − sh.

3. H +  − c

d + 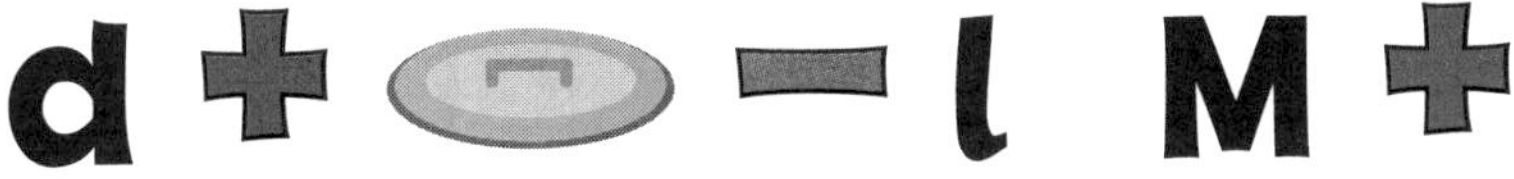 − l M +

 − b get 2  ?

4. 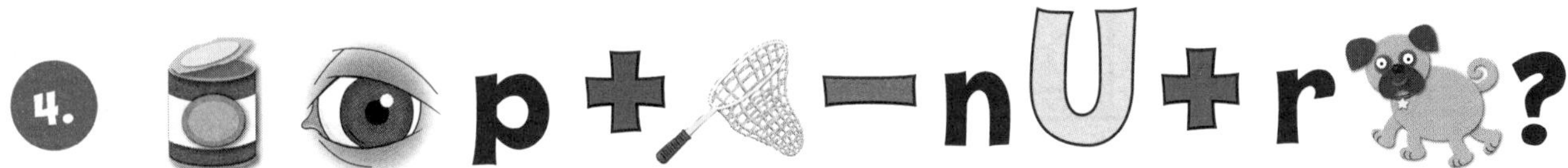 p + − n U + r ?

5. M + is a + tor.

ALPHA-CHALLENGE

Skills: Adjectives, Adverbs

Write an adjective and an adverb that begin with each letter shown. Some have been done for you.

	Adjective	Adverb
Letter: a		
Letter: r	red	
Letter: m		
Letter: t		
Letter: s		sadly
Letter: b		
Letter: d		
Letter: h	hot	
Letter: p		
Letter: q		quickly

Skill: Simple Sentences

Sentence Scramble

A simple sentence contains a subject and a verb. Draw a line to connect the words and form a simple sentence. Write it on the lines. Underline the noun that the sentence is about. Underline the verb.

Skills: Prefixes, Suffixes, Word Roots

Read the prefix or suffix on each cloud. On the raindrops, write four words that contain that prefix or suffix.

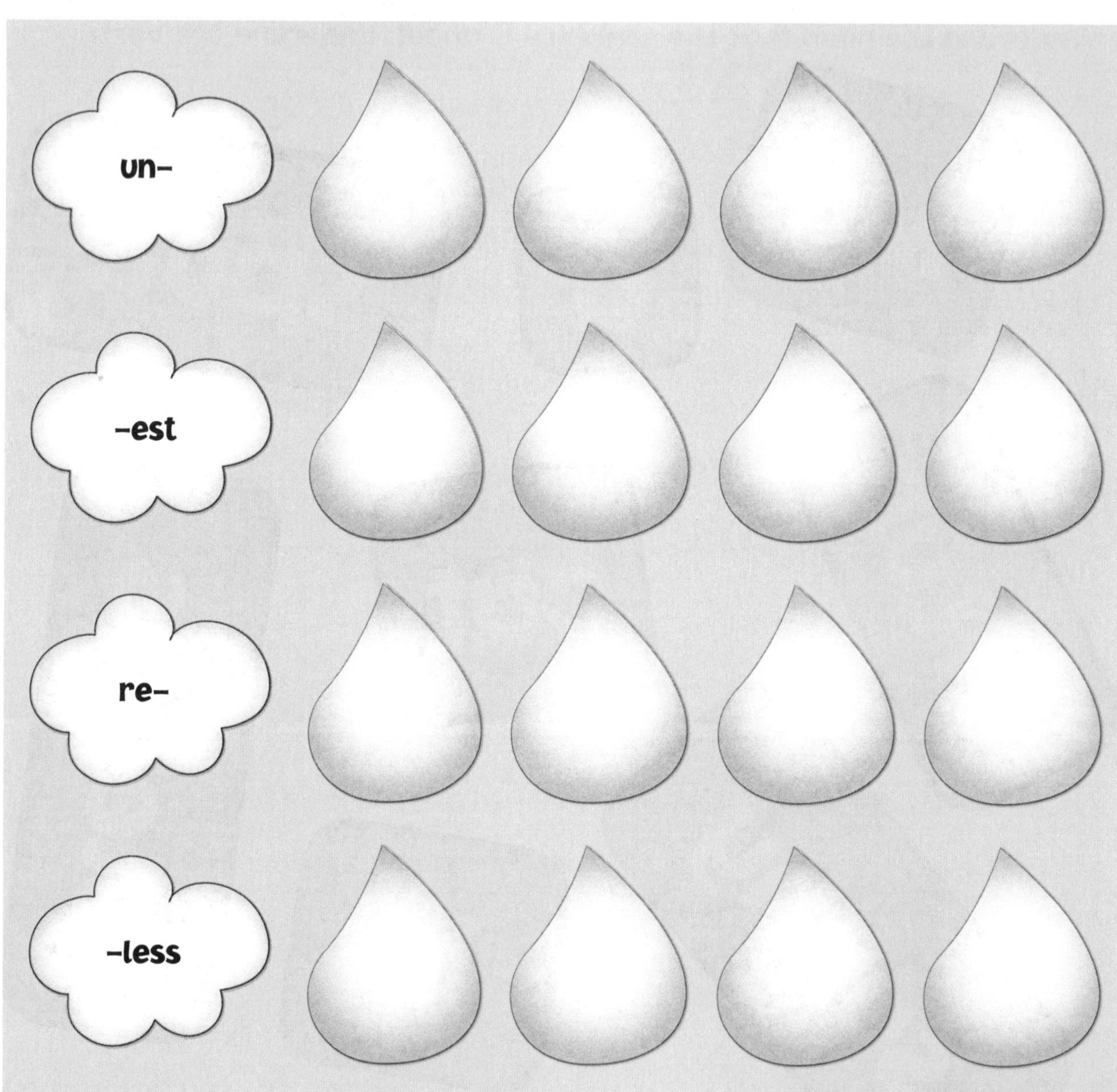

Picture This!

CODE BREAKER

Skill: Short and Long Vowel Sounds

Use the code to find the vowels that complete the words. Write the words in the blanks. Circle the words with long vowel sounds.

1. c  k  

2. g  m 

3. tw  tch 

4. sn  w

5. l   p 

6. sh   p

7. cl  p 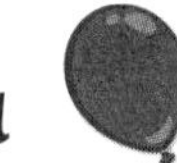

8. dr   n 

Code Key

a	e	i	o	u

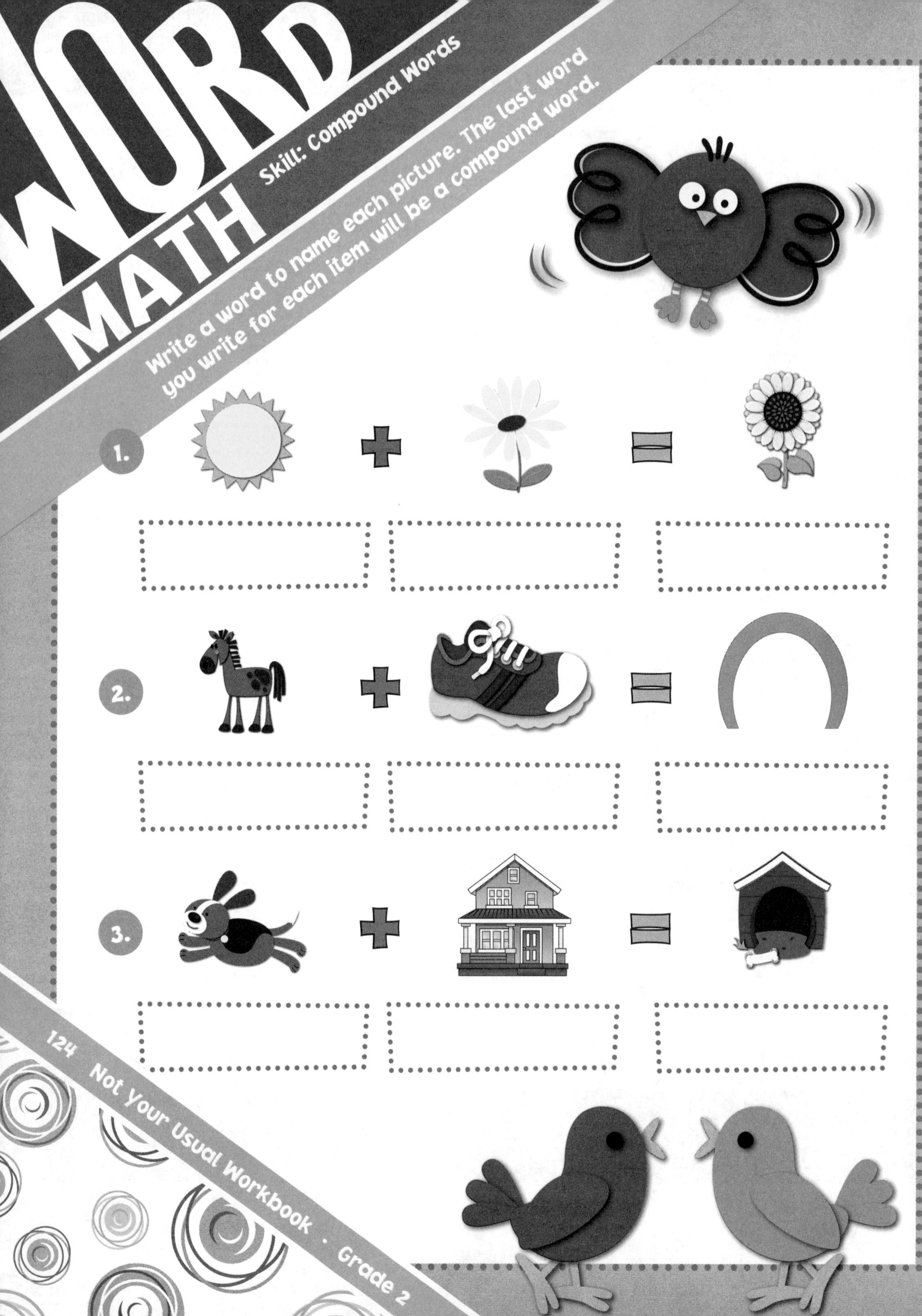
WORD MATH
Skill: Compound Words
Write a word to name each picture. The last word you write for each item will be a compound word.
1.
2.
3.

4.
5.
6.
7.

Sudoku for You

U			
			B
	L		
		E	

Skill: Vocabulary

Write letters in the boxes so that each row and column has the letters to spell a word that means "feeling very sad." No letter should appear twice in the same row or column. Do not guess. Use logic!

In Search Of

Skill: Contractions

Find and circle the pair of words that forms each contraction. For example, for the contraction "they're," look for "they are" in the puzzle.

can't

won't

he'll

it's

I'm

aren't

you've

don't

W

P X L

J R R C X

A D J C X G W

N Y V H A V V H R

A P P Y J L R U A U H

M U P U N L O P Y U B A A

C I W W T S E Z C E W Q D H L

A L M X F I O R A Z A P F S N I T

I W K P Q T J L N G P Z K T E V N N I

A F X E M I C C N L E I H K O G I G H T R

W Q Z Q H O H M O L J N R B D N J T P L C K N

E D L T W I P V O A E O M K P

H O V F G O F O D K T T D D B O L

S F Z T C V D Z Q K B K N K K X M I P

J C S S N F G R W A W P J L G E K I C S I

D P W L K P E U X H U U N R N S F G L K E E H

H A F G O F O D G N L F N P A

I B Y L L I W E H N X L B Y W Z S

R C N U U J U A K C H R F E O U L S E

U Y P K Q I A M S A W G W T R U K Y C X V

K J S N M C B R X Y P O M O Y Z H F U L A X L

F X E J T K O X A O Q K A F Z

Q Z H O P E F U L I P D Y V M D A

G T L P Z W H X X D M A D S E O S R T

L D F S E R G F T P M J J A O Z E R T Q E

L K X C V B N M A D Q U N I O K U P D F G H P

JUMBLED UP

Skill: Collective Nouns

A collective noun names a group, like a PRIDE of lions or a SCHOOL of fish. Unscramble the jumbled letters to write a collective noun that matches each picture.

1. a MARWS ______ of

2. a CHBNU ______ of

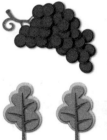

3. a EROFST ______ of

4. a PKCA ______ of

5. a OLCFK ______ of

6. a ERLTTI ______ of

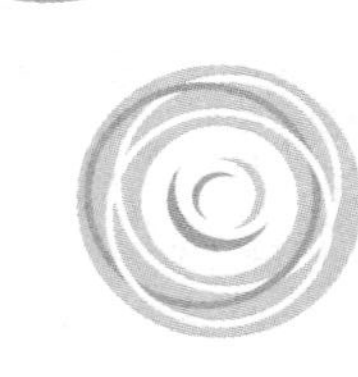

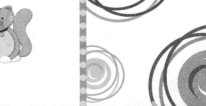

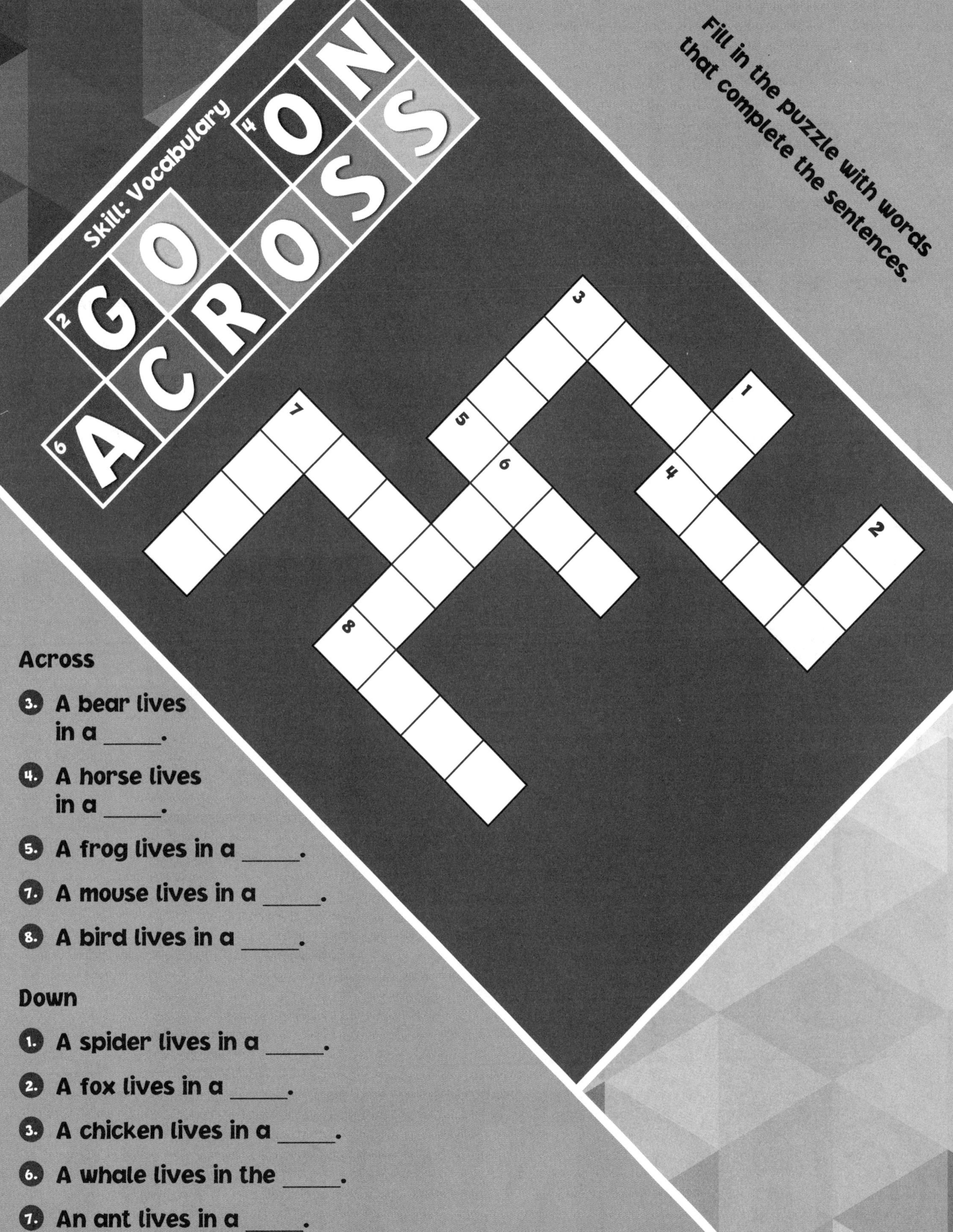

Across

3. A bear lives in a _____.
4. A horse lives in a _____.
5. A frog lives in a _____.
7. A mouse lives in a _____.
8. A bird lives in a _____.

Down

1. A spider lives in a _____.
2. A fox lives in a _____.
3. A chicken lives in a _____.
6. A whale lives in the _____.
7. An ant lives in a _____.

PREST-O CHANGE-O!

Skill: Vocabulary

How can you change a dog into a cat? One letter at a time! Write a word to match each clue. Each word should be the same as the word above it except for one changed letter.

what you do to make a hole

like a mountain

it can hold something

it hits a ball

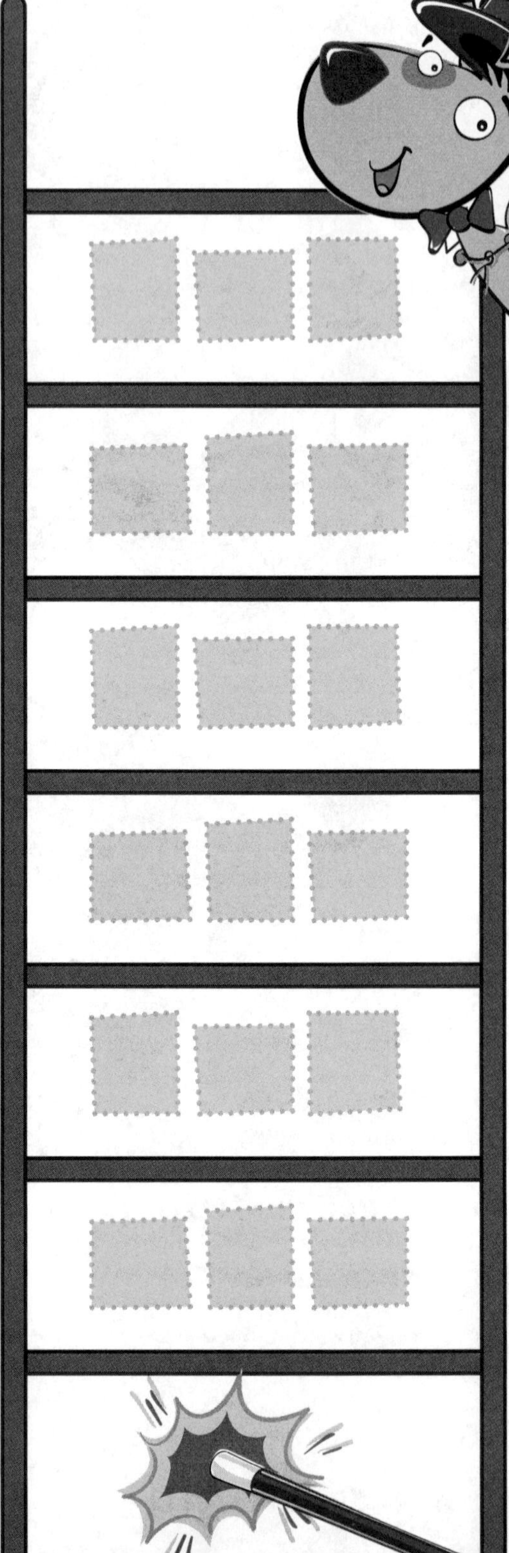

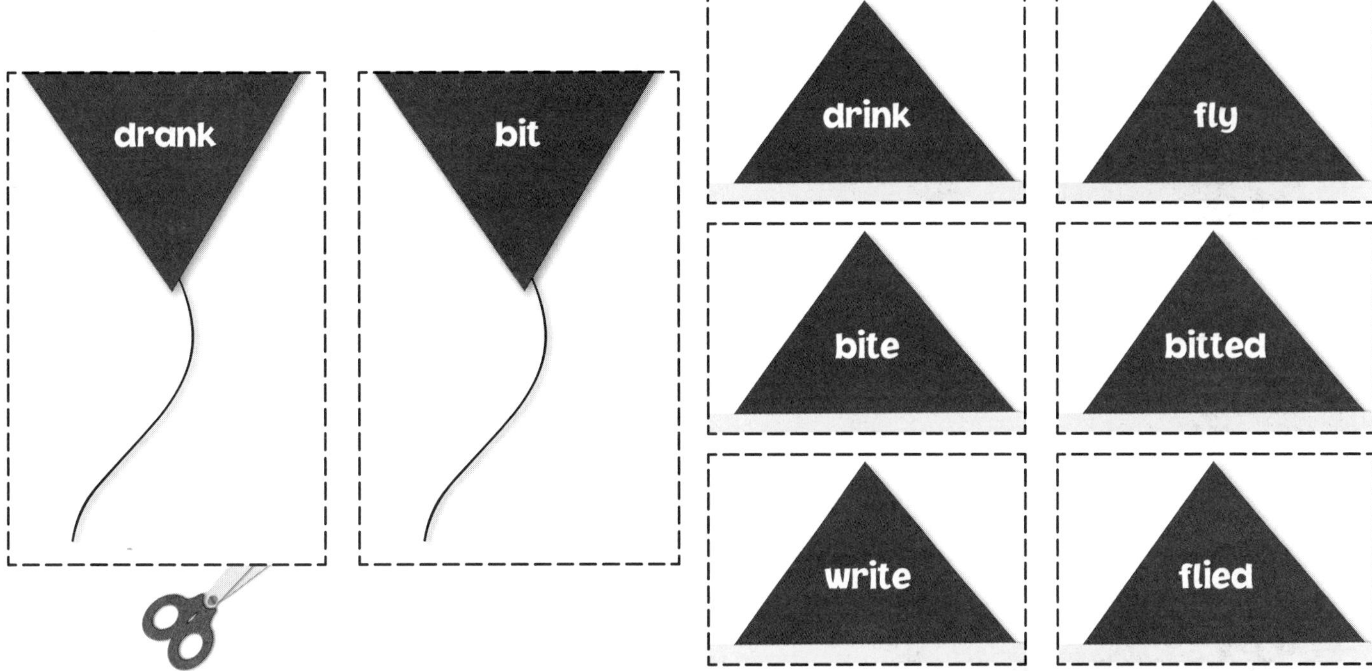

Skill: Irregular Verbs

IN PIECES

Cut out the puzzle pieces. Put them together to match the present-tense verbs with past-tense verbs. You will not use all the pieces.

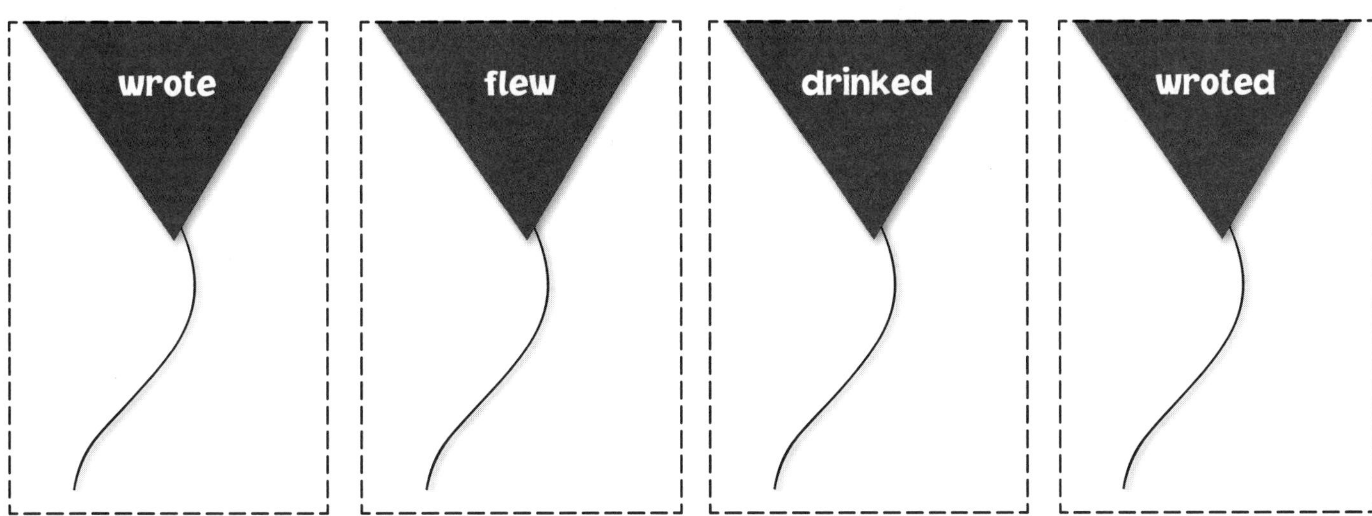

MAZE CRAZE

Skills: Short and Long Vowel Sounds, Spelling

Move from letter to letter to find words hidden in the puzzle. How many words with long vowel sounds can you find? Write them on the lines.

T	A	N	S
R	K	E	P
O	E	I	O
S	M	L	H

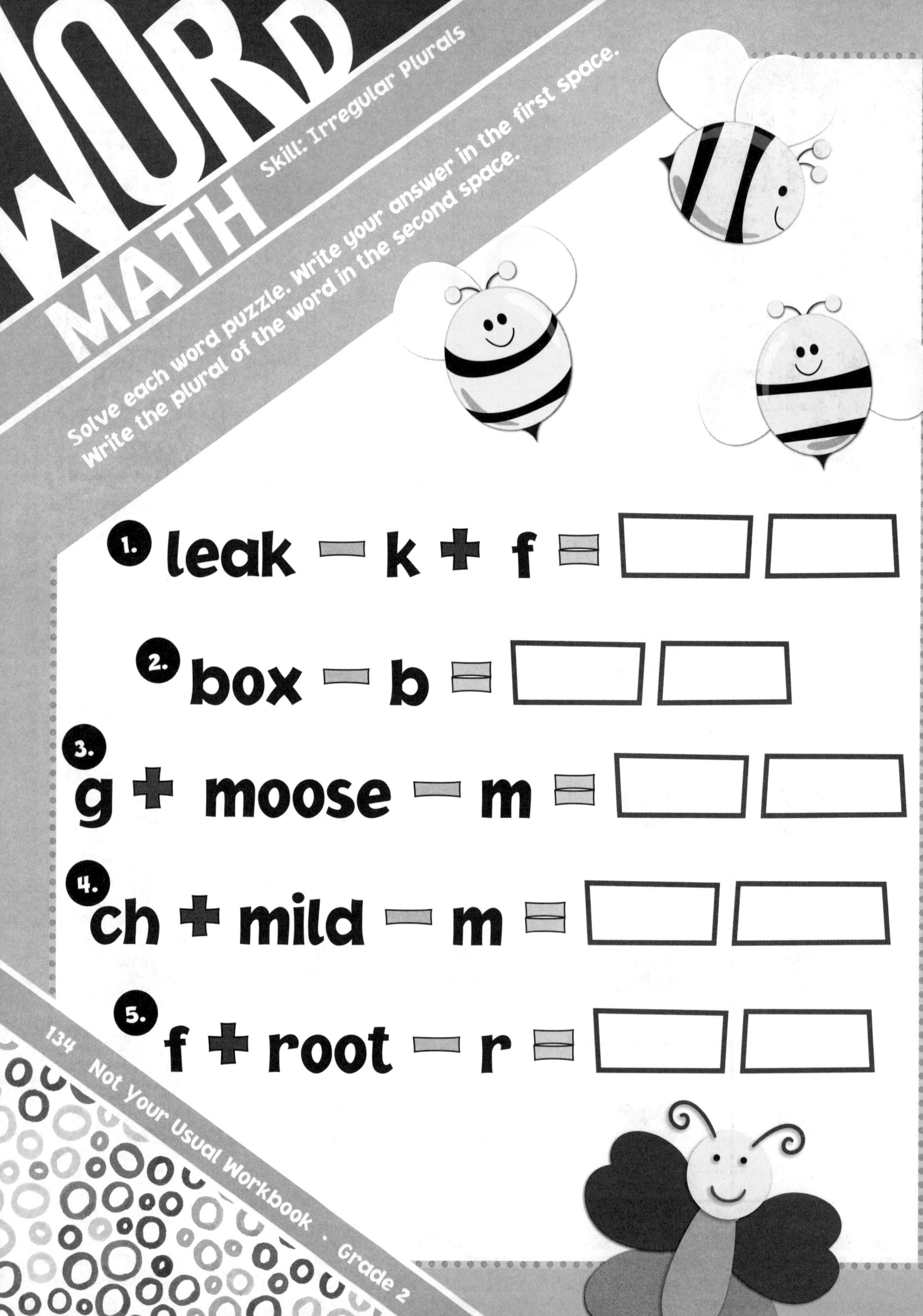

WORD MATH

Skill: Irregular Plurals

Solve each word puzzle. Write your answer in the first space. Write the plural of the word in the second space.

1. leak − k + f = ☐ ☐

2. box − b = ☐ ☐

3. g + moose − m = ☐ ☐

4. ch + mild − m = ☐ ☐

5. f + root − r = ☐ ☐

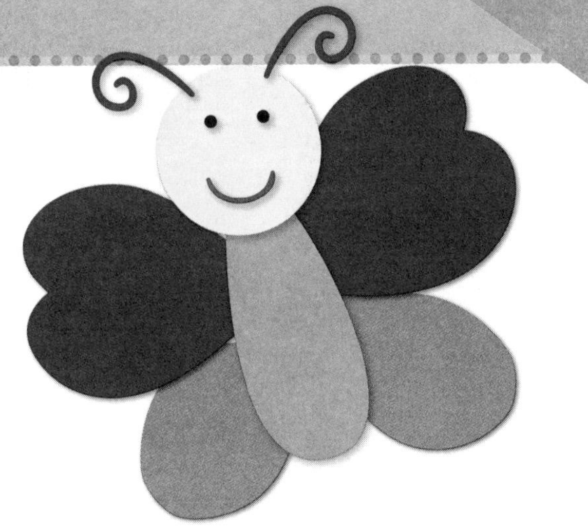

6. m + house − h = [ ] [ ]

7. sh + sleep − sl = [ ] [ ]

8. toots − s + h = [ ] [ ]

9. mat − t + n = [ ] [ ]

10. kn + life − l = [ ] [ ]

JUMBLED UP

Skill: Spelling

How many words can you make from the letters in "elephant"? Write them on the lines.

ELEPHANT

Write a sentence using only three-letter words.

Write a sentence that is five words long.

Write a sentence that contains two color words.

Use the letters in your name to make a word. Use that word in a sentence.

How good are you at following directions? Write the sentences described above to find out!

Skill: Writing Sentences

QUIZ WHIZ

CODE BREAKER

Skill: Capitalization

Decode the words that name special days of the year. Begin important words in each name with a capital letter.

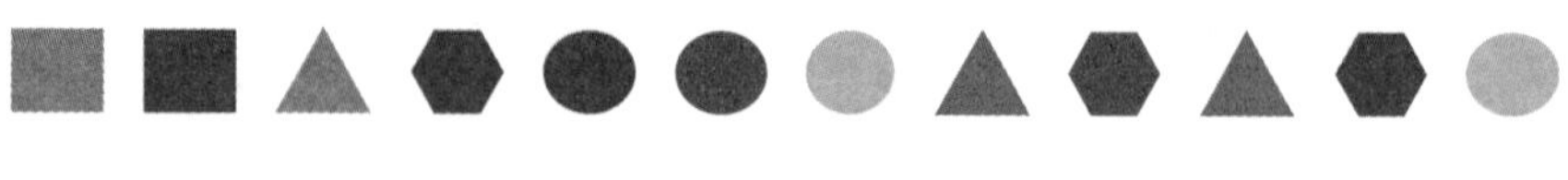

Code Key

A	B	C	D	E	F	G	H	I	J	K	L	M

N	O	P	Q	R	S	T	U	V	W	X	Y	Z

Skill: Possessives

The world is a colorful place! Answer each question with a phrase that includes a possessive noun ending with an apostrophe (') and s. For example, you might write "the girl's hair."

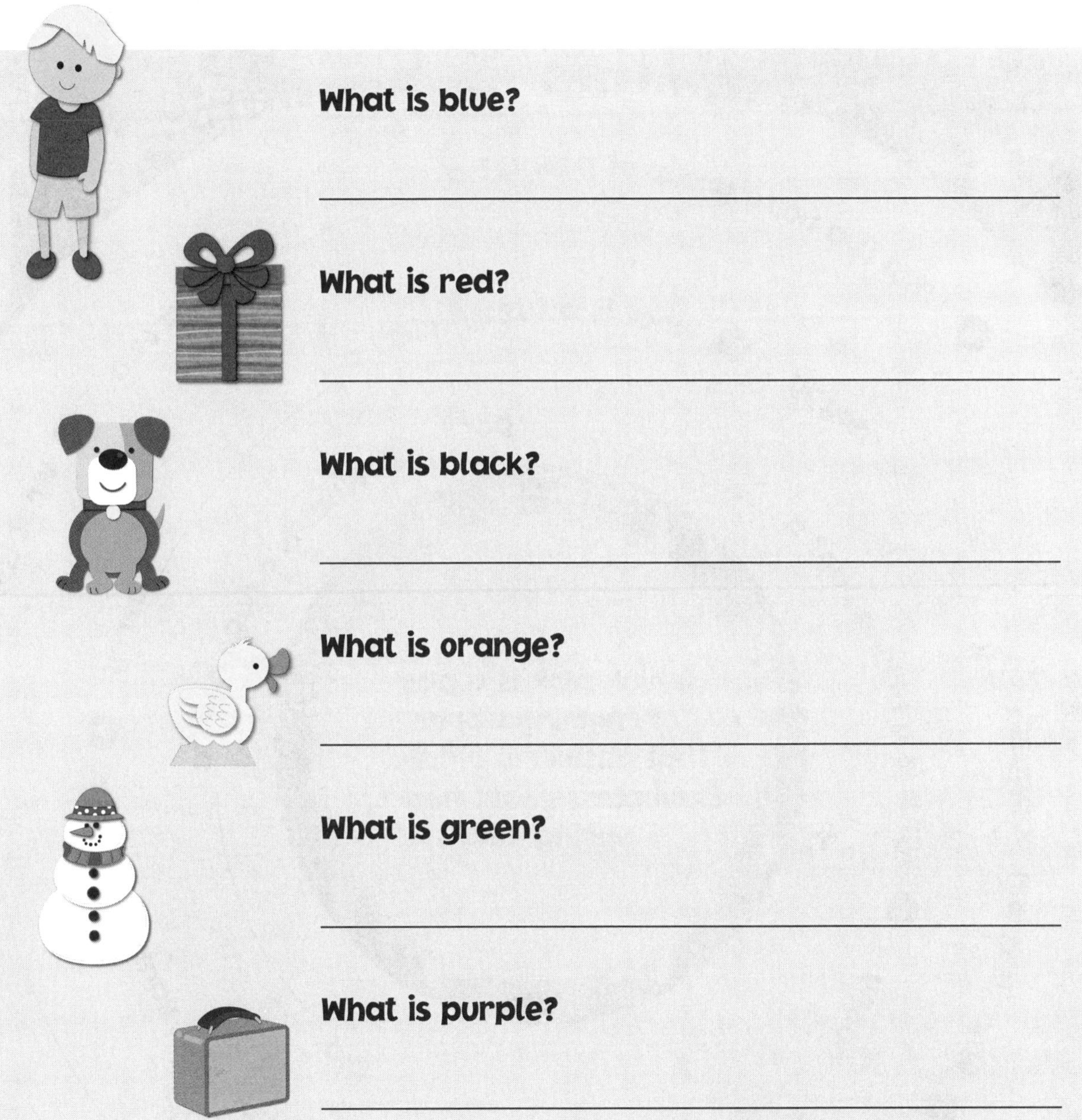

What is blue?
What is red?
What is black?
What is orange?
What is green?
What is purple?

Picture This!

RIDDLE ME

Write the adjective that completes each hink pink.

Skills: Adjectives, Context Clues

A hink pink is a pair of rhyming words that answer a riddle. Examples: smart heart, spring king

1. What is a noisy group of people? a ______________ crowd
2. What is a happy father? a ______________ dad
3. What is a fake horse? a ______________ pony
4. What is a wet puppy? a ______________ doggy
5. What is a fuzzy fruit? a ______________ berry
6. What is a rabbit that has a sense of humor? a ______________ bunny
7. What is a boiling pan? a ______________ pot
8. What is a huge hog? a ______________ pig

MIRROR

Skill: Irregular Verbs

1. say — said
2. know — knowed
3. tell — told
4. bring — brung
5. feel — feeled
6. give — gave
7. grow — grew
8. choose — choosed

Read each present-tense verb. Then, hold the page up to a mirror to read the word beside it. If the word in the mirror is the correct past-tense form, draw a smiley face (☺) in the circle. If it is not the correct past-tense form, draw a sad face (☹).

Skill: Compound Sentences

Sentence Scramble

What a mess! These sentences got scrambled. Draw lines to match the sentence parts and make four compound sentences.

Did you pick the tomatoes,

and I love lettuce.

I love tomatoes,

or are they still green?

but it didn't eat the spinach.

but they have not come up.

The bunny ate the carrots,

Mom planted seeds,

Sudoku for You

Skill: Irregular Plurals

Write letters in the boxes so that each row and column has the letters to spell the plural of "ox." No letter should appear twice in the same row or column. Do not guess. Use logic!

	E		
X			O
		N	

ALPHA-CHALLENGE

Skill: Spelling

Look at the scene. How many words can you think of to describe it? Try to write one word that begins with each letter of the alphabet. Read each word you wrote. Is it spelled correctly?

A ______________ J ______________ S ______________

B ______________ K ______________ T ______________

C ______________ L ______________ U ______________

D ______________ M ______________ V ______________

E ______________ N ______________ W ______________

F ______________ O ______________ X ______________

G ______________ P ______________ Y ______________

H ______________ Q ______________ Z ______________

I ______________ R ______________

PREST-O CHANGE-O!

Skill: Compound Words

Name each picture by writing a compound word. Write each half of the word in a box. One half of each compound word you write will be used in the next compound word.

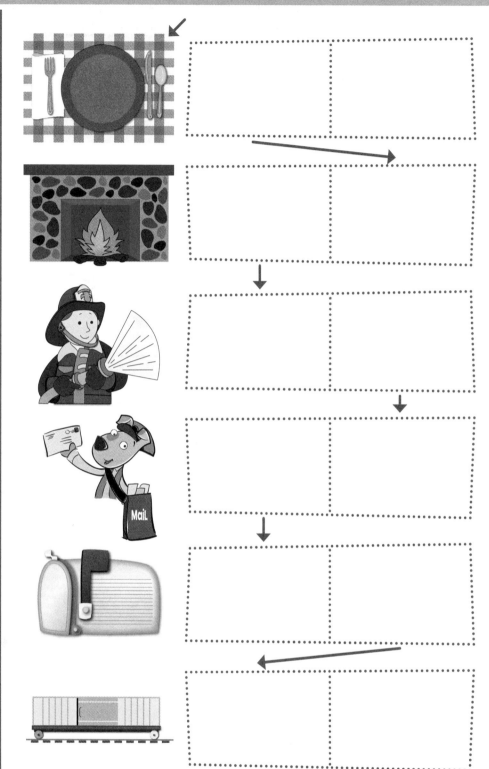

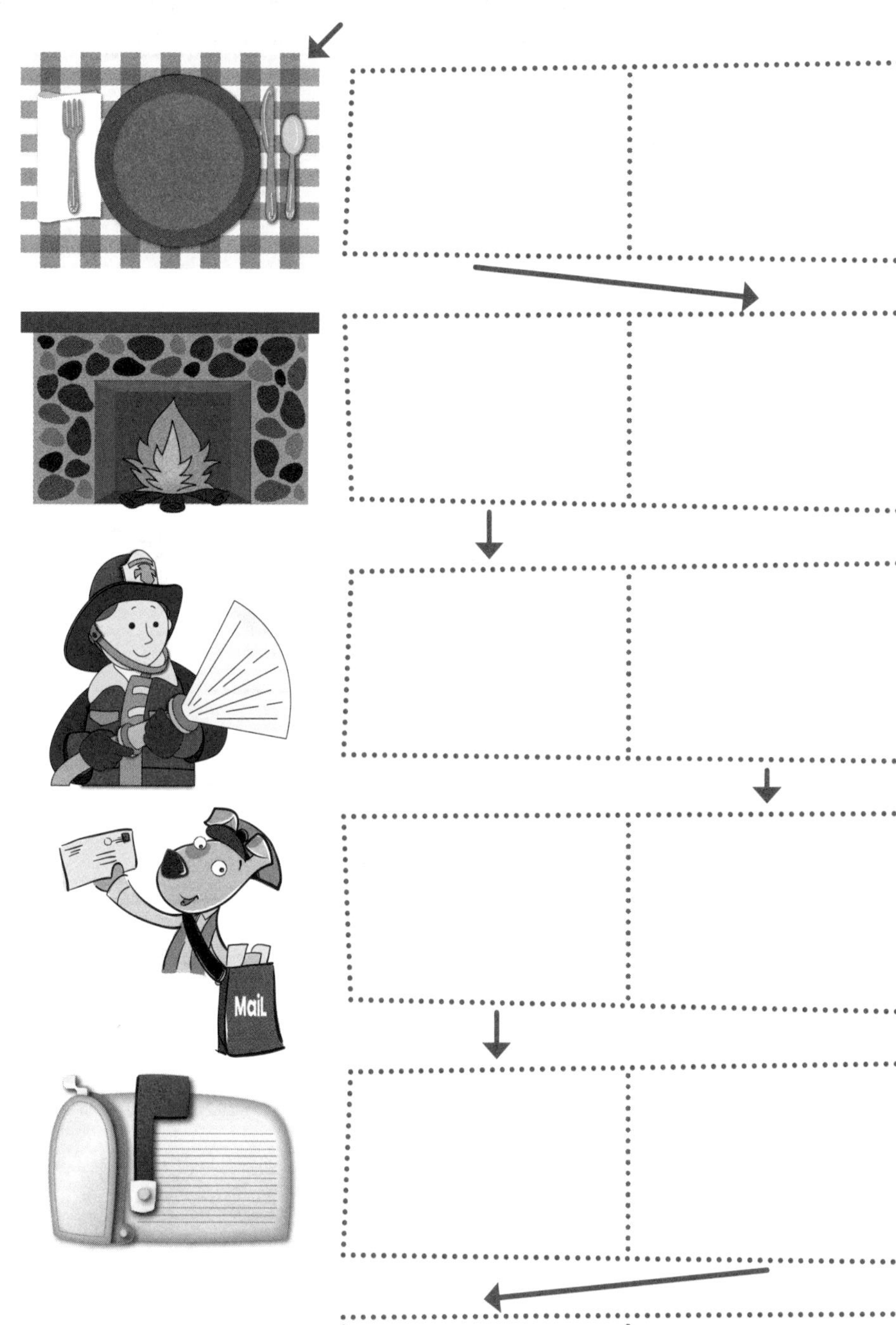

Choose an animal from the word box. Write five sentences that give clues about the animal. Read your clues to a friend. Can he or she guess the animal?

1. ______________________________

2. ______________________________

3. ______________________________

4. ______________________________

5. ______________________________

Word Box

polar bear	kangaroo
elephant	penguin
dolphin	turtle

Skill: Writing Sentences

QUIZ WHIZ

In Search Of

A reflexive pronoun refers back to the subject of the sentence. It often includes "self." Circle each reflexive pronoun. Find it in the puzzle.

1. I dropped the cup myself.
2. Ellen was late herself.
3. Let's give ourselves a pat on the back!
4. You said yourself that you were sorry.
5. They were excited themselves.
6. The night itself was hot and humid.

Skill: Reflexive Pronouns

B G H G Y E A V X N H V H R A V C O K L
T B U F P M H Y A P J R U H L U Q A Z D
G A E M U M M N U P L P B A O Y A U S S
A L E P B Z F T Z L O R Y J J K X F M R
D M U S L S W H O D U Y U H H S K L I C
P Q E X X C E E J Z R B M T E I H E L T
S A C A S L Q M I L S O U V R Q N S I T
R I I W Y K V S F Y E C F Y S K V Y N N
Q Z H I O E J E U J L B N A E S I M G A
Q J D Q U H J L N F V R I Y L D T N P L
T A S Z R E T V A N E T Y C F P K K P Y
V J C F S O U E Z R S P R A S N B Z O D
D P W W E G Q S O E K L G S J B G R H F
L W I Q L H B L L R G O E I F U L X K W
K E G L F H B D E F M M T C L T Y O A E
H G P I J B Y K T H L S R Y O H W Y Z S
H P R C U N U A U J E H E E C R U F L S
K J S N X M C Y B L P M Z J O O F Y U L
J G L P T F X K F J O A K M X O F Q Z M
C D W Q E Z H F O P U I Y D L P M D D A

Skills: Prefixes, Suffixes, Word Roots

Write each word on the tree that shows its prefix or suffix.

unfair
cheerful
resell
reuse
unwise
useful
joyful
refill
uneven

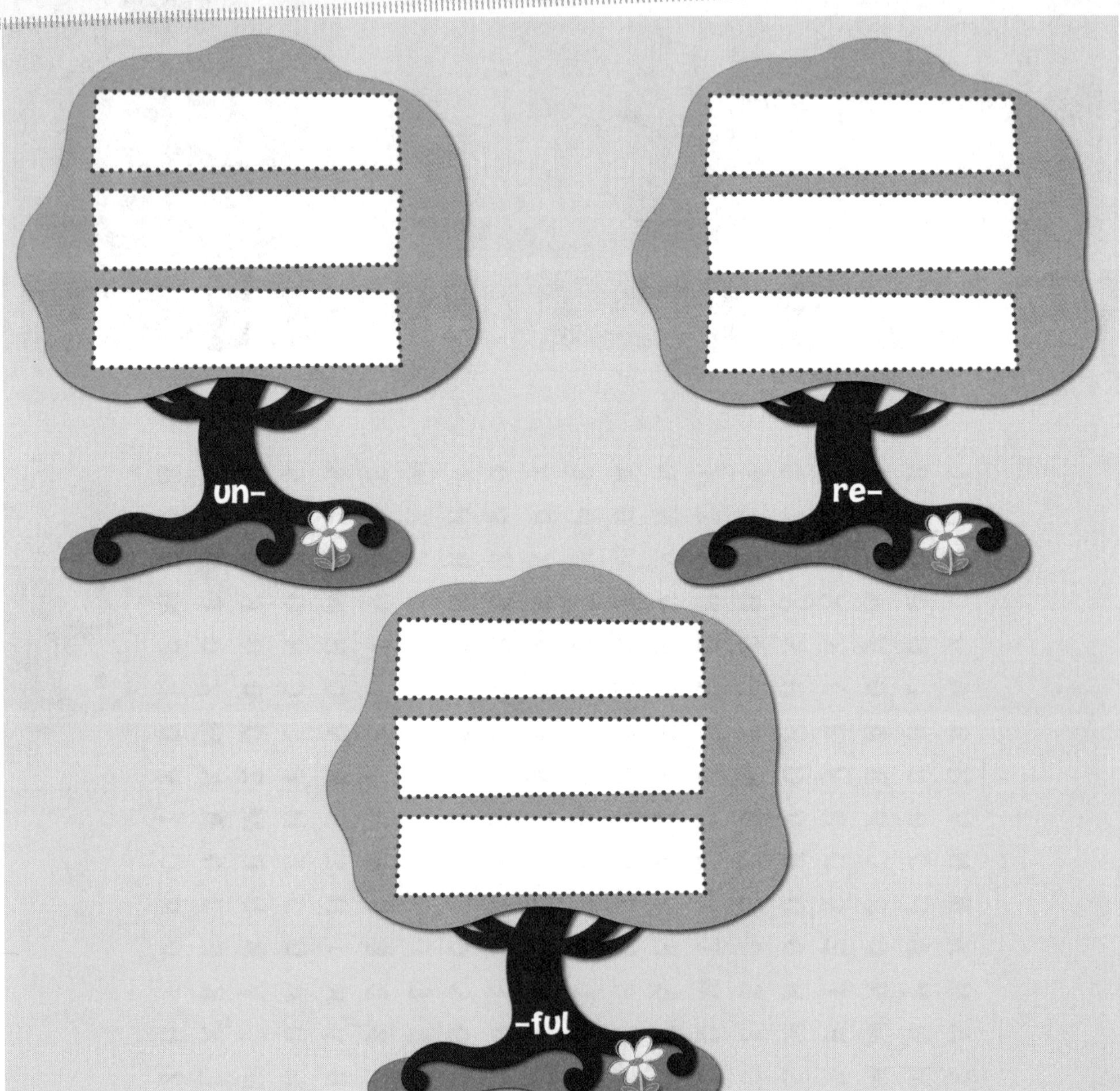

Picture This!

RIDDLE ME

Write a letter for each clue. Write the letters in order to spell the name of a holiday. Begin each important word in the name of a holiday with a capital letter.

Skills: Capitalization, Spelling

1. This letter is found in "hill," "hat," "shed," and "hug." ____
2. This letter is the first letter of the alphabet. ____
3. This letter is the last letter in ____.
4. This letter is the same as the one before it. ____
5. This letter spells both a short and a long vowel sound in ____.
6. This letter looks like an upside-down "m." ____
7. This letter spells the long vowel sound in ____.
8. This letter is the same as the one before it. ____
9. This letter comes at the end of ____.

Don't be spooked! Write the name of the mystery holiday.

JUMBLED UP

Skills: Short and Long Vowel Sounds, Spelling

Use the letters and letter pairs in the chicken to spell words. Each word should have a "long a" sound. Use each letter or letter pair only once. Write the words on the eggs.

d ai tr e n ay

a k ai tr m n a

d e ay a c

e pl sh n

MAZE CRAZE

Skill: Adverbs

Help the alien find its spaceship. Follow the adverbs through the maze. Write a sentence on the lines that includes one of the adverbs you found.

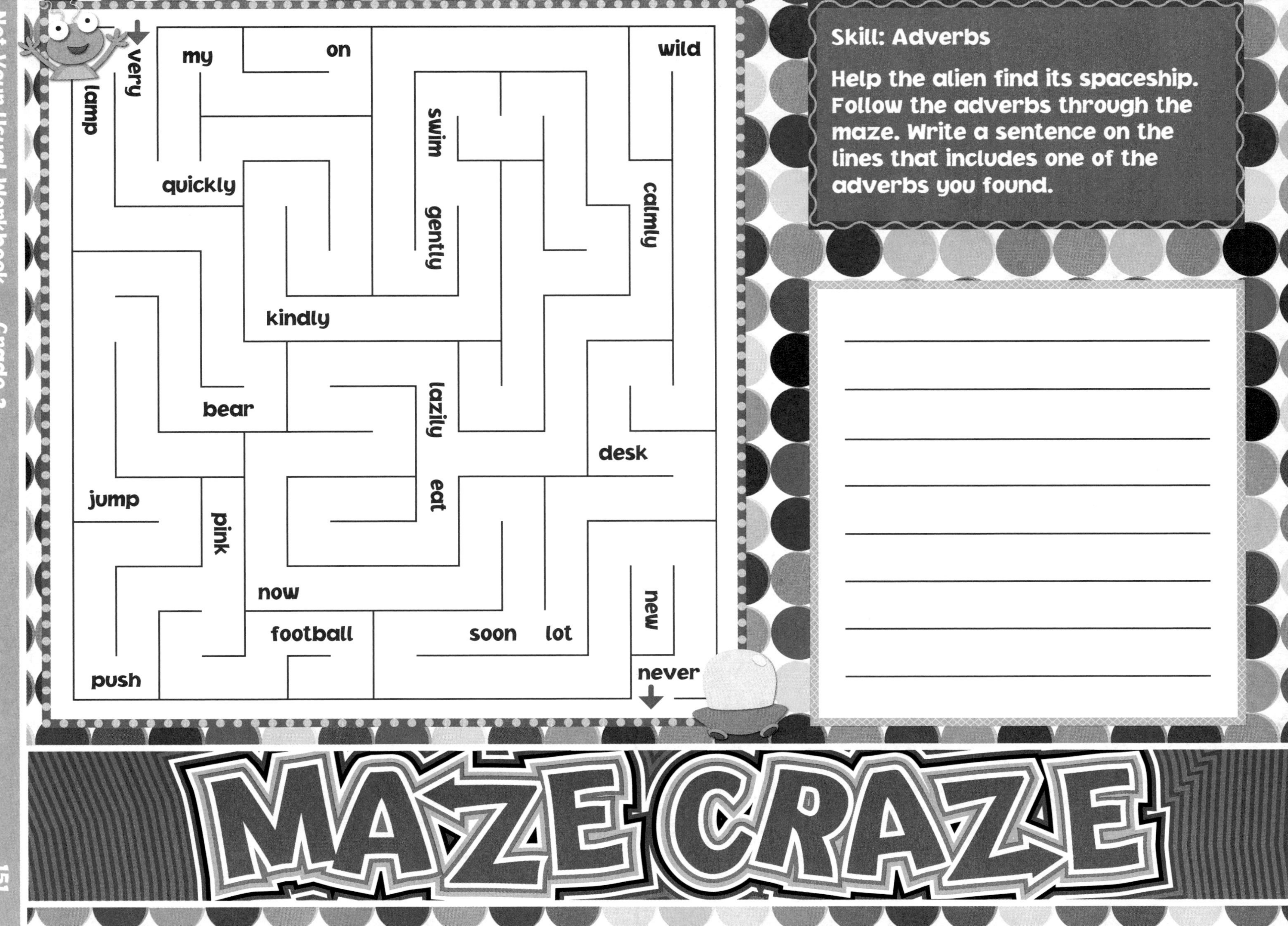

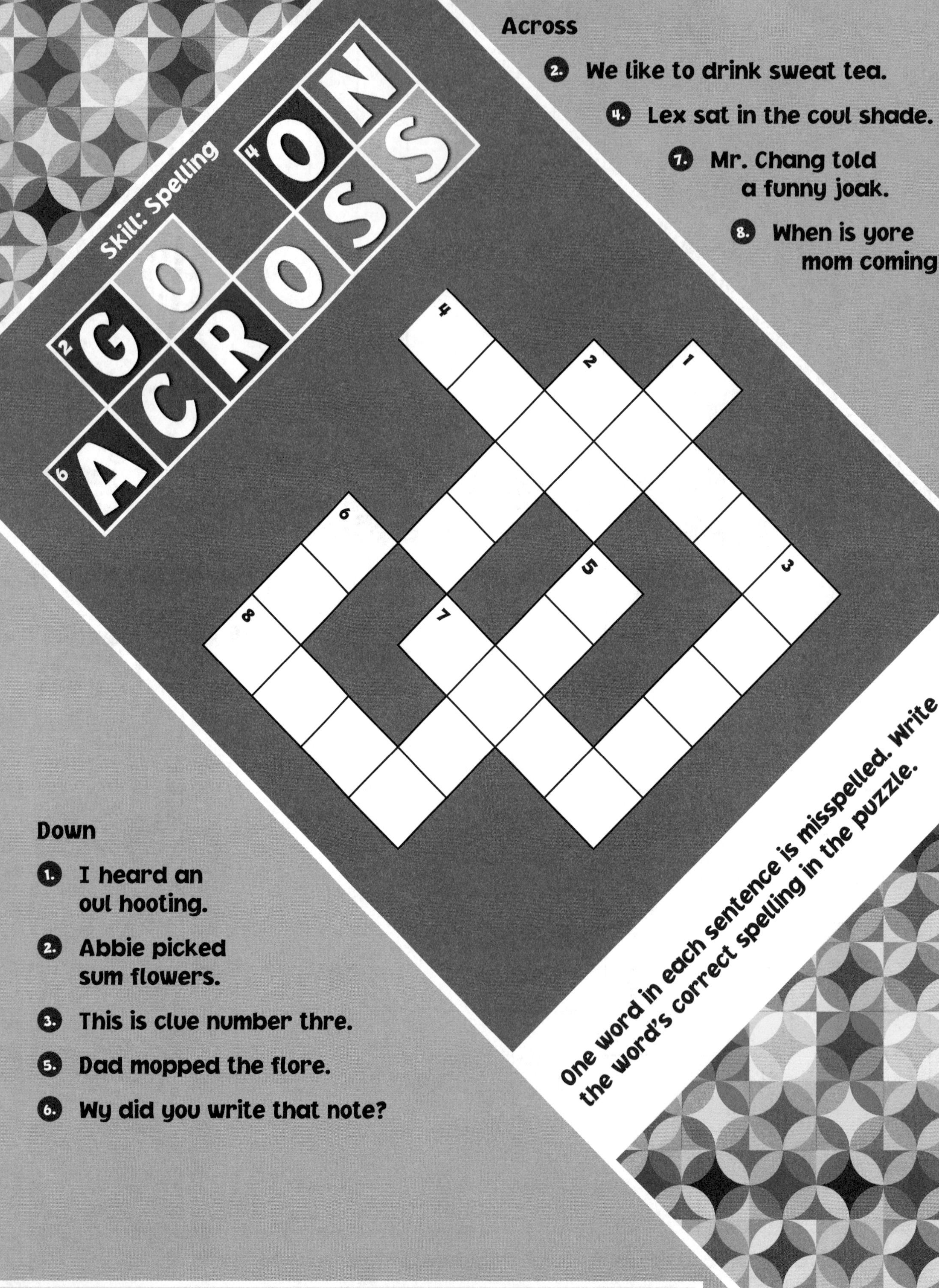

Across

2. We like to drink sweat tea.

4. Lex sat in the coul shade.

7. Mr. Chang told a funny joak.

8. When is yore mom coming?

Down

1. I heard an oul hooting.

2. Abbie picked sum flowers.

3. This is clue number thre.

5. Dad mopped the flore.

6. Wy did you write that note?

One word in each sentence is misspelled. Write the word's correct spelling in the puzzle.

MIRROR

Skill: Capitalization

1. grand canyon
2. omaha, nebraska
3. amazon river
4. blue ridge mountains
5. great salt lake
6. swiss alps
7. death valley
8. mississippi river

Hold the page up to a mirror to read the names of specific places. Write them on the lines. Use a capital letter to begin each word.

Skill: Contractions

Read the word on each baseball. On the baseball bats, write contractions made from the word. Some are done for you.

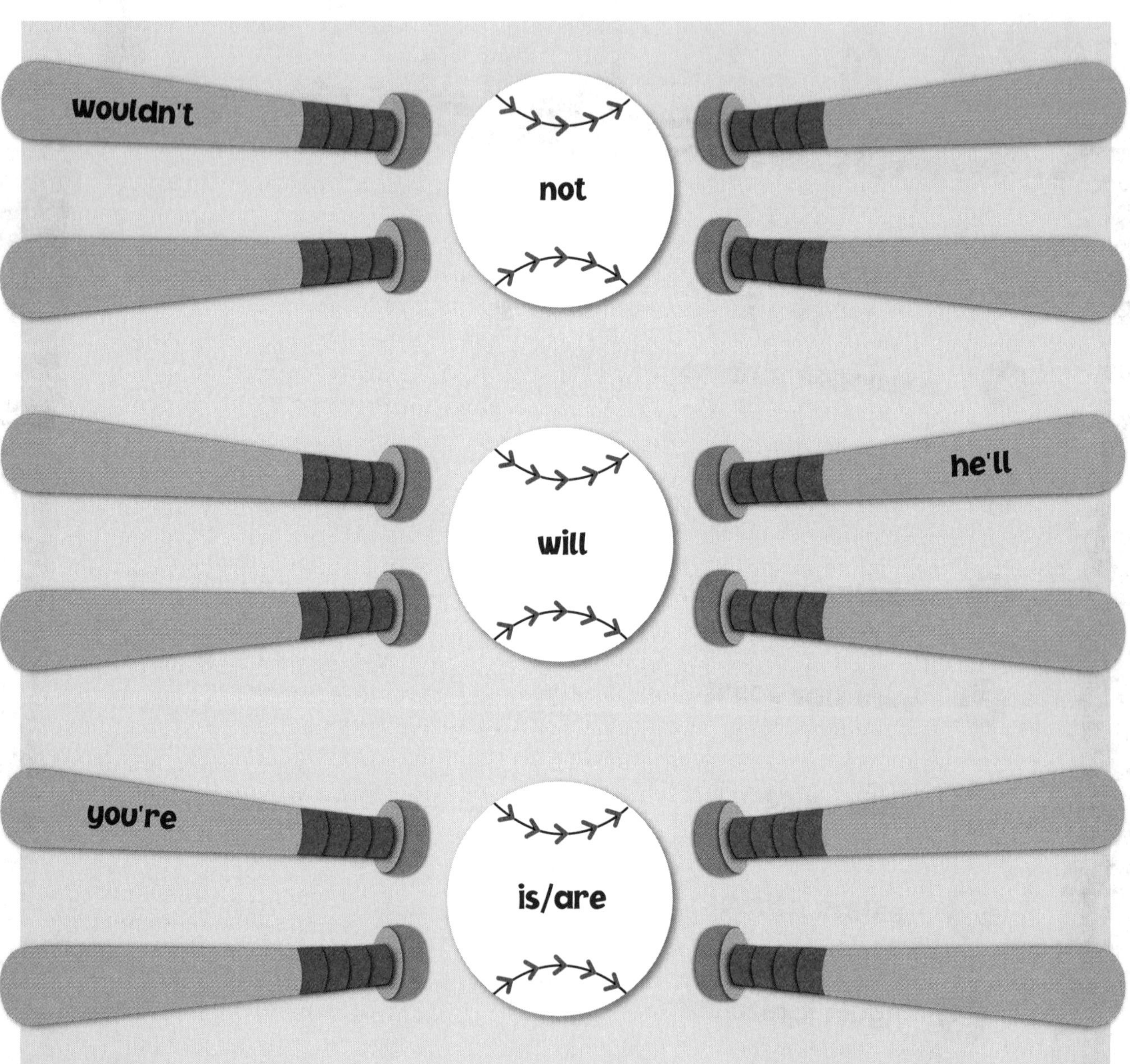

Picture This!

ALPHA-CHALLENGE

Skill: Capitalization

Fill in the chart. First, write the name of an item that begins with each letter shown. Then, write an imaginary product name for the item that you might see at the store. Begin each important word in the brand name with a capital letter. Some are done for you.

	Item	Brand Name
Letter p:	peanut butter	Lots o' Nuts peanut butter
Letter s:		
Letter m:		
Letter t:	tissue	
Letter a:		
Letter r:		
Letter n:		
Letter f:		
Letter b:		
Letter d:	dog food	

Use the code to find the secret message. Write the sentence on the lines. Hint: You will need to add two apostrophes, two capital letters, and one period to write the sentence correctly.

8385 1964 95 97 29645 5048

Code Key

a	b	d	e	h	i	k	m	n	s
3	1	8	4	0	9	6	2	7	5

Frogs don't drink water,

or frogs can survive in the water.

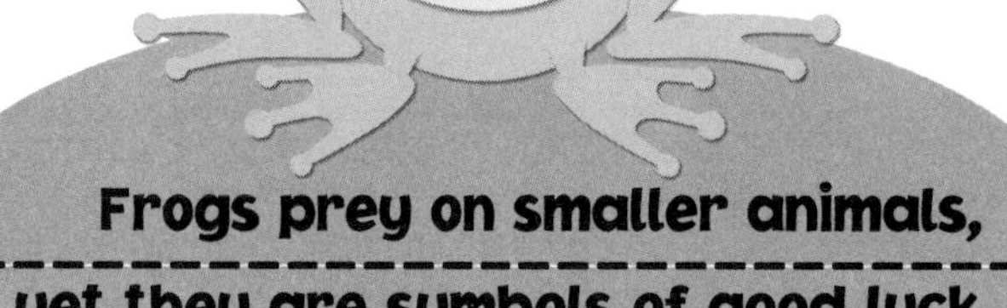

Frogs prey on smaller animals,

yet they are symbols of good luck.

Skill: Compound Sentences

IN PIECES

Cut out the puzzle pieces. Match them to form four compound sentences.

Frogs can survive on land,

but they absorb it through their skin.

Some people think frogs are ugly,

and larger animals prey on frogs.

Skill: Simple Sentences

Sentence Scramble

A simple sentence contains a subject and a verb. Draw a line to connect the words and form a simple sentence. Write it on the lines. Circle the noun or pronoun that the sentence is about. Underline the verb.

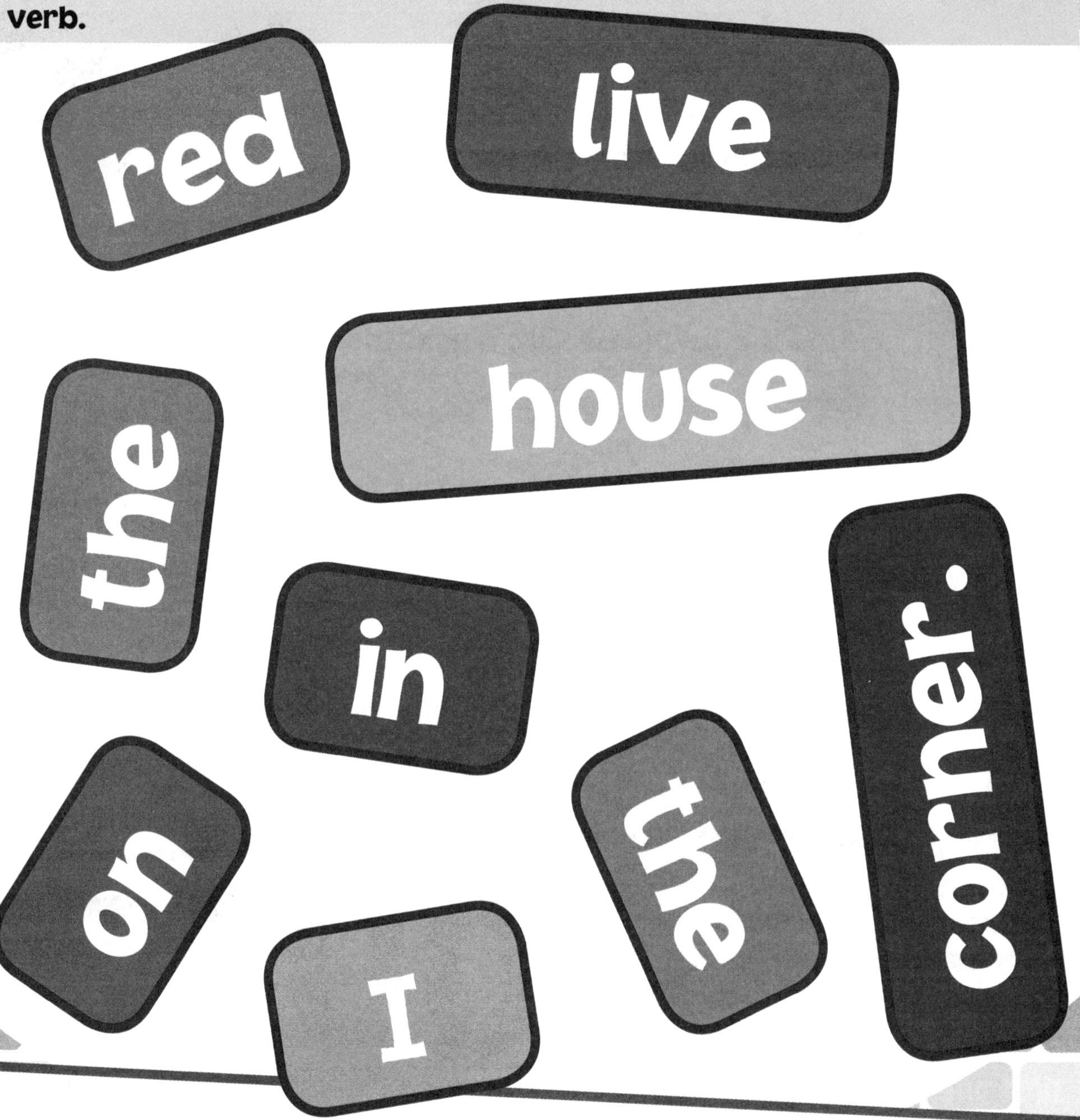

____

____

1. Q: What is a cupcake?

A: It is a small cake baked in a cup.

2. Q: ______________________________

A: It is a frozen ball you can make outside in the snow.

3. Q: ______________________________

A: It is a ring you can wear in your ear.

4. Q: ______________________________

A: It is a tall house with a light that guides ships to safety.

5. Q: ______________________________

A: It lets you pack things inside and carry them on your back.

6. Q: ______________________________

A: It is a small light that keeps your room from being too dark at night.

Read each answer. Write a question to match it. Each question you write should contain a compound word that combines two words found in the answer. The first one is done for you.

Skill: Compound Words

QUIZ WHIZ

Skill: Short and Long Vowel Sounds

Cut out each dog bone. If the word has a short vowel sound, tape or glue it on the short dog. If it has a long vowel sound, tape or glue it on the long dog.

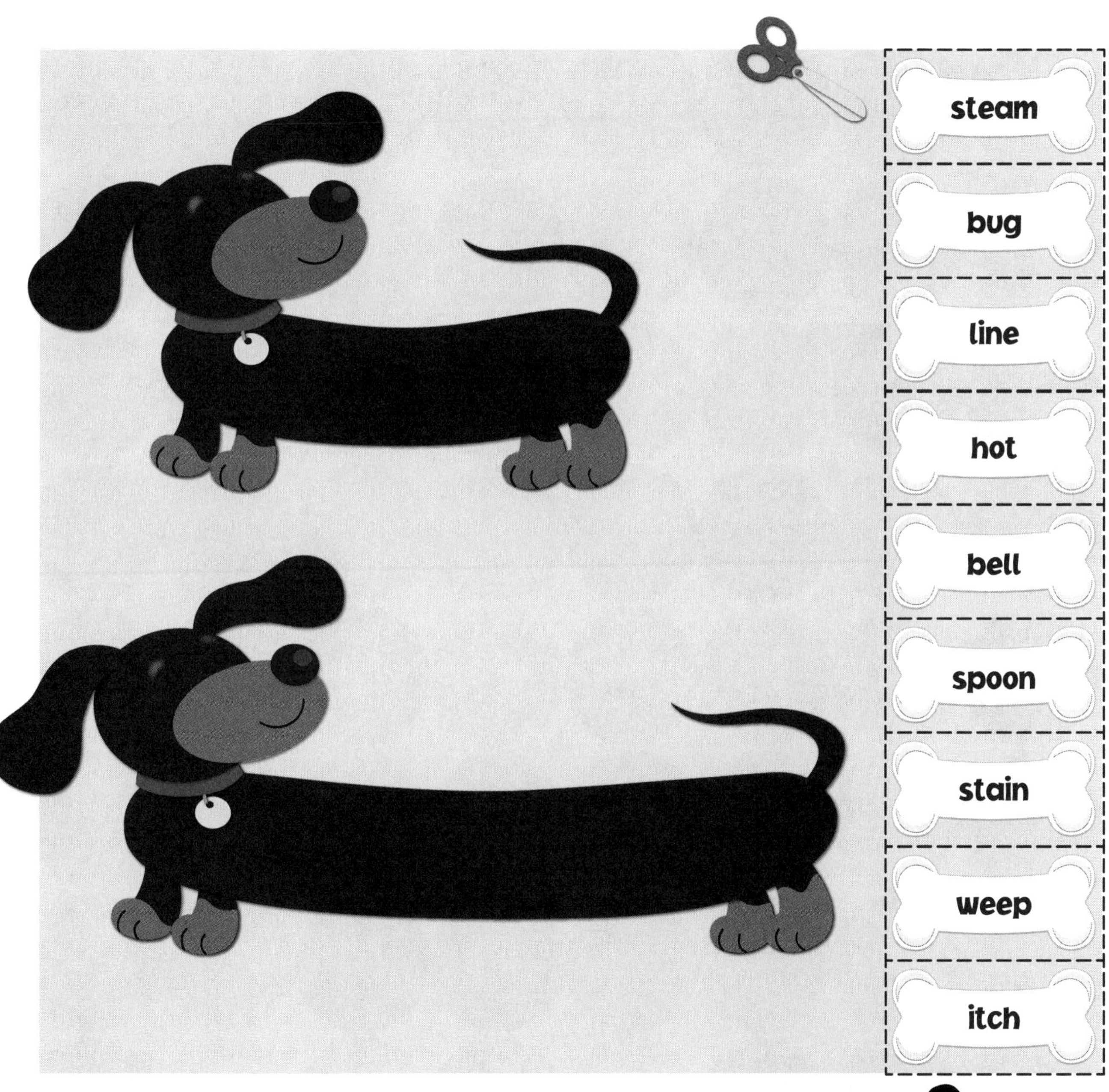

Picture This!

In Search Of

Skill: Irregular Verbs

Solve the puzzle by finding and circling the past-tense form of each verb below. For example, if the word is "win," search for "won" in the puzzle.

say

feel

write

take

grow

drive

buy

wear

```
         A X N Y V H A V H R V O C
         V M V T Q S R G E X F T Q
         T E U H E O A T Y T E L A
         N N C G Y H O I O P L B X
         W G Q U E R D O D H T O K
         W Z D O W F K N G U A B H
         Z V L B D W E R G Z H X N
         E L B J B G D T Z H X F V
         Y R V J A H X B C M C I I
         F S O C R I F B P L M S T
         R L E W A T G D R O V E K
         Q B N M M A G Z O O R T B
         Z I P J N A A D J C D B G
         E S F D K N H K A H M T L
         F B H J D S N M L P W Y T
P I B Y M K H G F Y D V X A R W Z S B
R C N U U J U A K C H E E R F U L S E
S N M C B R X Y P O M Z J O Y F U L A
L P F X E J T K O X A K M O Q F Z M T
```

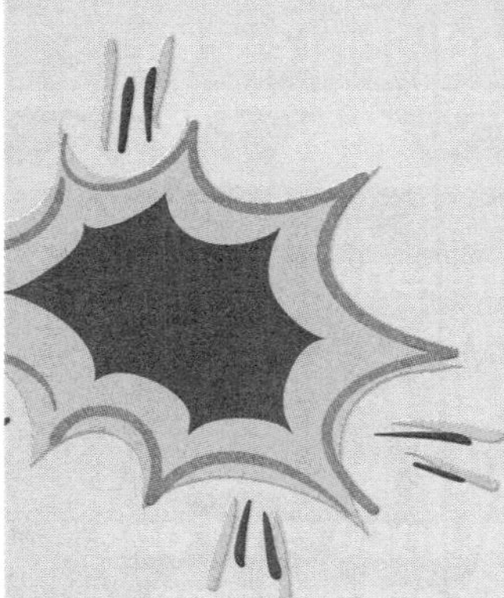

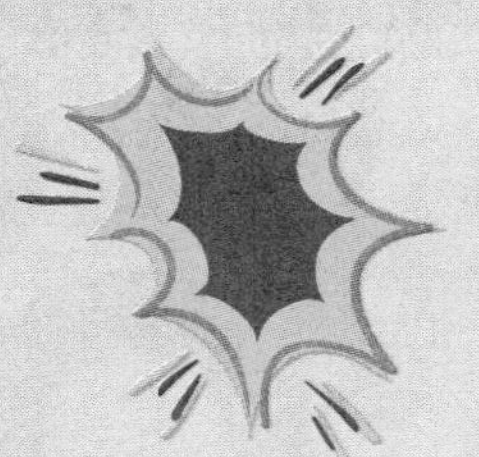

JUMBLED UP

Skill: Simple and Compound Sentences

Oh, no! Someone knocked over a dictionary, and all these words fell out. Use the words to write one simple sentence and one compound sentence on the lines. You may reuse words. Don't forget to add capital letters and punctuation marks.

buried fence so it need dog

in someone a bone dug yard

over up I pack

bee threw a ball the an

me but stung

ice

Simple Sentence: ____________________

____

Compound Sentence: ____________________

____

PRESTO-CHANGE-O!

Skills: Spelling, Vocabulary

Does it take magic to turn a cab into a bus? No, you just need to change one letter at a time! Write a word to match each clue. Each word should be the same as the word above it except for one changed letter.

a baby bear

to clean or pet something

it's under your feet

to bother

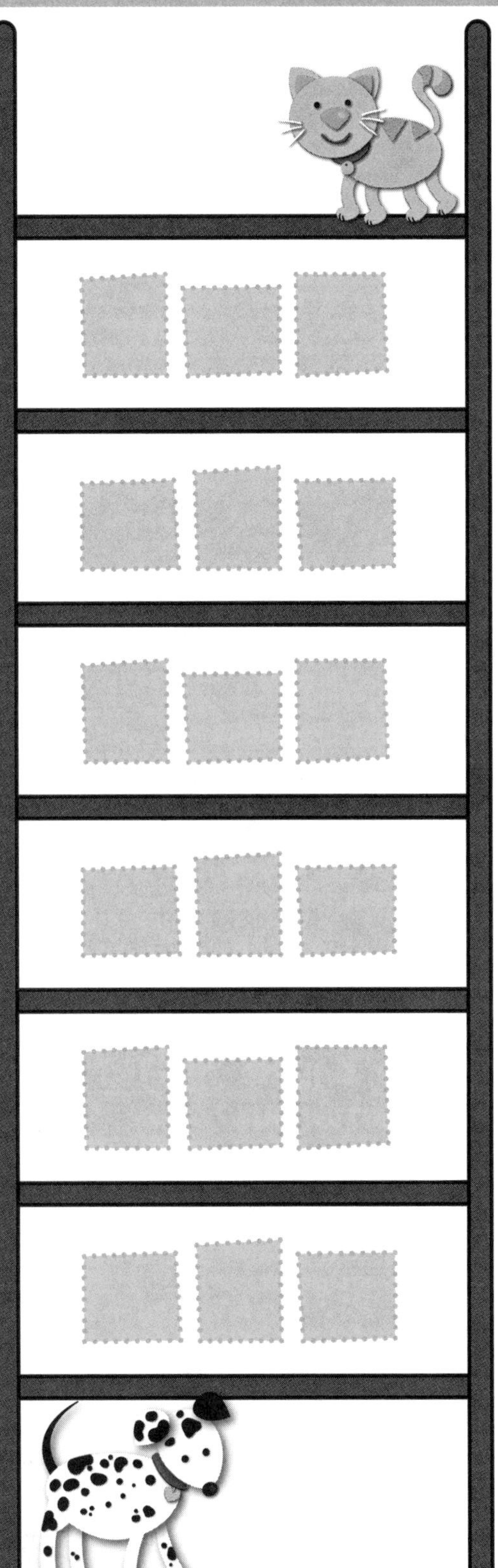

Sudoku for you

		y	o
z	c		

Skill:
Vocabulary

Write letters in the boxes so that each row and column has the letters to spell a word you might use to describe these things: a blanket, a home, a bed, a chair, a room. No letter should appear twice in the same row or column. Do not guess. Use logic!

Skill: Collective Nouns
GO ACROSS
bunch
Write a collective noun that describes a large group of each item shown. Then, fit the collective nouns you wrote into the puzzle. One is done for you.

JUMBLED UP

Skill: Possessives

Draw lines between the owners in Column A and the things they own in Column B. Then, for each pair, write a phrase that includes a possessive noun. For example, if the pair showed a girl named Rosa and her book, you would write "Rosa's book."

Column A | **Column B**

Madison  

Dad  

Marcus  

Romeo  

Skill: Short and Long Vowel Sounds

Cut out the words. Tape or glue them inside the Venn diagram.

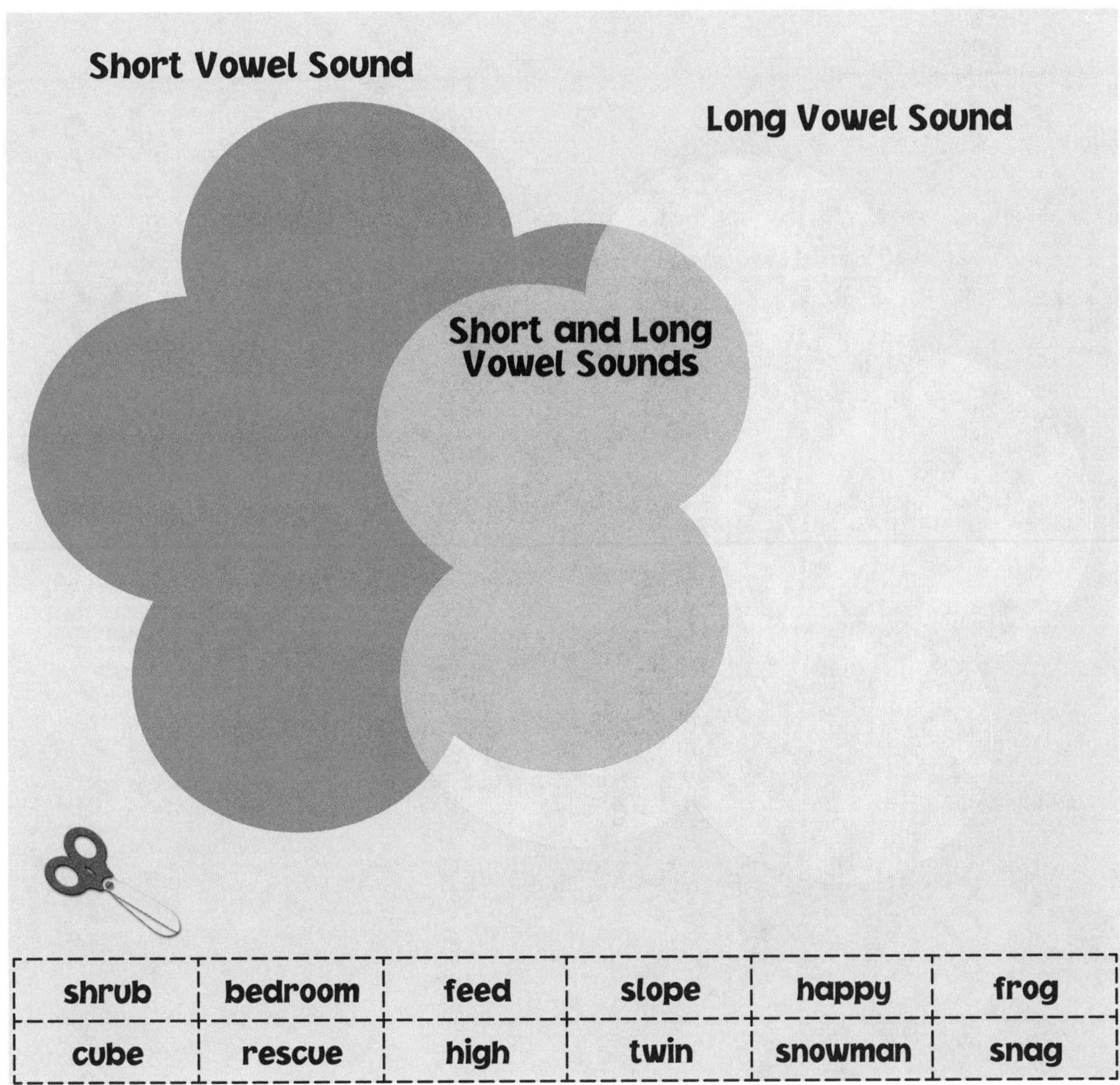

shrub	bedroom	feed	slope	happy	frog
cube	rescue	high	twin	snowman	snag

Picture This!

MAZE CRAZE

S	O	D	F
H	T	A	C
U	M	R	E
P	I	Y	N

Skill: Spelling

Move from letter to letter to find words hidden in the puzzle. How many words can you find that have at least three letters? Write them on the lines.

WORD MATH

Skill: Contractions

Solve each puzzle to find a pair of words. In the last blank, write the contraction for the words.

1.  − f − h

+ =

2. U R

+ =

3. th +  − gr − t + ve

+ =

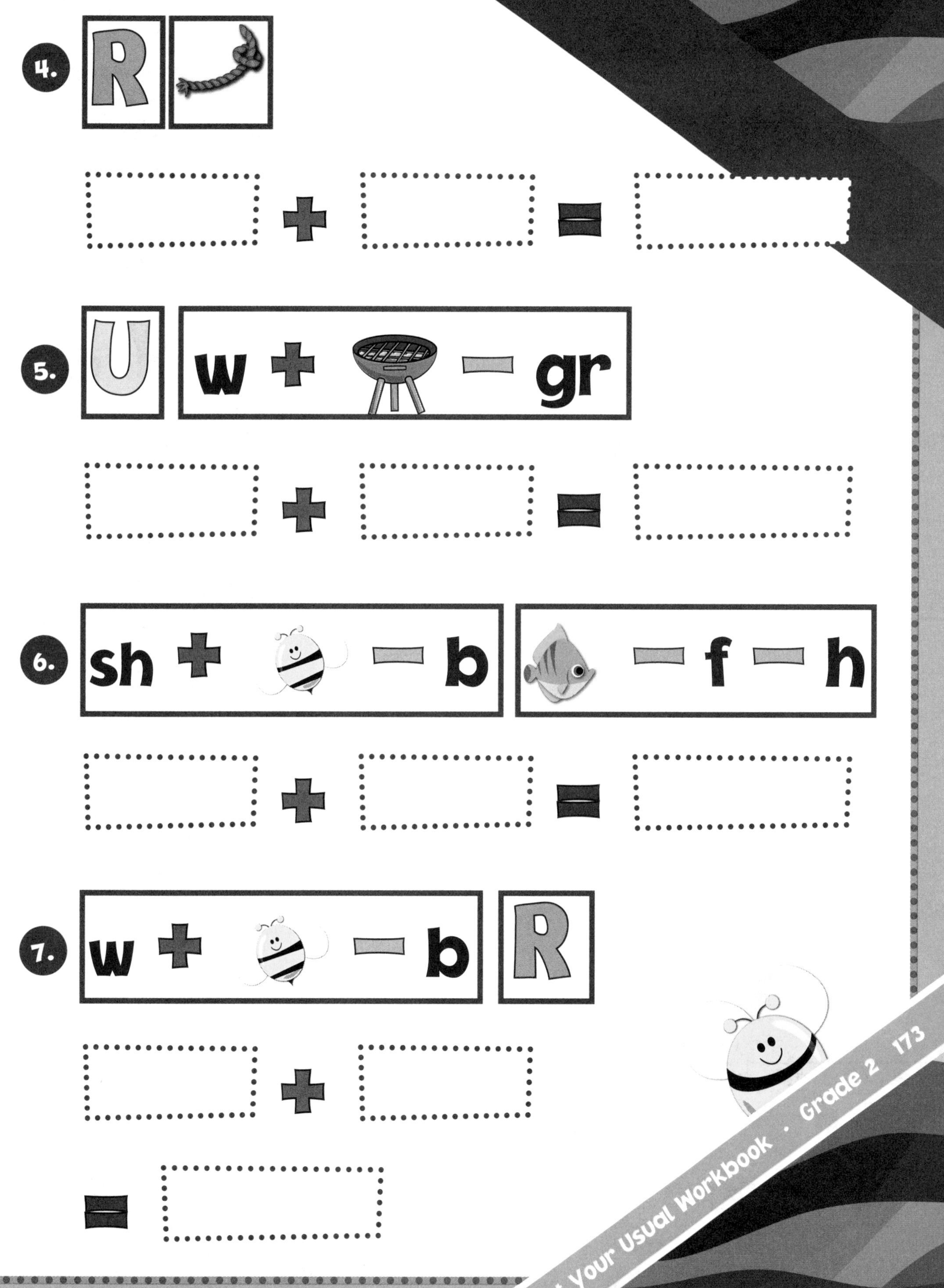
4.
R
+
=
5.
U
w
+
-
gr
+
=
6.
sh
+
-
b
-
f
-
h
+
=
7.
w
+
-
b
R
+
=

CODE BREAKER

Skill: Irregular Verbs

Use the code to find the past-tense forms of the verbs. Write them in the blanks.

1. begin
2. stand
3. write
4. tell
5. draw
6. break

Code Key

a	b	d	e	g	k	l	n	o	r	s	t	w

PRESTO CHANGE-O!

Skill: Long Vowel Sounds

How can you make food zoom? By changing one letter at a time! On each rung of the ladder, complete a word with a long vowel sound. Each word should be the same as the word above it except for one changed letter.

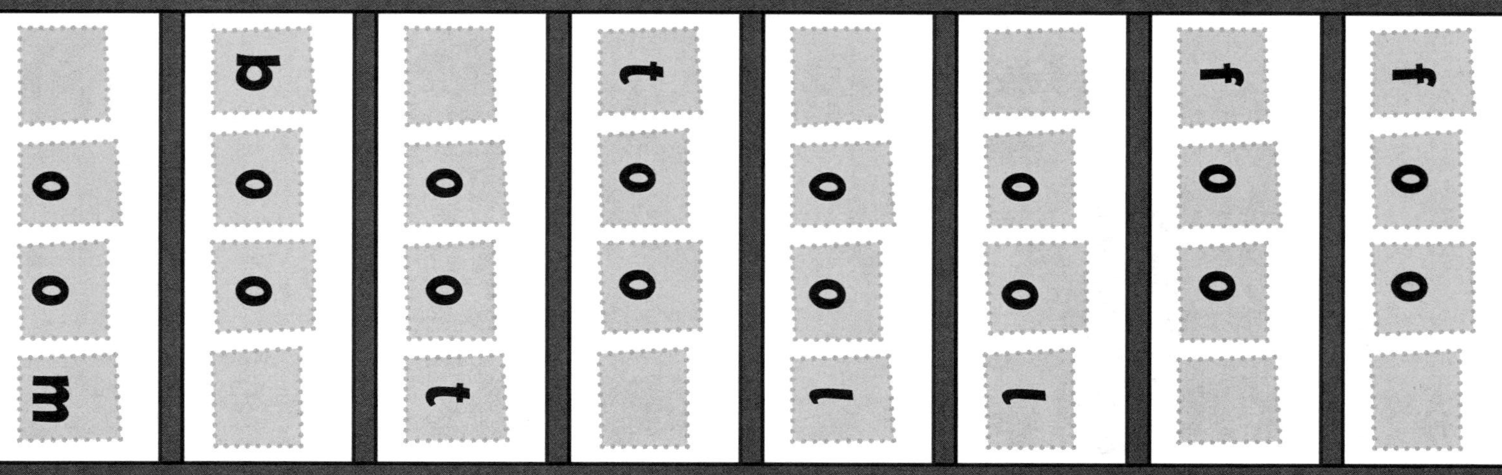

Skills: Adjectives, Vocabulary

Read the adjective on each nest. On each egg, write a noun that the adjective could be used to describe.

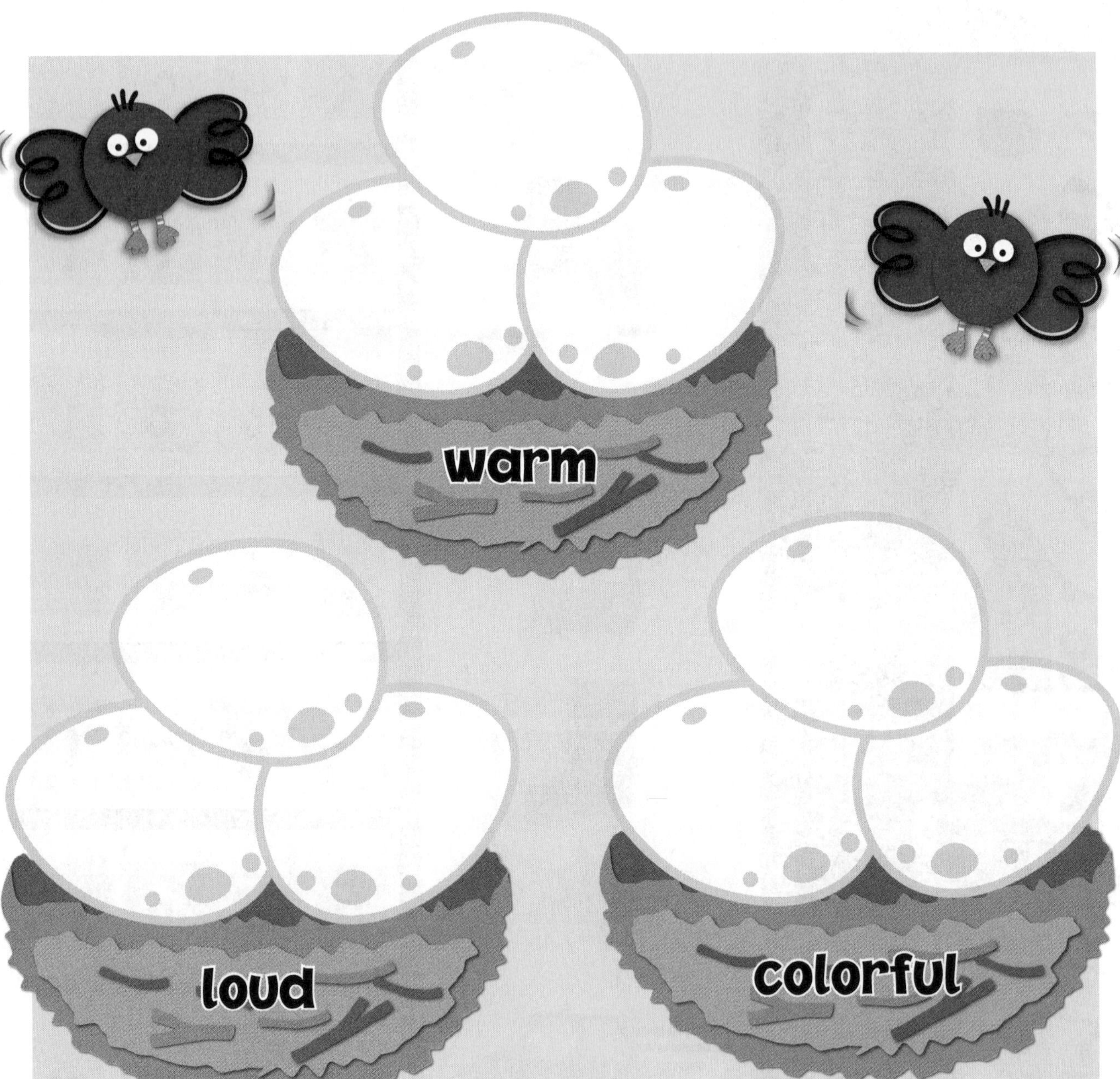

Picture This!

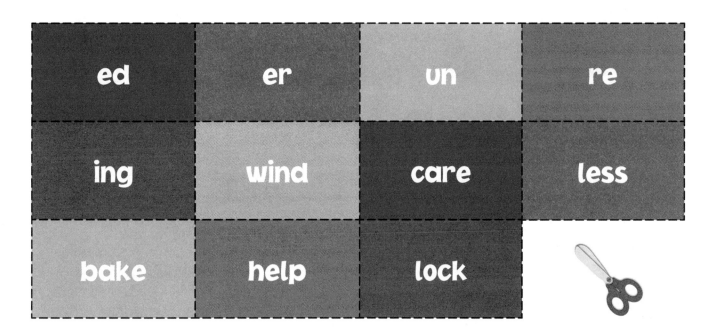

ed	er	un	re
ing	wind	care	less
bake	help	lock	

Skills: Prefixes, Suffixes, Word Roots

IN PIECES

Are you ready to build words? Cut out the word parts. On a tabletop, combine, reuse, and overlap the word parts to make new words. Use the lines to write the new words you made. You may need to change the spelling of the base word.

RIDDLE ME

Write a word to complete each hink pink.

Skill: Context Clues

1. What is a clean road? a neat ______
2. What is a library thief? a book ______
3. What is a house for chickens? a ______
4. What is a large branch? a ______ twig
5. What is a fast choice? a ______ pick
6. What is a rodent's cap? a rat ______
7. What is an odd mustache? a weird ______
8. What is a reptile dessert? a snake ______

pen

A hink pink is a pair of rhyming words that answer a riddle. Examples: smart heart, spring king

WORD MATH

Skill: Compound Words

Write a compound word to solve each puzzle.

1. d + rug + store

= ______

2. clever − cl + green

= ______

3. moat − m + meal

= ______

4. dice − d + berg

= ______

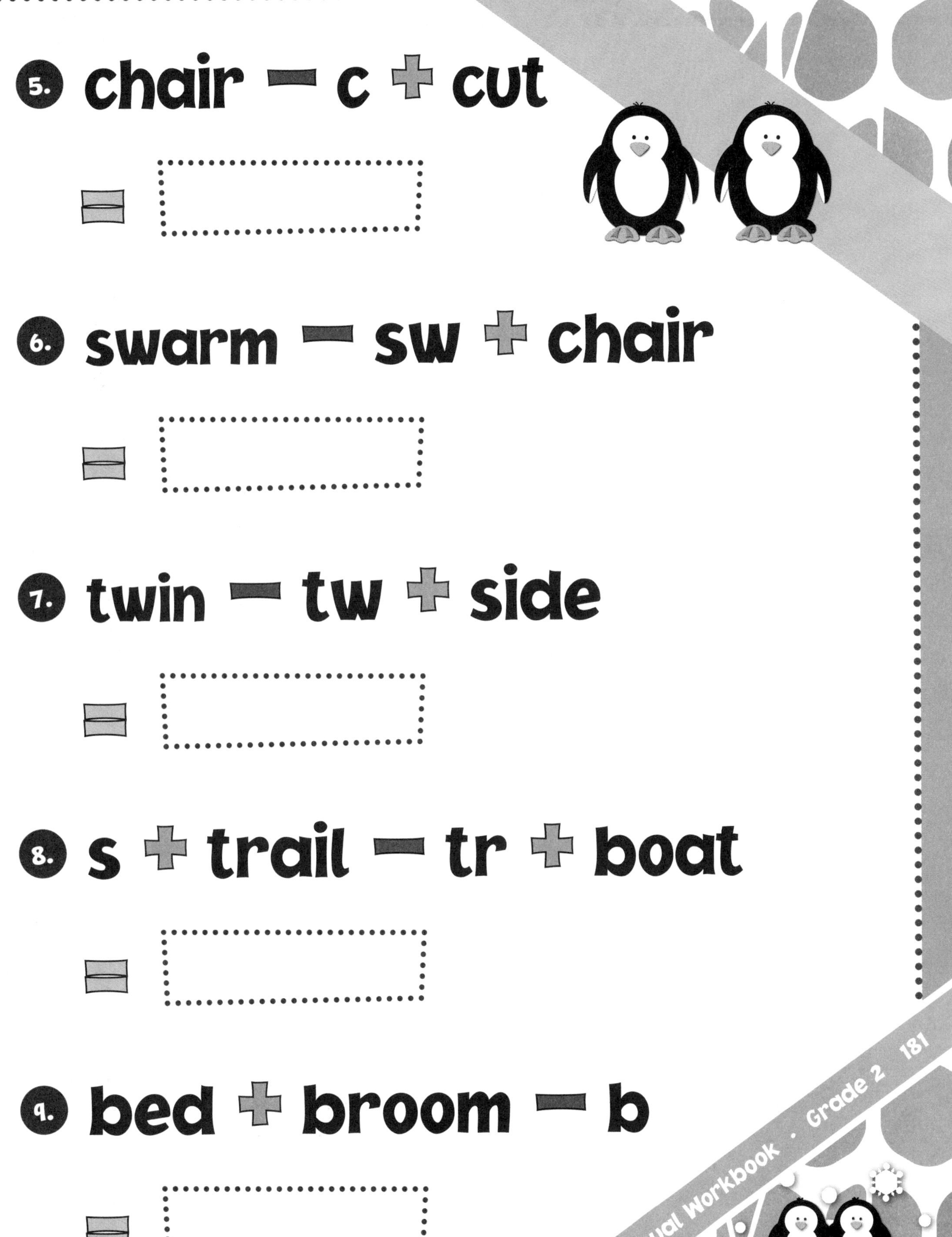
5. chair − c + cut
=
6. swarm − sw + chair
=
7. twin − tw + side
=
8. s + trail − tr + boat
=
9. bed + broom − b
=

JUMBLED UP

Skill: Compound Sentences

Rearrange the tiles to make a compound sentence. Write it on the lines.

om, and

okout.

we boug

ht everythi

t to the

for the co

grocery st

ore with M

ng we need

I wen

In Search Of

Skill: Adverbs

Find the adverb in each phrase. Circle it in the puzzle.

asked politely   found it easily   dove deeply into the pool

divided them fairly   always remembers

arrives soon   smiles proudly   finally laughs

B U F M H A P P Y J L R U H U A Q Z D G J
M U P O L I T E L Y N S G Z Q M F J C Q C
A E M R M U P F N L O F B A Y U A S S P P
L E P Z O G Z I Y I X G P O H V W Y R B D
Q E X C I U G N L W M N T I C Y L P E E D
A C A L M R D A M I U B D L B X L U T N N
I I W K P M G L H Z S Z M R R Q S R O S H
Z H I E M F H L Y O T J X L K I Y O I Y Z
J D Q H O G Y Y X J E O K W E K S E L A A
A S Z E D E K D B O H L Y E U L W F Y W F
J C D O V L P V J H O V A O J Y L C T L K
P W D W P S X P S R V S H U G R A H H A E
W I Q A D S H H J Y I H X X M O K R W U A
E G L H M Q O H W L U E Z E T P X H E P O
G P I B Y P L M Y Z W Y T K H F W Z S B L
P R C N U U J U A K C H E E R F U L S E C
J S N M C B R X Y P O M Z J O Y F U L A X

RIDDLE ME

Write a letter for each clue. Write the letters in order to form a secret word that has a common suffix. Then, write two other words that contain that suffix.

Skill: Suffixes

1. My capital looks like one rung of a ladder. ______
2. I am a one-letter word that means "me" or "myself." ______
3. There are two of me in "cuddle." ______
4. I spell the long vowel sound in "icicle." ______
5. I am the first letter of the second half of the alphabet. ______
6. You have to double me to write the past-tense form of "hug." ______

The secret word is:

1	2	3	4	5	6

______

______

CODE BREAKER

Skill: Contractions

Use the clues and the code to find the letters that spell each contraction. Write the complete contraction in the blank. Don't forget to include the apostrophe in each word you write.

1. after m ☐ before w ☐
   before s ☐ after m ☐ ,
   before n ☐ = ______

2. after h ☐ before c ☐ ,
   before i ☐ before i ☐
   = ______

3. before m ☐ , after r ☐
   before c ☐ = ______

4. before o ☐ before s ☐
   after s ☐ , before h ☐
   = ______

5. after n ☐ after c ☐
   before d ☐ , after y ☐
   before c ☐ = ______

Code Key

l i m t h w e c o a s n y r v u d

1. lots
2. finished
3. wish
4. touch
5. healthy
6. actual
7. trip
8. snug

MIRROR

Skill: Reflexive Pronouns

him self

her self

your self

our selves

it self

them selves

my self

your selves

Reflexive pronouns refer back to a noun. They end with "self" or "selves." Hold the page up to a mirror to read the first part of each reflexive pronoun. Write the whole word on the line.

MAZE CRAZE

Skills: Simple Sentences, Possessives

Follow the arrows through the maze to spell the words in a secret sentence. Write the sentence on the lines. To write the sentence correctly, you will need to add a capital letter, an apostrophe, and a period.

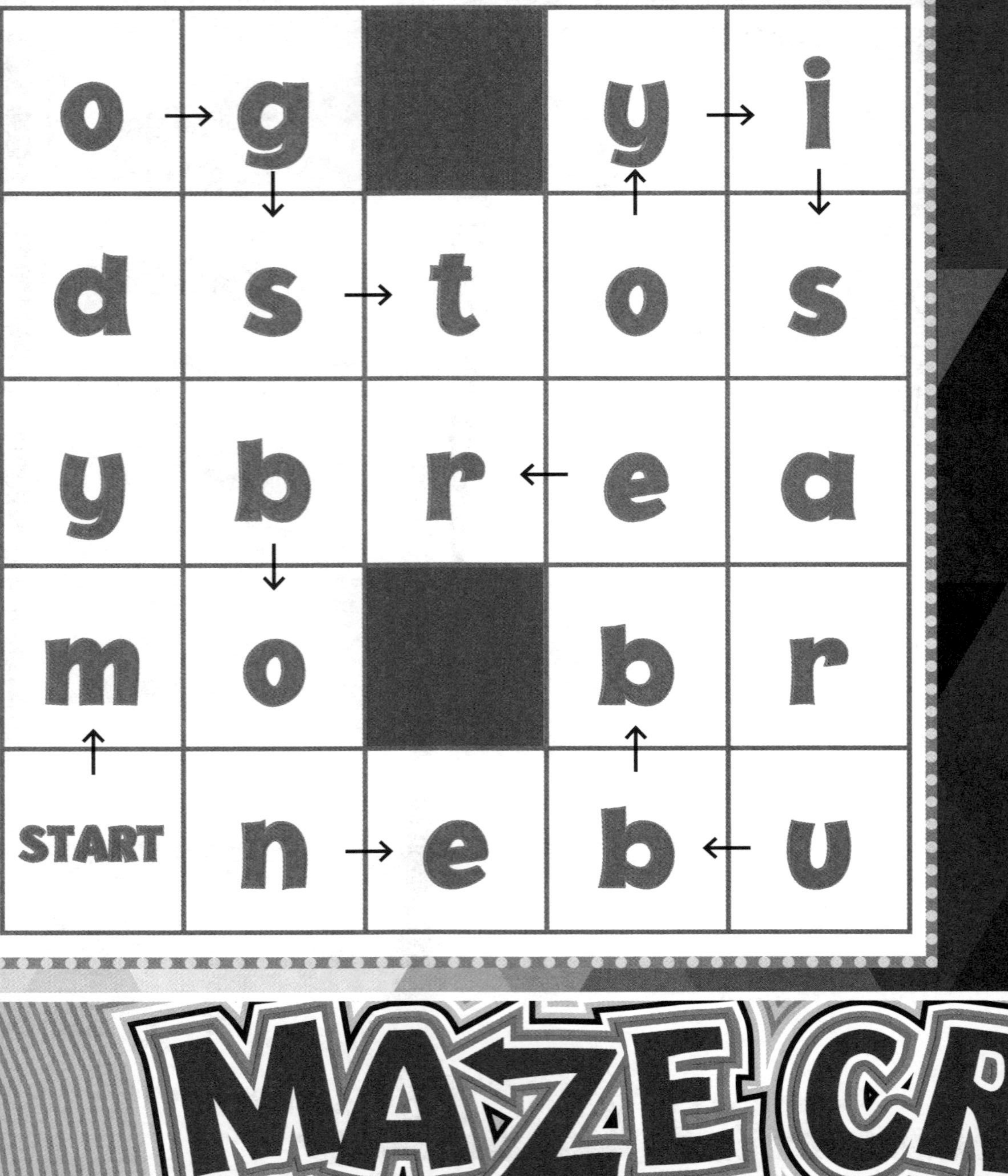

Sudoku for You

O			S
	W	L	

Skill: Central Message or Moral

Remember the story "The Tortoise and the Hare"? The moral of the story is:

"______ and steady wins the race."

Write letters in the boxes so that each row and column has the letters to spell the missing word. No letter should appear twice in the same row or column. Do not guess. Use logic!

ALPHA-CHALLENGE

Skill: Compound Words

Fill in the chart by writing a compound word that fits each category. Some compound words are given for you.

Category	Compound Word
Fruit	
Animal	
Food	
Relative	
Room	bedroom
Sport	
Insect	
Number	
Body Part	fingernail
Vehicle	

JUMBLED UP

Skills: Prefixes, Suffixes, Word Roots

Match word parts on the lock and the keys to form words. Write the new words on the lines.

Write a word to match each clue.

1. I have a long a sound, but there is no "a" in me!

2. I have a short u sound spelled "u."

3. My long e sound is spelled with two different vowels.

4. I have a long a sound spelled "a-consonant-silent e."

5. I have a long i sound and end with a silent letter.

6. I have a long o sound. I begin with a consonant blend.

7. My long e sound is spelled with a double letter.

8. If you added "e" to me, I would rhyme with "line."

9. I end with a long a sound.

Word Box

grub	peach	pin
wife	eight	float
space	sweep	gray

Skills: Short and Long Vowel Sounds, Spelling

PREST-O CHANGE-O!

Skills: Prefixes, Suffixes, Irregular Verbs

How many ways can you write the verb "write"? Write letters in the blanks to change "write" to fit each clue.

doing it now — writ_ _ _

did it yesterday — wr_ _ _

do it again — _ _write

does it — write_

did it again — _ _wr_te

it has been done — writ_ _ _

Skill: Word Roots

Read the base word in the center of each pinwheel. On the lines, write four words that use the base word. Hint: You may need to change the spelling of the base word before adding a prefix or suffix.

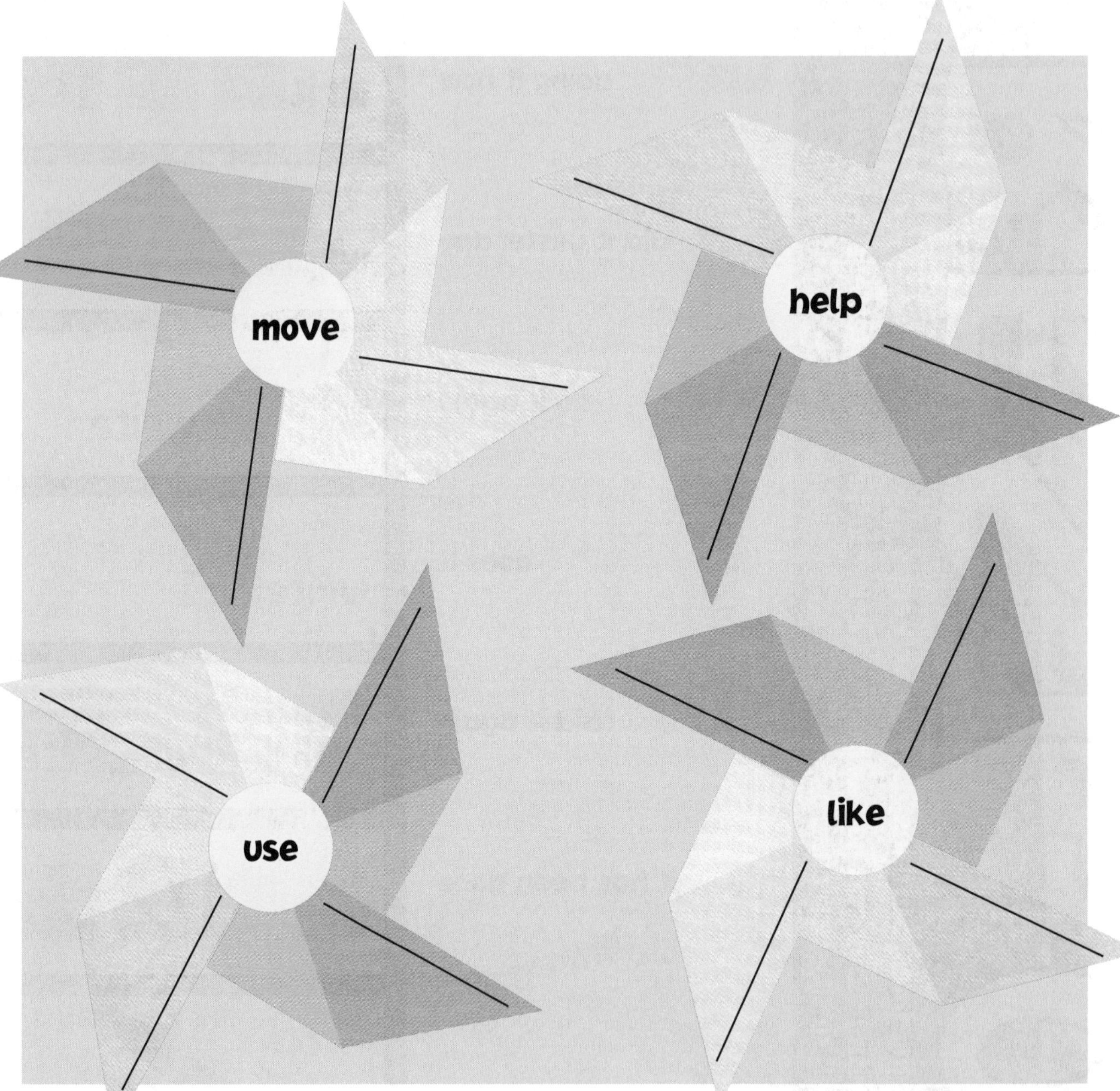

Picture This!

Skill: Compound Sentences

Sentence Scramble

A compound sentence has two subjects (each with a noun or pronoun) and two verbs. It has a comma after the joining word. Draw a line to connect the words and make a compound sentence. Write the sentence at the bottom of the page.

The

mouse

cracker.

snuck

and

into

it

____

____

WORD MATH

Skills: Adjectives, Adverbs

Decode the words. Write them on the lines to complete the sentence. Then, find adjectives and adverbs in the sentence and write them in the blanks.

1. sh + tiny − t 2. [picture] 3. sp + [picture] − b 4. [picture] − n + r 5. d + [picture] − br 6. [picture] 7. [picture] − c + ly 8. scr + speech − sp + ed 9. 2 10. h + [picture] − s 11. ch + [picture] − d + ful 12. b + [picture] − sh + ing 13. [picture]

The _____ _____ car _____
1. 2. 3.

_____ _____ the _____
4. 5. 6.

and _____ _____ _____
7. 8. 9.

a _____ by the _____
10. 11.

_____ _____.
12. 13.

Adjectives

Adverbs

RIDDLE ME

Write a letter for each clue. Write the letters in order to form a secret word that is a common verb. Then, write the past-tense form of the verb on the line.

Skill: Irregular Verbs

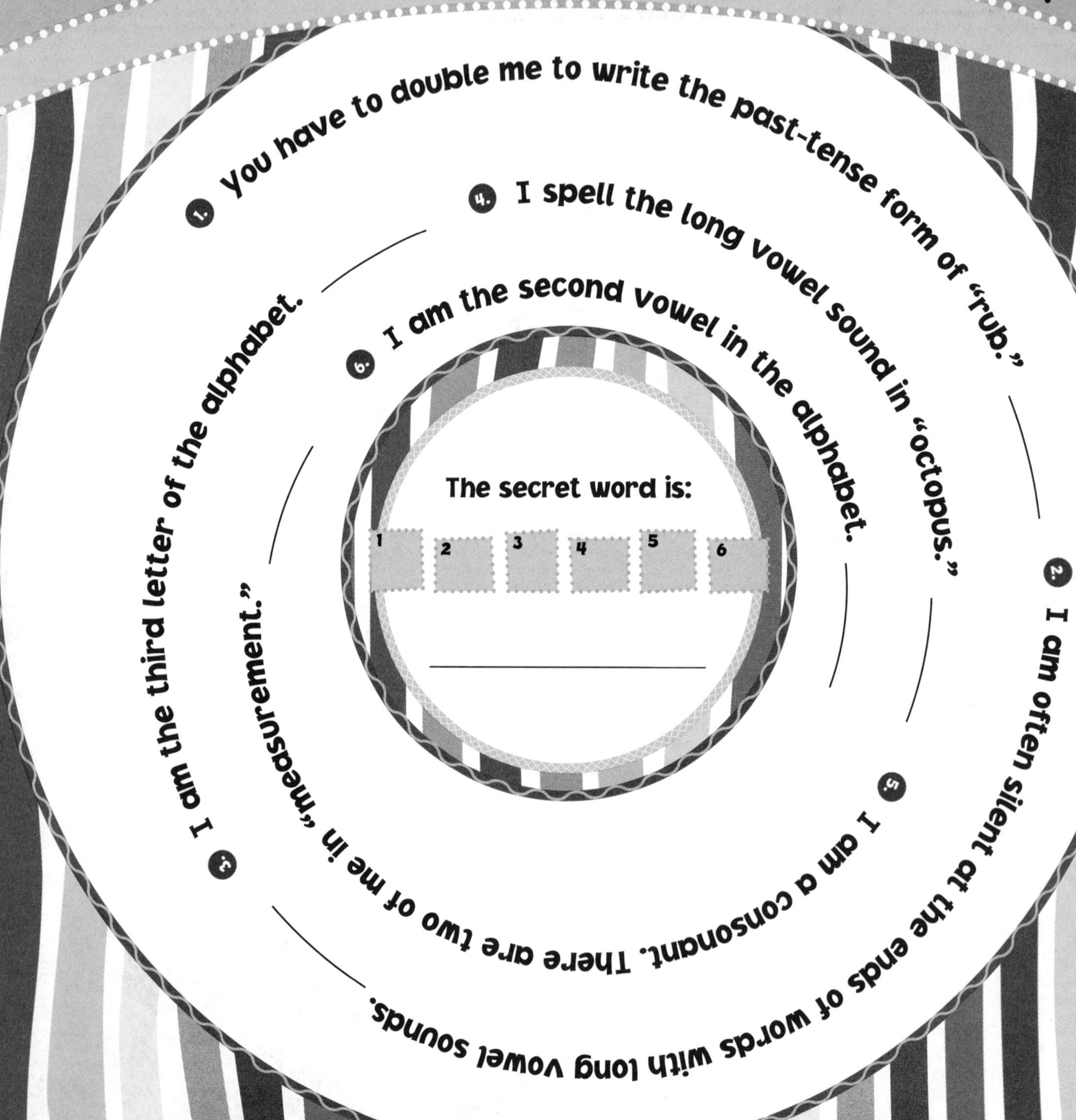

D	E	T	V
L	W	Y	A
C	U	H	R
S	N	I	O

Skill: Contractions

Make as many contractions as you can using the letters in the boxes. Write them on the lines. You may use letters more than once. Be sure to add an apostrophe (') to each word you write.

Skill: Irregular Plurals

MIRROR

1. person people
2. moose meese
3. elf elfs
4. man men
5. mouse mice
6. sheep sheep
7. goose gooses
8. wolf wolfs

Read each word. Hold the page up to a mirror to read the word beside it. If it is the correct plural of the first word, draw a smiley face ( ) in the circle. If it is not correct, draw a sad face ( ).

In Search Of

Skill: Compound Words

Find eight compound words in the puzzle. Use the clues to help you figure out what each word is.

1. space for animals at a farm
2. chunk of ice in Arctic waters
3. red and black bug
4. library book kept too long
5. man who works on a ranch
6. arch of colors in the sky
7. food from the ocean
8. it lights up the road

JUMBLED UP

Skills: Short and Long Vowel Sounds, Compound Words

Fill in the chart. Find a word hiding inside each word shown. Write the hidden word. Use the clues to help you.

Beginning Word	Clue to Hidden Word	Hidden Word
oatmeal	It has a long o sound.	
midnight	It has a long i sound.	
handkerchief	It has a long e sound.	
quicksand	It has a short a sound.	
teapot	It has a short o sound.	
yesterday	It has a long a sound.	
rainbow	It has a long a sound.	
broomstick	It has a short i sound.	

Skill: Simple and Compound Sentences

Use the words in each box. Write simple sentences or compound sentences that contain the words. Use capital letters and punctuation marks correctly in each sentence you write.

Picture This!

Write the name of a text feature to match each set of clues.

- at the back
- like a dictionary
- tells how to pronounce words

What am I?

- at the beginning
- a list of page numbers

What am I?

- taken with a camera
- a real-life image

What am I?

- in a nonfiction book
- at the back
- a list of topics and page numbers

What am I?

- under a picture
- gives information

What am I?

Word Box

index photograph

caption glossary

table of contents

QUIZ WHIZ

Skill: Text Features

ANSWER
KEY

Skill: Odd and Even

ODD

EVEN

Oh, no! You're in a traffic jam! Starting with car 2, move through the jam counting by twos. Did you move through an odd or an even number of cars? Circle the answer.

Math path

8 Not Your Usual Workbook · Grade 2

Page 8

PATTERN POWER

Skill: Telling Time

What time is it? It's time for patterns! The times shown on the clocks in each row follow a pattern. Draw hands on the last clock in each row to complete the pattern.

Not Your Usual Workbook · Grade 2 9

Page 9

DARE TO DECODE

Skills: Addition, Subtraction

The equations below are written in code. Each shape stands for a digit 1 to 9. Crack the code by using what you know about doubles.

5 1 9 2 4 7 6 8 3

10 Not Your Usual Workbook · Grade 2

Page 10

STORY STUMPERS

Read each problem carefully. Use logic and math skills to find the answers.

Skill: Word Problems

1. Twelve students are going on a field trip to the zoo. There are 4 more girls going on the trip than boys. How many boys and how many girls are going?

4 boys 8 girls

2. Dr. Lewis treated 10 animals this morning. Half of the animals were dogs. She saw 2 fewer cats than dogs. She saw 1 fewer rabbit than she saw cats. How many of each animal did Dr. Lewis treat?

5 dogs 3 cats 2 rabbits

3. Manuel has a bag of fruit. There are 4 apples in the bag. There are 3 more oranges than apples in the bag. There are 5 fewer pears than oranges. How many fruits are in the bag?

13 fruits

Not Your Usual Workbook · Grade 2 11

Page 11

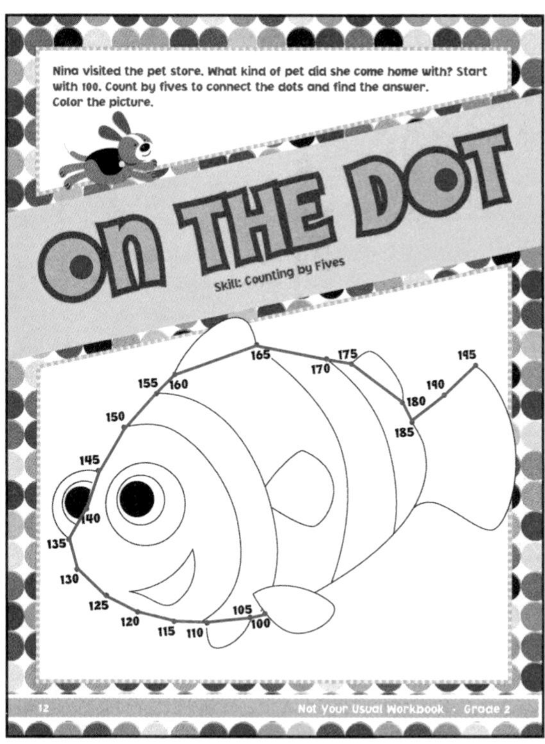

Page 12

Skill: Counting Money
Cut out the coins. Beside each item, glue or tape the coins needed to buy it.
A Show of Hands
Answers may vary. Possible answers shown.

Page 13

Draw a square and a triangle. The sides of each shape should be 3 inches long. Then, decorate each shape with a colorful pattern.
QUICK DRAW
Skills: Drawing Shapes, Measuring Length
Not Your Usual Workbook · Grade 2
15

Page 15

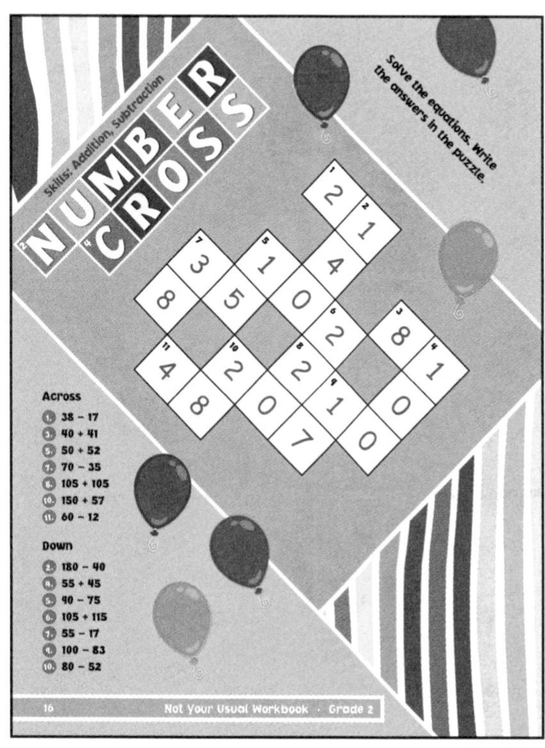

NUMBER CROSS
Skills: Addition, Subtraction
Solve the equations. Write the answers in the puzzle.
Across
38 – 17
40 + 41
50 + 52
70 – 35
105 + 105
150 + 57
60 – 12
Down
180 – 40
55 + 45
90 – 75
105 + 115
55 – 17
100 – 83
80 – 52
16
Not Your Usual Workbook · Grade 2

Page 16

Page 17

Magic Square
The numbers shown by the dice in each row and column add up to the same number.
Can you draw the missing dice?
18
Not Your Usual Workbook · Grade 2

Page 18

Page 19

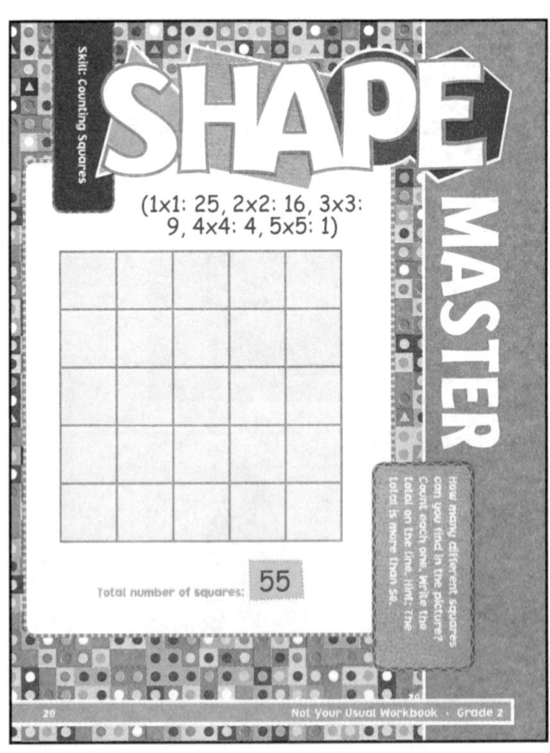

Page 20

Page 21

Page 22

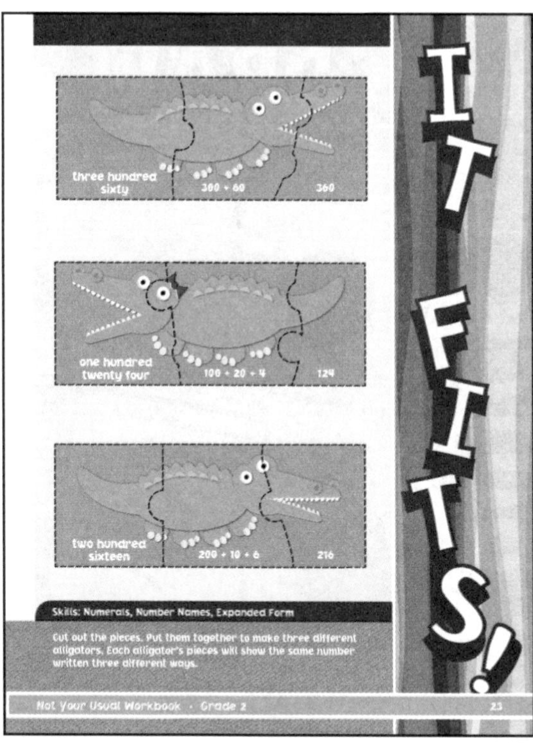

IT FITS!
three hundred sixty
300 + 60
360
one hundred twenty four
100 + 20 + 4
124
two hundred sixteen
200 + 10 + 6
216
Skills: Numerals, Number Names, Expanded Form
Cut out the pieces. Put them together to make three different alligators. Each alligator's pieces will show the same number written three different ways.
Not Your Usual Workbook · Grade 2 23

Page 23

Page 25

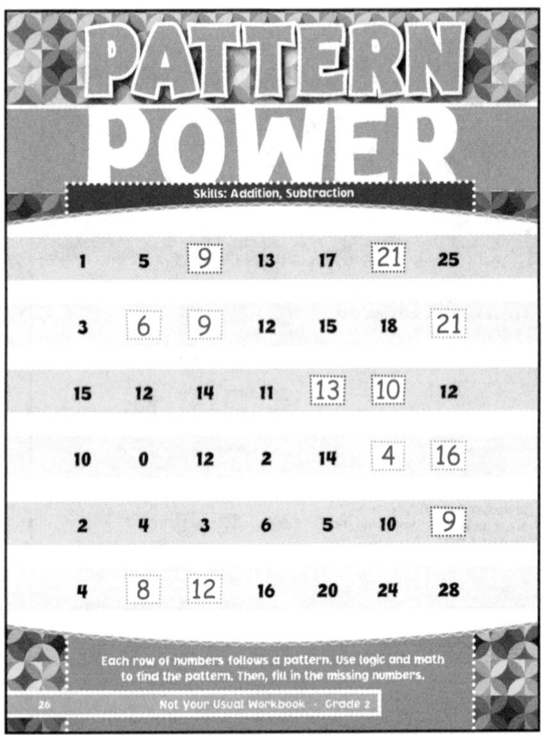

PATTERN POWER

Skills: Addition, Subtraction

1	5	9	13	17	21	25
3	6	9	12	15	18	21
15	12	14	11	13	10	12
10	0	12	2	14	4	16
2	4	3	6	5	10	9
4	8	12	16	20	24	28

Each row of numbers follows a pattern. Use logic and math to find the pattern. Then, fill in the missing numbers.

26 Not Your Usual Workbook · Grade 2

Page 26

Skill: Counting by Fives, Tens, and Hundreds

START	25	30	40	100
10	100	35	50	200
20	200	40	60	300
30	50	45	75	85
60	55	60	65	END

START	100	50	60	100
50	200	300	400	500
60	70	80	700	600
90	110	200	800	900
70	75	80	90	END

START	20	25	30	40
40	30	100	45	60
50	60	70	80	90
90	95	75	85	100
70	75	80	90	END

START	100	105	200	300
90	120	110	210	400
80	70	115	450	500
130	125	120	500	600
135	140	145	150	END

Find a path through each puzzle from START to END. Decide whether to count by fives, tens, or hundreds to find the path.

Math path

Not Your Usual Workbook · Grade 2 27

Page 27

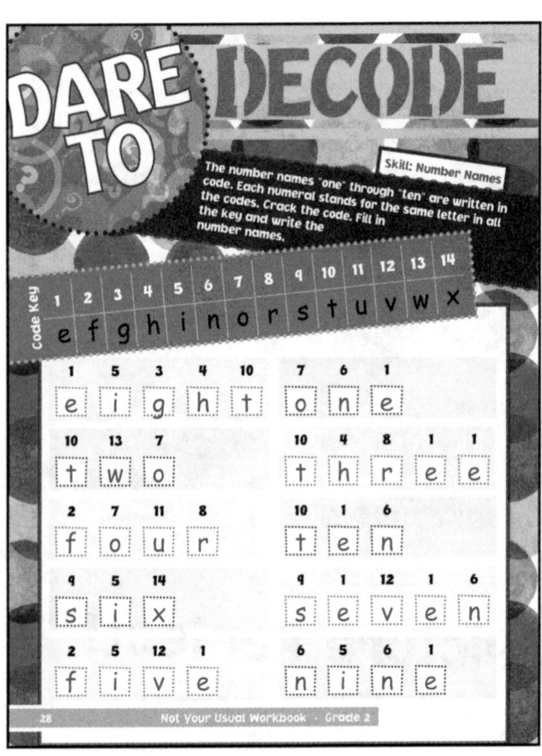

DARE TO DECODE

Skill: Number Names

The number names "one" through "ten" are written in code. Each numeral stands for the same letter in all the codes. Crack the code. Fill in the key and write the number names.

Code Key	1	2	3	4	5	6	7	8	9	10	11	12	13	14
	e	f	g	h	i	n	o	r	s	t	u	v	w	x

1 5 3 4 10 — eight
7 6 1 — one
10 13 7 — two
10 4 8 1 1 — three
2 7 11 8 — four
10 1 6 — ten
9 5 14 — six
9 1 12 1 6 — seven
2 5 12 1 — five
6 5 6 1 — nine

28 Not Your Usual Workbook · Grade 2

Page 28

Follow the directions to draw four different shapes.

QUICK DRAW

Skill: Drawing Shapes

Draw the shape you find at each end of a cylinder.

Draw a shape that has three sides and three angles.

Draw a quadrilateral that has four equal sides.

Draw a shape that has five sides.

Not Your Usual Workbook · Grade 2 29

Page 29

PATTERN POWER
Skill: Telling Time
Find the pattern formed by the times shown on the clocks in each row. Draw the missing hands on the clock faces to complete the patterns.
30 Not Your Usual Workbook · Grade 2

Page 30

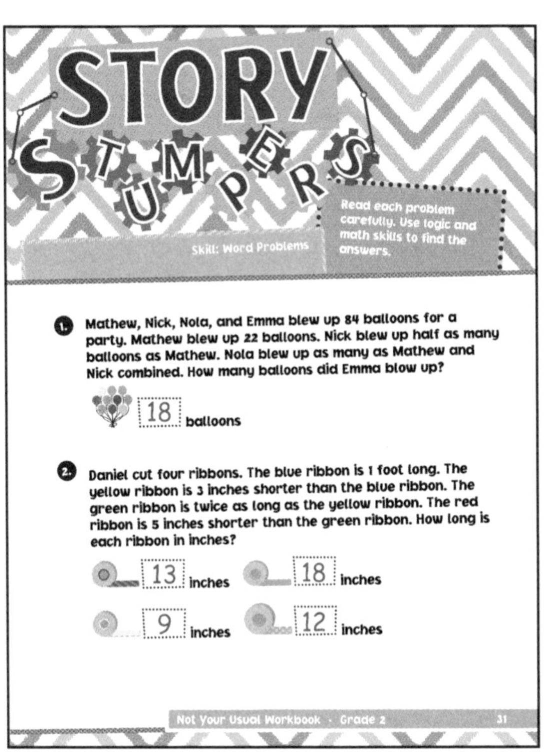

Page 31

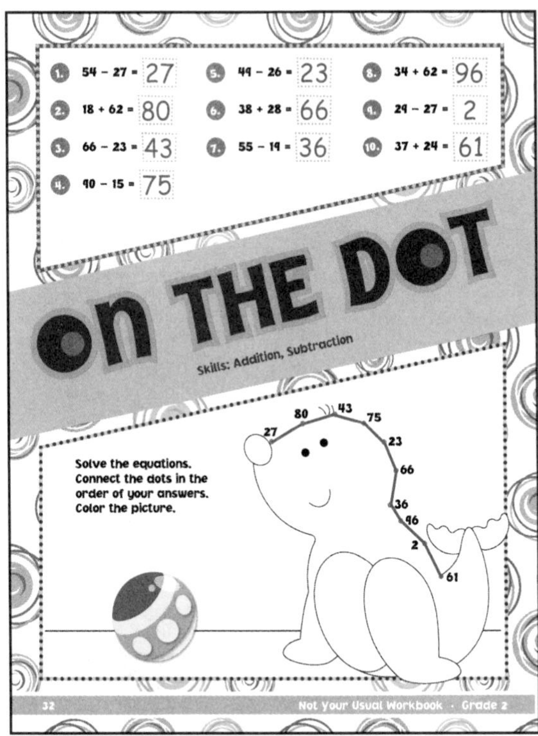

1. 54 − 27 = 27
2. 18 + 62 = 80
3. 66 − 23 = 43
4. 90 − 15 = 75
5. 49 − 26 = 23
6. 38 + 28 = 66
7. 55 − 19 = 36
8. 34 + 62 = 96
9. 29 − 27 = 2
10. 37 + 24 = 61
ON THE DOT
Skills: Addition, Subtraction
Solve the equations. Connect the dots in the order of your answers. Color the picture.
27
80
43
75
23
66
36
96
2
61
32 Not Your Usual Workbook · Grade 2

Page 32

Page 33

Page 35

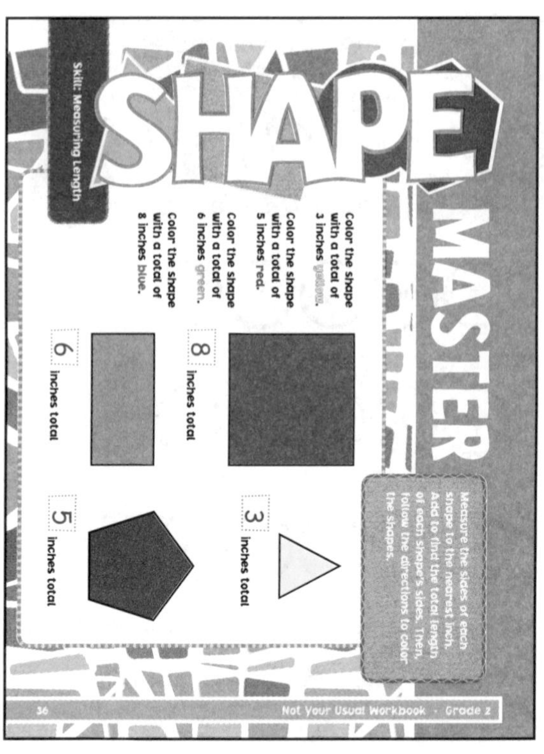

Page 36

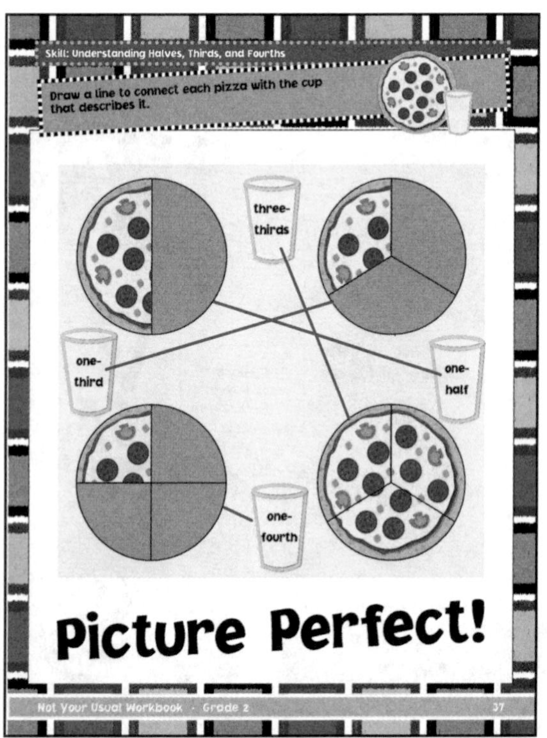

Skill: Understanding Halves, Thirds, and Fourths
Draw a line to connect each pizza with the cup that describes it.
three-thirds
one-third
one-half
one-fourth
Picture Perfect!
Not Your Usual Workbook · Grade 2 37

Page 37

Page 38

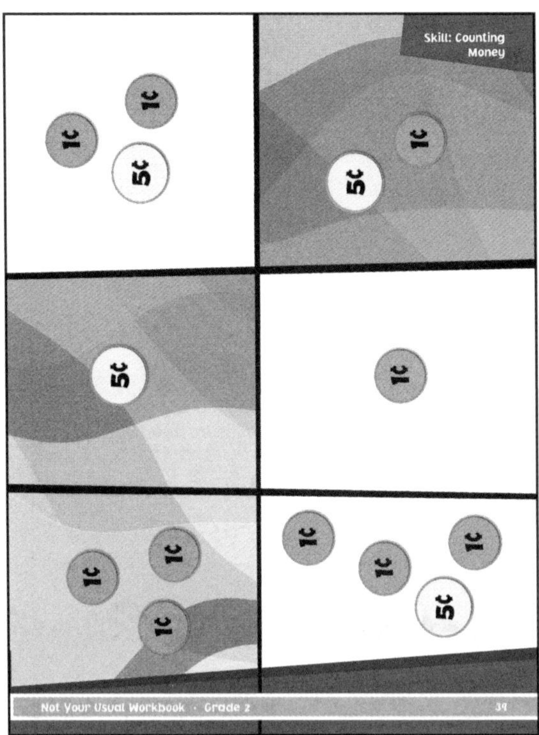

Page 39

Page 40

e(quation) sen+sation
Some numbers are missing from the math problems.
Use the blocks to help you complete the equations.
Skills: Place Value, Addition, Subtraction
2 12 – 1 0 5 = 1 0 7
1 8 3 + 4 5 = 2 2 8
1 9 7 – 1 6 2 = 3 5
Not Your Usual Workbook · Grade 2
41

Page 41

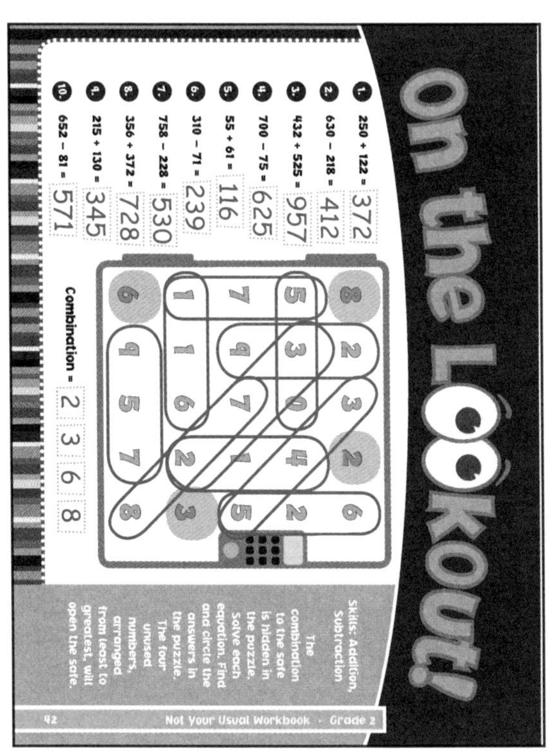

Page 42

Page 43

Skill: Place Value
How much money is in the bag? It depends on how you arrange the numbers! Make the four highest numbers you can using digits shown on the bag. Use each digit only once.
Answers may vary. Possible answers shown.
$953
$952
$841
$741
Picture Perfect!
Not Your Usual Workbook · Grade 2
45

Page 45

Skill: Addition
14
11
20
18
Answers may vary. Possible answers shown.
Begin each puzzle at the arrow. Find a path by adding numbers until you reach the sum shown above the puzzle. The path for each puzzle should include at least four squares.
Math path
46
Not Your Usual Workbook · Grade 2

Page 46

Page 47

STORY STUMPERS

Read each problem carefully. Use logic and math skills to find the answers.

Skills: Word Problems, Counting Money

1. Hailey has 57¢. None of the coins are quarters. The number of nickels equals the number of dimes and pennies combined. How many of each coin does she have?

1¢ 2 pennies 5¢ 5 nickels 10¢ 3 dimes

2. Robbie bought a toy car for 69¢. He paid with one dollar. He received three different coins as change. Circle the coins that made up his change. Write the amount.

1¢ 5¢ 10¢ 25¢ 31 ¢

69¢

3. A yo-yo costs 45¢. Lexi paid using two different types of coins. She used an equal number of each coin. How many of which coins did she use?

1¢ 0 pennies 5¢ 3 nickels

10¢ 3 dimes 25¢ 0 quarters

48 Not Your Usual Workbook · Grade 2

Page 48

PATTERN POWER

Skill: Adding 10 or 100

1. 156 256 356 456 556 656
2. 400 500 600 700 800 900
3. 26 36 46 56 66 76
4. 128 138 148 158 168 178

Find the pattern shown by the numbers in each row. Then, fill in the missing digits.

Not Your Usual Workbook · Grade 2 49

Page 49

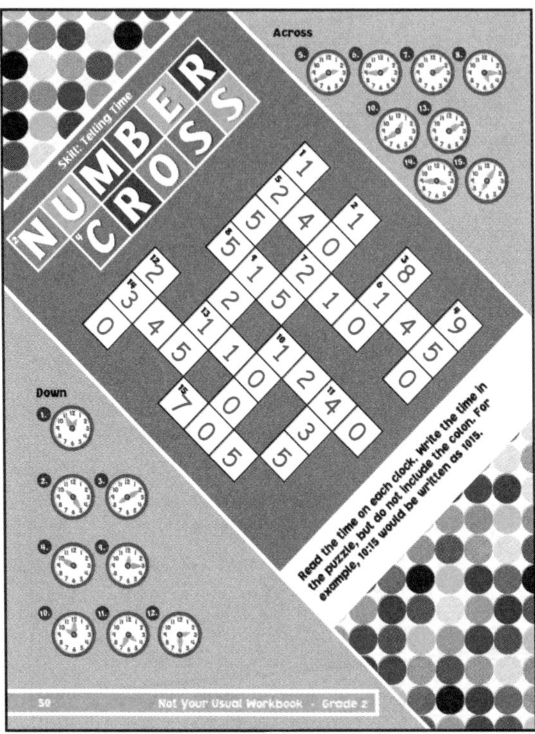

NUMBER CROSS

Skill: Telling Time

Across

Down

Read the time on each clock. Write the time in the puzzle, but do not include the colon. For example, 10:15 would be written as 1015.

50 Not Your Usual Workbook · Grade 2

Page 50

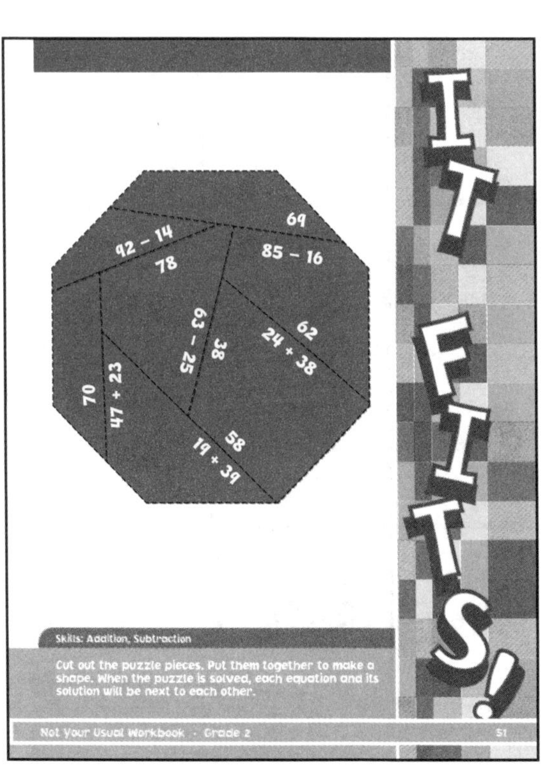

IT FITS!

Skills: Addition, Subtraction

Cut out the puzzle pieces. Put them together to make a shape. When the puzzle is solved, each equation and its solution will be next to each other.

Not Your Usual Workbook · Grade 2 51

Page 51

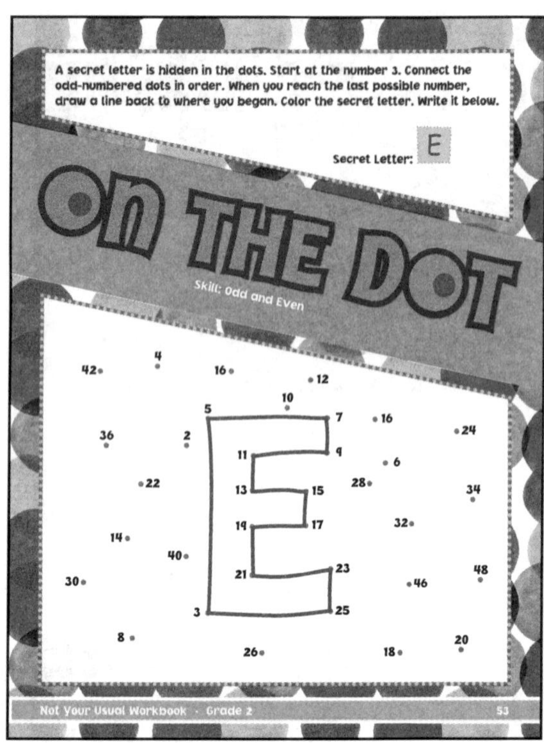

Page 53

Page 54

Page 55

Page 56

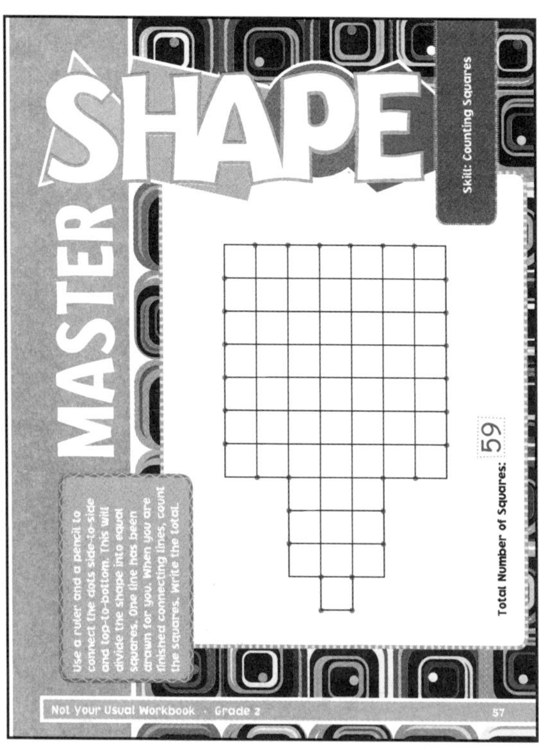
MASTER SHAPE

Skill: Counting Squares

Use a ruler and a pencil to connect the dots side-to-side and top-to-bottom. This will divide the shape into equal squares. One line has been drawn for you. When you are finished connecting lines, count the squares. Write the total.

Total Number of Squares: 59

Not Your Usual Workbook · Grade 2 57

Page 57

e(quation) sen+sation

Skills: Addition, Subtraction

Write + or – on each balloon to make the equation true.

1. 16 − 5 + 2 = 13
2. 8 + 9 − 11 = 6
3. 5 + 10 + 3 = 18
4. 2 + 19 − 5 = 16
5. 7 + 12 − 1 = 18
6. 18 − 1 − 5 = 12

58 Not Your Usual Workbook · Grade 2

Page 58

DARE TO DECODE

Skill: Counting Money

The coins of Animalonia are worth the same amounts as American coins. Draw a line to match the coins with the same values. Use the amounts shown below as clues.

= 51¢
= 40¢
= 21¢
= 35¢

1¢ 5¢ 10¢ 25¢

Not Your Usual Workbook · Grade 2 59

Page 59

QUICK DRAW

Make a drawing to illustrate each story problem. In the blanks, use doubles to write an equation that shows the solution.

Skills: Using Arrays, Word Problems

Aunt Minnie planted 4 rows of bean plants. She planted 4 bean plants in each row. How many bean plants are in Minnie's garden? Use doubles in your equation.

8 + 8 = 16

In a parking lot, cars were parked in 4 rows. There were 5 cars in each row. How many cars were parked in the lot? Use doubles in your equation.

10 + 10 = 20

60 Not Your Usual Workbook · Grade 2

Page 60

Page 61

On the LOOKout!
Skills: Numerals, Expanded Form
Read the expanded forms. Find the matching numerals in the puzzle.
1. 100 + 50 + 6 = 156
2. 400 + 30 + 5 = 435
3. 300 + 70 + 5 = 375
4. 500 + 40 + 3 = 543
5. 400 + 80 + 2 = 482
6. 200 + 20 + 9 = 229
7. 100 + 90 + 6 = 196
8. 700 + 10 + 5 = 715
9. 800 + 50 + 3 = 853
10. 300 + 60 + 4 = 364

Page 63

Page 64

Page 65

Page 66

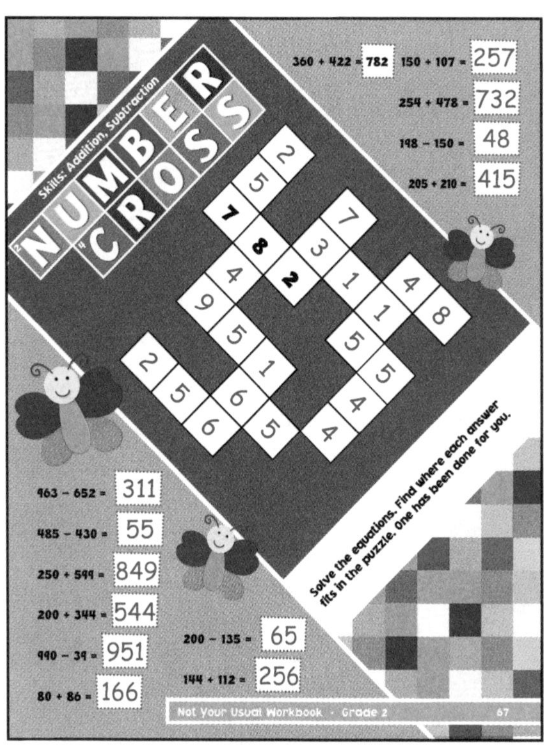

Page 67

Page 68

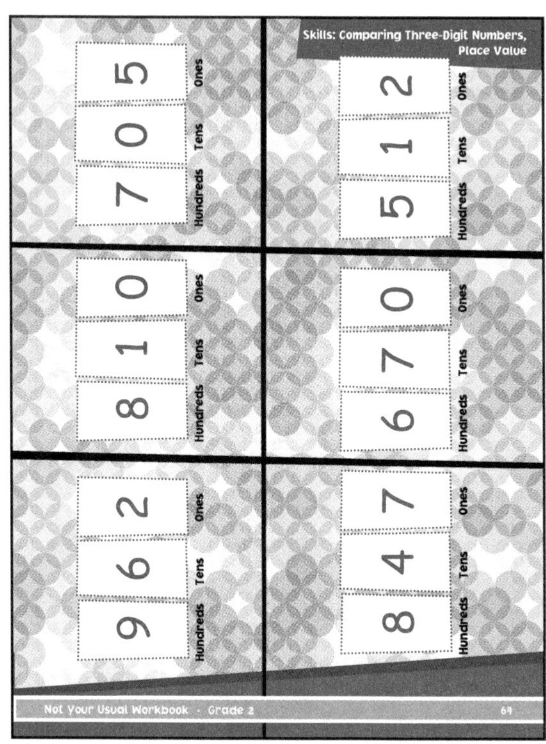

Page 69

Page 70

Page 71

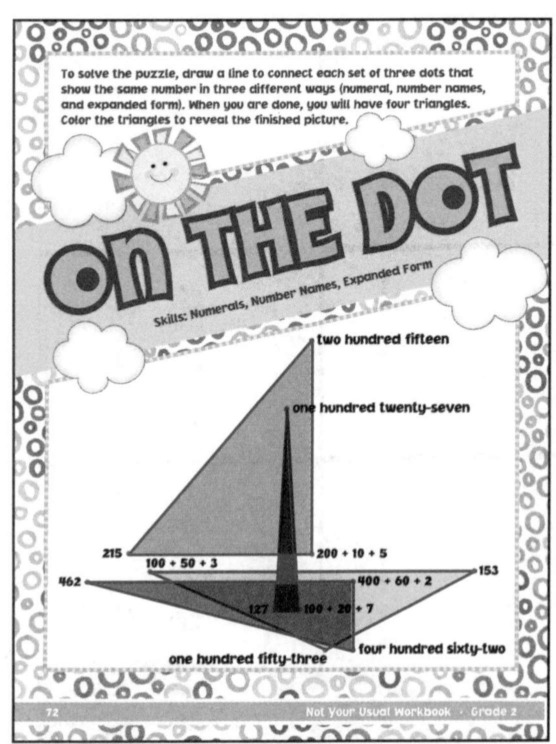

Page 72

Page 73

Page 75

e(quation) sen+sation
Skill: Using Arrays
Look at each group of dots. Solve the equations beside it. Then, circle all the equations that describe the dots.
4 + 4 + 4 = 12
3 + 3 + 3 + 3 = 12
4 + 3 + 4 = 11
6 + 6 = 12
12 + 12 = 24
5 + 5 + 5 + 5 + 5 = 25
10 + 10 + 5 = 25
12 + 12 + 1 = 25
5 + 5 + 5 + 5 = 20
4 + 4 + 4 + 4 + 4 = 20
8 + 10 = 18
10 + 10 = 20
5 + 5 + 5 = 15
7 + 7 = 14
7 + 7 + 1 = 15
3 + 3 + 3 + 3 + 3 = 15
76
Not Your Usual Workbook · Grade 2

Page 76

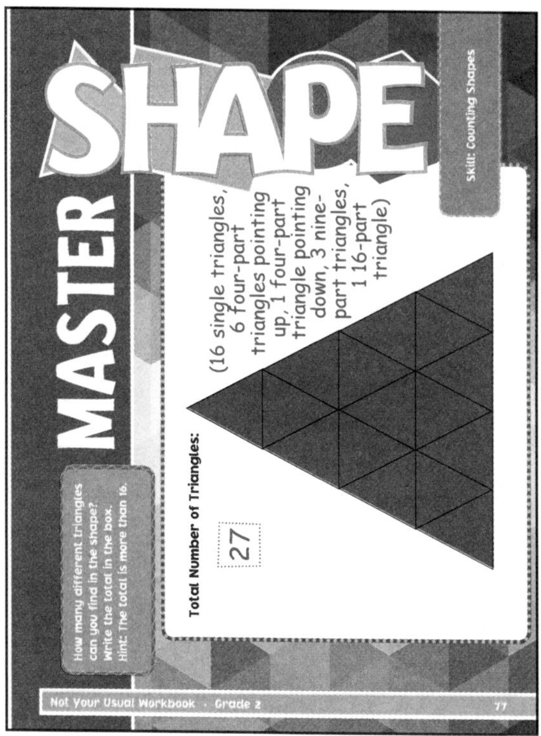

MASTER SHAPE
Skill: Counting Shapes
(16 single triangles, 6 four-part triangles pointing up, 1 four-part triangle pointing down, 3 nine-part triangles, 1 16-part triangle)
Total Number of Triangles:
27
How many different triangles can you find in the shape? Write the total in the box. Hint: The total is more than 16.
Not Your Usual Workbook · Grade 2
77

Page 77

Page 78

Draw a picture that includes a tree that is 18 feet tall, an adult who is 6 feet tall, a child who is 4 feet tall, and a dog that is 2 feet tall. Use the ruler to help you.
QUICK DRAW
Skill: Measuring Length
tree
Drawings will vary.
adult
child
dog
Not Your Usual Workbook · Grade 2
79

Page 79

Page 80

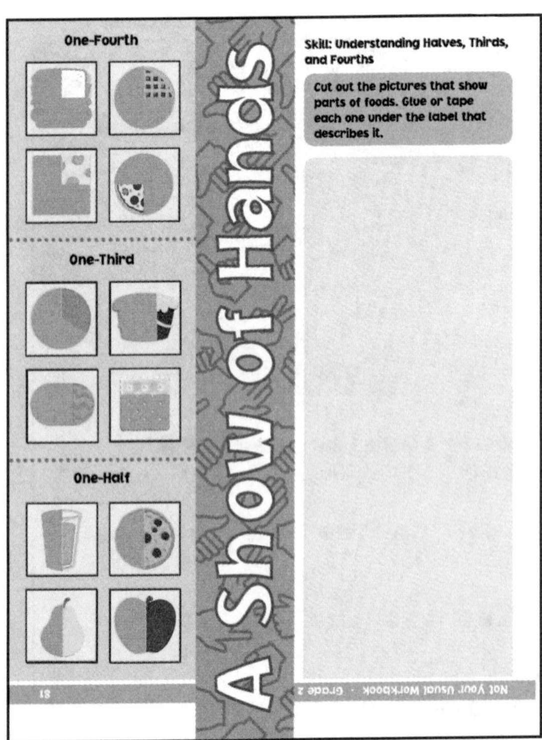

One-Fourth
One-Third
One-Half
A Show of Hands
Skill: Understanding Halves, Thirds, and Fourths
Cut out the pictures that show parts of foods. Glue or tape each one under the label that describes it.

Page 81

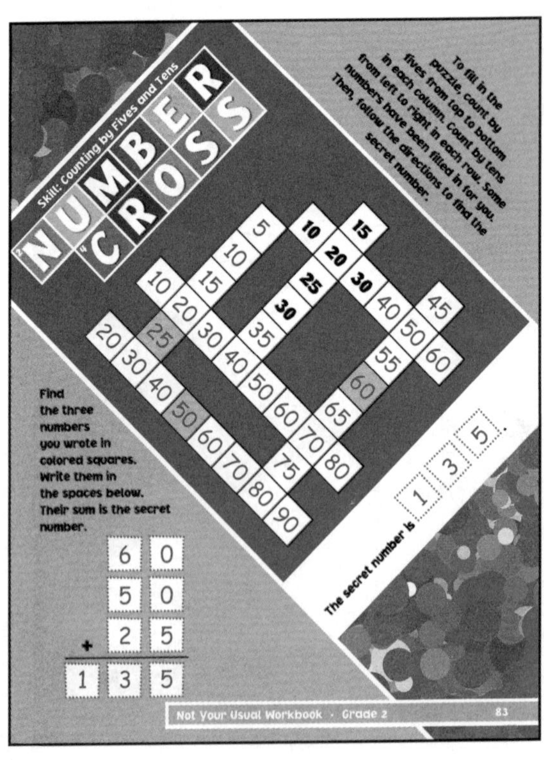

Page 83

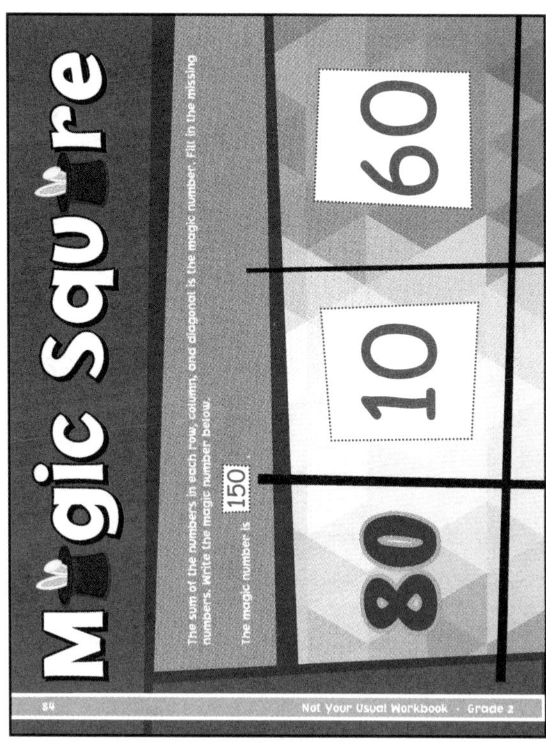

Page 84

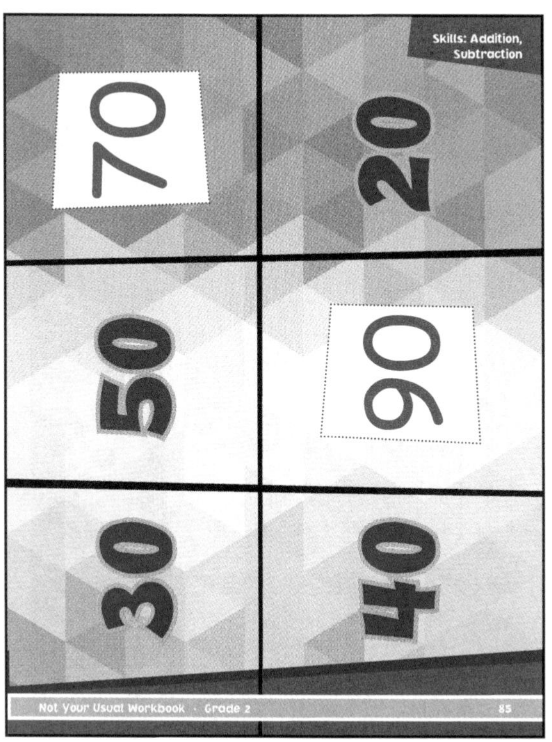

Page 85

Page 86

Page 87

Page 88

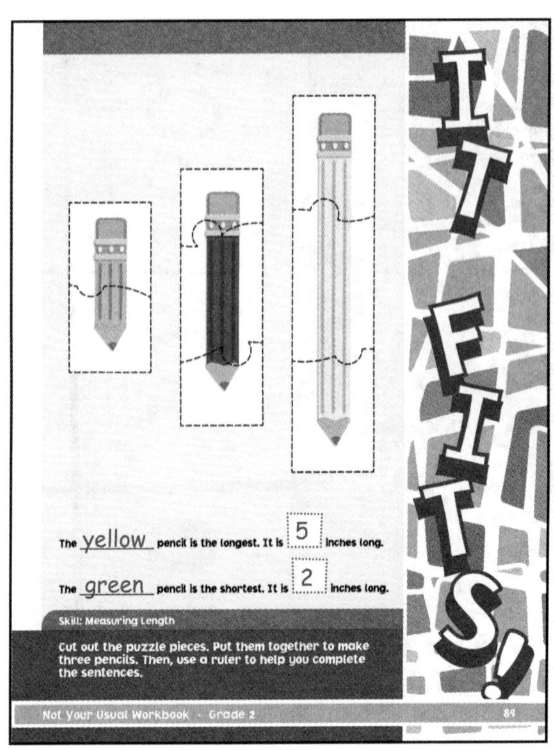

It Fits!
The yellow pencil is the longest. It is 5 inches long.
The green pencil is the shortest. It is 2 inches long.
Skill: Measuring Length
Cut out the puzzle pieces. Put them together to make three pencils. Then, use a ruler to help you complete the sentences.
Not Your Usual Workbook · Grade 2 89

Page 89

Pattern Power
Skills: Addition, Subtraction
12 24 36 48 60 72 84
75 65 55 45 35 25 15
9 18 27 36 45 54 63
2 4 8 16 32 64 128
84 74 64 54 44 34 24
Find the pattern in each row of numbers. Fill in the missing numbers.
Not Your Usual Workbook · Grade 2 91

Page 91

Page 92

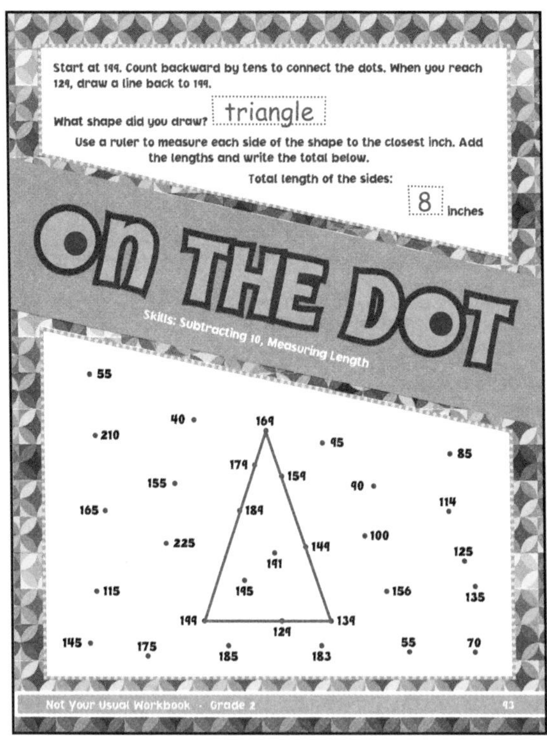

Start at 199. Count backward by tens to connect the dots. When you reach 129, draw a line back to 199.

What shape did you draw? triangle

Use a ruler to measure each side of the shape to the closest inch. Add the lengths and write the total below.

Total length of the sides: 8 inches

ON THE DOT

Skills: Subtracting 10, Measuring Length

Not Your Usual Workbook · Grade 2 93

Page 93

e(quation) sen+sation

Skills: Addition, Subtraction

Someone stole numbers from these equations! Use logic and math to write in the missing digits.

115 + 147 = 262

306 + 244 = 550

412 + 293 = 705

282 + 519 = 801

94 Not Your Usual Workbook · Grade 2

Page 94

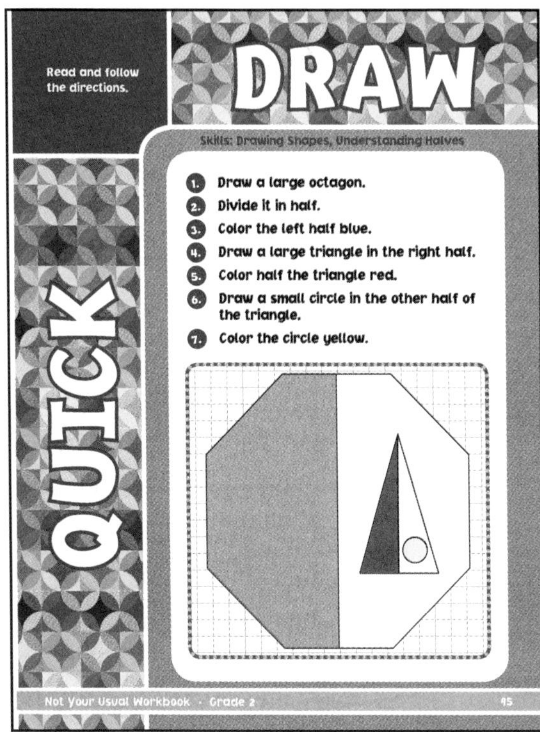

Read and follow the directions.

QUICK DRAW

Skills: Drawing Shapes, Understanding Halves

1. Draw a large octagon.
2. Divide it in half.
3. Color the left half blue.
4. Draw a large triangle in the right half.
5. Color half the triangle red.
6. Draw a small circle in the other half of the triangle.
7. Color the circle yellow.

Not Your Usual Workbook · Grade 2 95

Page 95

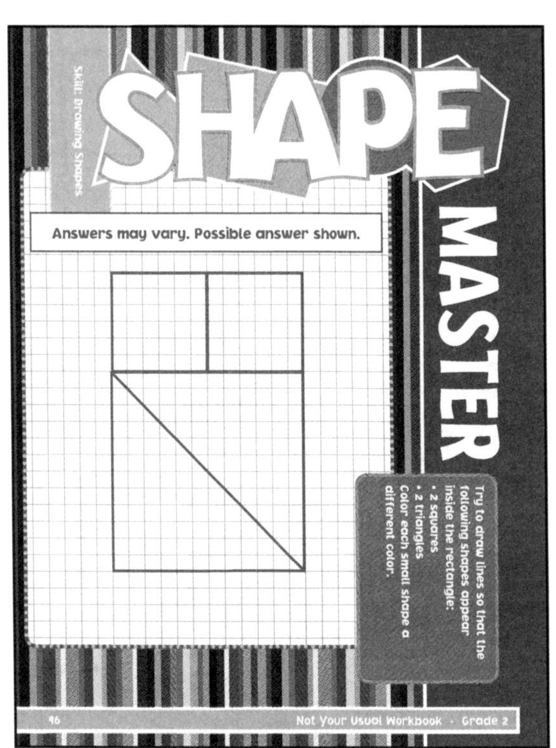

SHAPE MASTER

Skill: Drawing Shapes

Answers may vary. Possible answer shown.

Try to draw lines so that the following shapes appear inside the rectangle:
- 2 squares
- 2 triangles

Color each small shape a different color.

96 Not Your Usual Workbook · Grade 2

Page 96

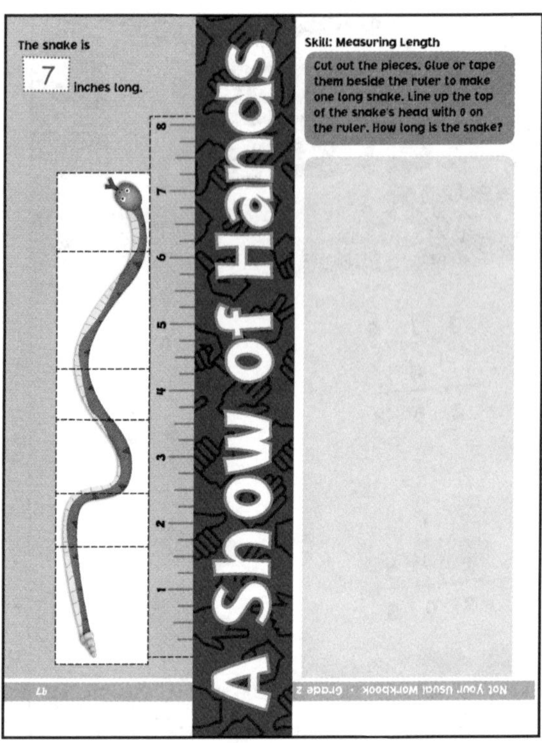
The snake is
7
inches long.
A Show of Hands
Skill: Measuring Length
Cut out the pieces. Glue or tape them beside the ruler to make one long snake. Line up the top of the snake's head with 0 on the ruler. How long is the snake?

Page 97

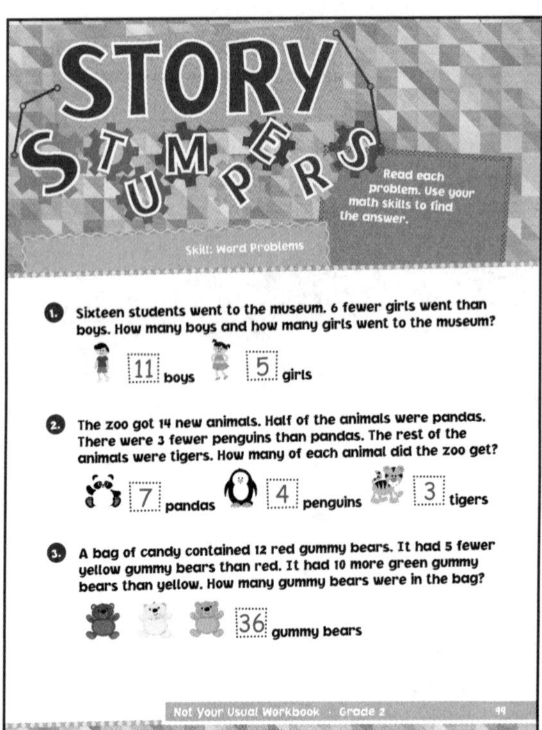
STORY STUMPERS
Read each problem. Use your math skills to find the answer.
Skill: Word Problems
1. Sixteen students went to the museum. 6 fewer girls went than boys. How many boys and how many girls went to the museum?
11 boys 5 girls
2. The zoo got 14 new animals. Half of the animals were pandas. There were 3 fewer penguins than pandas. The rest of the animals were tigers. How many of each animal did the zoo get?
7 pandas 4 penguins 3 tigers
3. A bag of candy contained 12 red gummy bears. It had 5 fewer yellow gummy bears than red. It had 10 more green gummy bears than yellow. How many gummy bears were in the bag?
36 gummy bears
Not Your Usual Workbook · Grade 2

Page 99

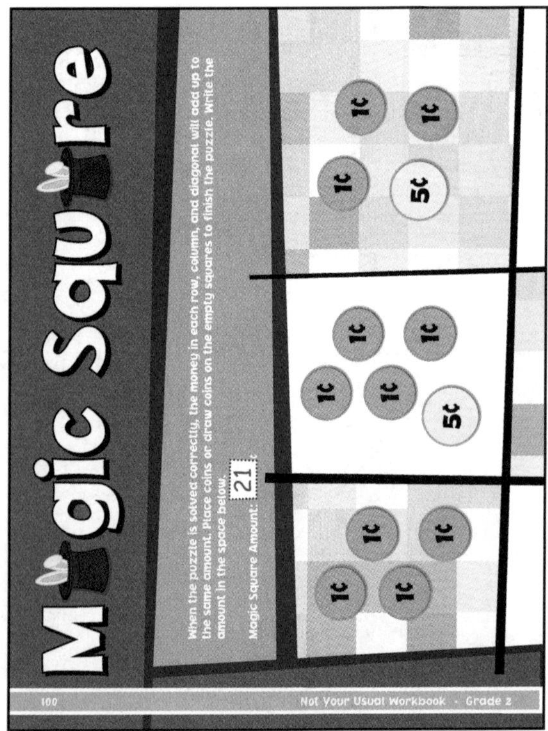
Magic Square
When the puzzle is solved correctly, the money in each row, column, and diagonal will add up to the same amount. Place coins or draw coins on the empty squares to finish the puzzle. Write the amount in the space below.
Magic Square Amount: 21
100 Not Your Usual Workbook · Grade 2

Page 100

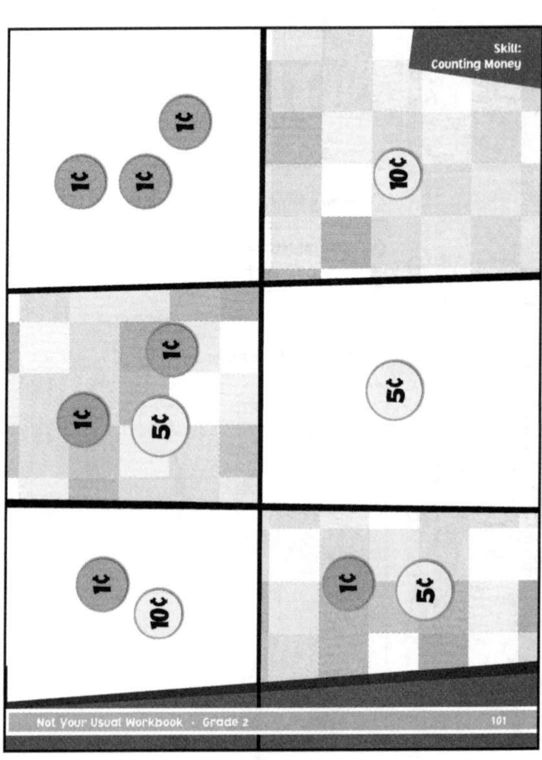
Skill: Counting Money
Not Your Usual Workbook · Grade 2 101

Page 101

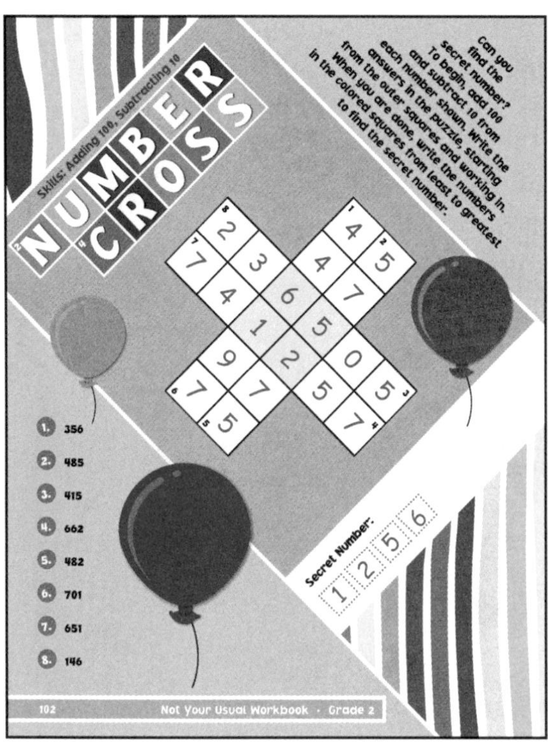

Page 102

Page 103

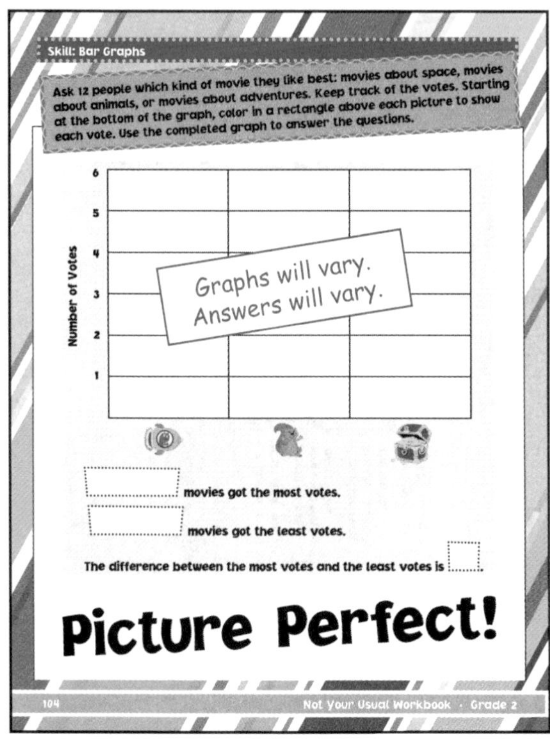

Page 104

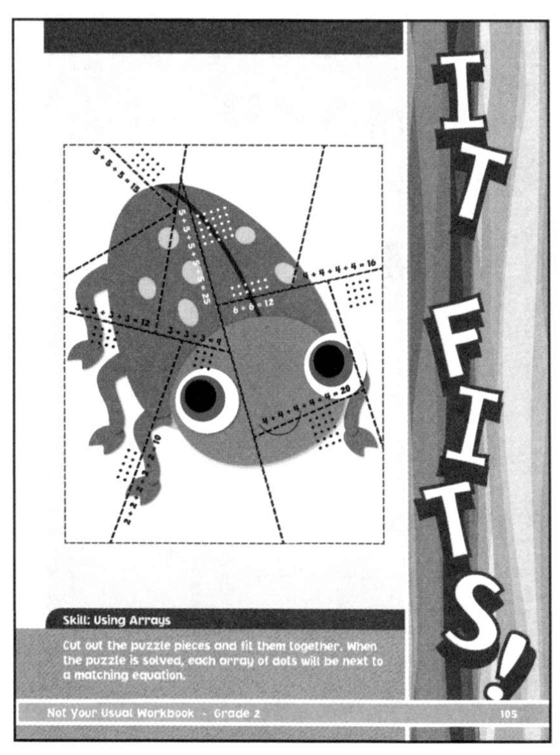

IT FITS!
Skill: Using Arrays
Cut out the puzzle pieces and fit them together. When the puzzle is solved, each array of dots will be next to a matching equation.
Not Your Usual Workbook · Grade 2 105

Page 105

Skill: Adjectives

In Search Of

Circle the adjective in each phrase. Find it in the puzzle.

a sweet peach · a full glass · the deep pool
the furry kitten · a chilly rain · a red pen
a sunny day · a safe place

108 Not Your Usual Workbook · Grade 2

Page 108

snow / ball · sun / flower · gold / fish

Skill: Compound Words

IN PIECES

Cut out the puzzle pieces. Match them to make ice cream cones that show compound words.

pan / cake · wheel / chair · flash / light

Not Your Usual Workbook · Grade 2 109

Page 109

Sudoku for You

E	M	C	I
I	C	E	M
M	E	I	C
C	I	M	E

Skill: Irregular Plurals

Write letters in the boxes so that each row and column has the letters to spell the plural of "mouse." No letter should appear twice in the same row or column. Do not guess. Use logic!

111 Not Your Usual Workbook · Grade 2

Page 111

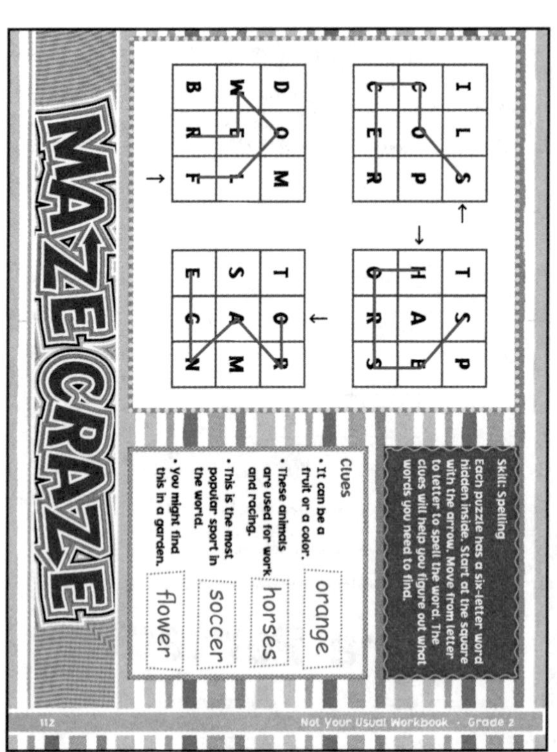

Maze Craze

Skill: Spelling

Each puzzle has a six-letter word hidden inside. Start at the square with the arrow. Move from letter to letter to spell the word. The clues will help you figure out what words you need to find.

Clues

- It can be a fruit or a color. orange
- These animals are used for work and racing. horses
- This is the most popular sport in the world. soccer
- You might find this in a garden. flower

112 Not Your Usual Workbook · Grade 2

Page 112

Page 113

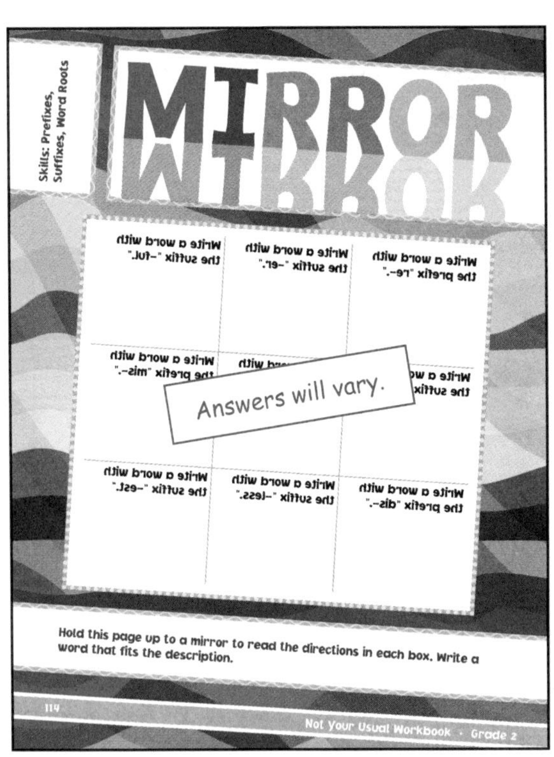

Page 114

Page 115

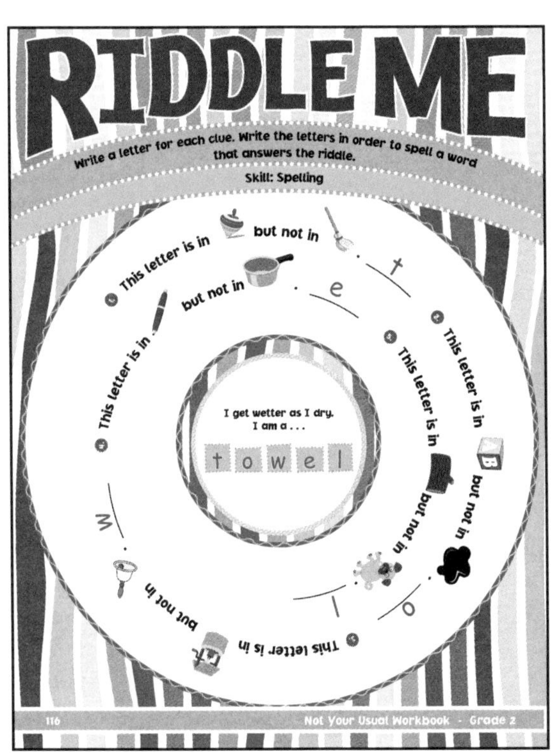

Page 116

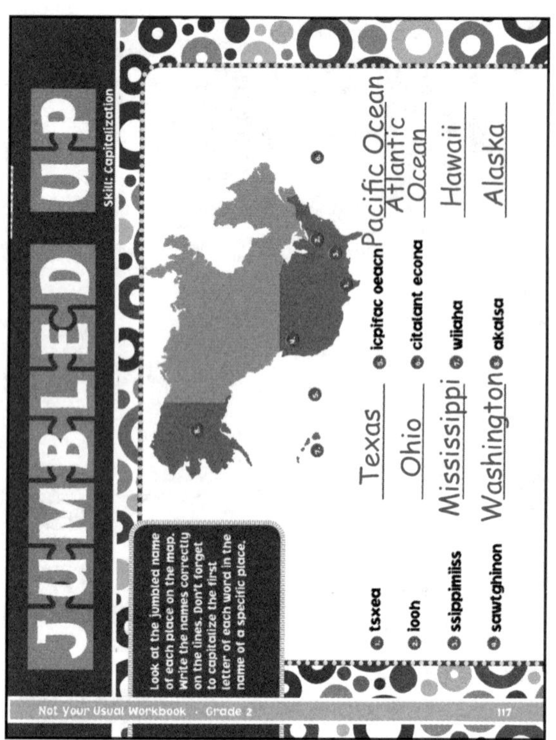
JUMBLED UP
Skill: Capitalization

Look at the jumbled name of each place on the map. Write the names correctly on the lines. Don't forget to capitalize the first letter of each word in the name of a specific place.

1. tsxea — Texas
2. iooh — Ohio
3. ssippimiss — Mississippi
4. sawtghinon — Washington
5. icpifac oeacn — Pacific Ocean
6. citalant econa — Atlantic Ocean
7. wiiaha — Hawaii
8. akaisa — Alaska

Not Your Usual Workbook · Grade 2 117

Page 117

WORD MATH
Skill: Point of View

Use the letters and pictures to decode each sentence. Write it in the blank. Is the sentence in first-person point of view? Write "F" in the box. Is it in third-person point of view? Write "T" in the box.

1. I like to play the drums. F
2. Max can meet his friend at the park. T

118 Not Your Usual Workbook · Grade 2

Page 118

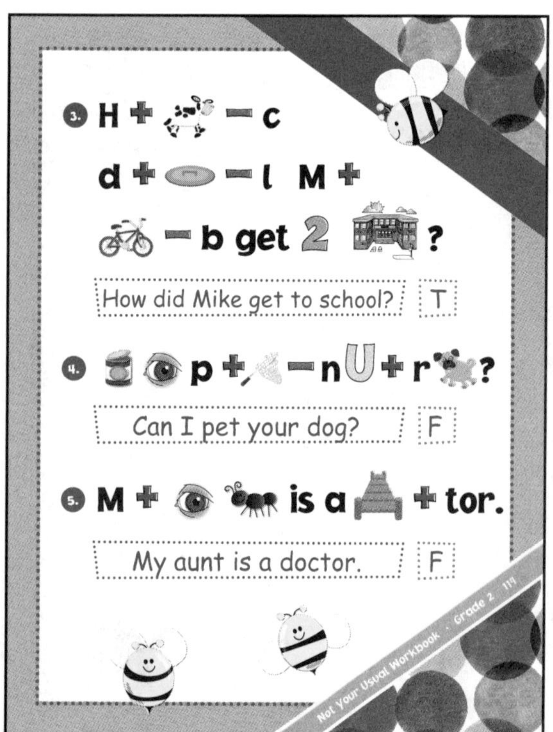
3. How did Mike get to school? T
4. Can I pet your dog? F
5. My aunt is a doctor. F

Not Your Usual Workbook · Grade 2 119

Page 119

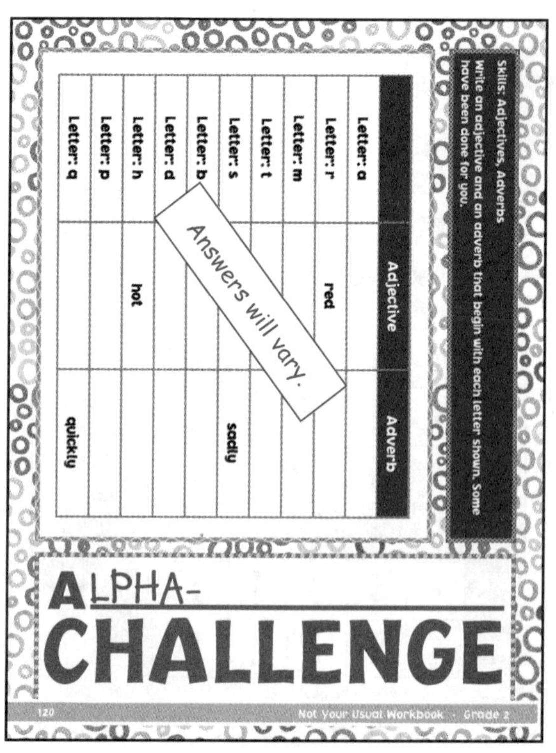
Skills: Adjectives, Adverbs

Write an adjective and an adverb that begin with each letter shown. Some have been done for you.

	Adjective	Adverb
Letter: a		
Letter: r	red	
Letter: m		
Letter: t		
Letter: s		sadly
Letter: b		
Letter: d		
Letter: h	hot	
Letter: p		
Letter: q		quickly

Answers will vary.

ALPHA-CHALLENGE

120 Not Your Usual Workbook · Grade 2

Page 120

Page 121

Skills: Prefixes, Suffixes, Word Roots
Read the prefix or suffix on each cloud. On the raindrops, write four words that contain that prefix or suffix.
un-
-est
re-
-less
Answers will vary.
Picture This!
122
Not Your Usual Workbook · Grade 2

Page 122

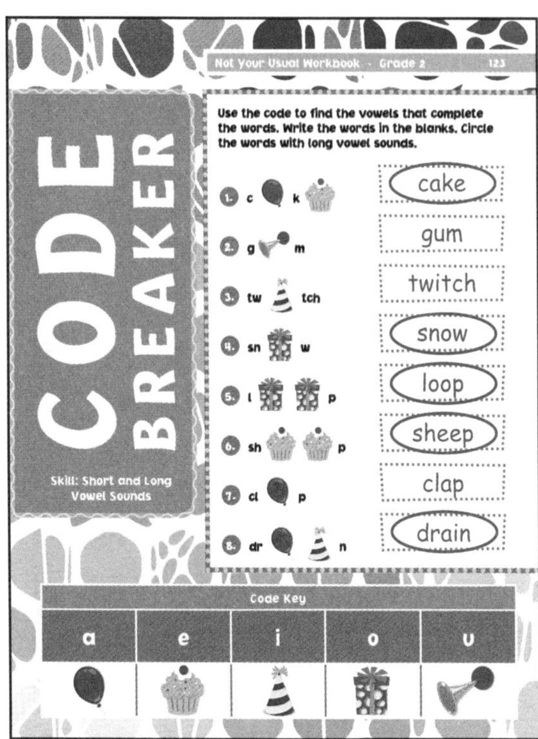

Not Your Usual Workbook · Grade 2
123
CODE BREAKER
Skill: Short and Long Vowel Sounds
Use the code to find the vowels that complete the words. Write the words in the blanks. Circle the words with long vowel sounds.
cake
gum
twitch
snow
loop
sheep
clap
drain
Code Key
a
e
i
o
u

Page 123

Page 124

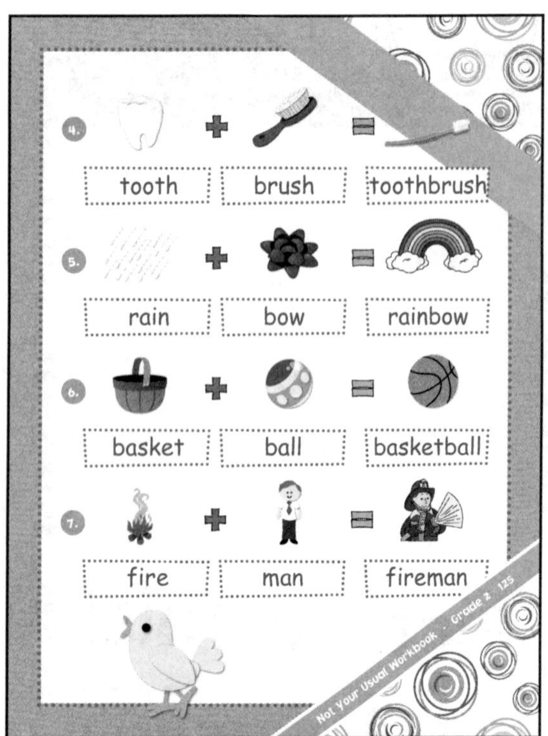

4. tooth + brush = toothbrush

5. rain + bow = rainbow

6. basket + ball = basketball

7. fire + man = fireman

Page 125

Sudoku for you

Skill: Vocabulary

Write letters in the boxes so that each row and column has the letters to spell a word that means "feeling very sad." No letter should appear twice in the same row or column. Do not guess. Use logic!

U	B	L	E
L	E	U	**B**
E	**L**	B	U
B	U	**E**	L

Page 126

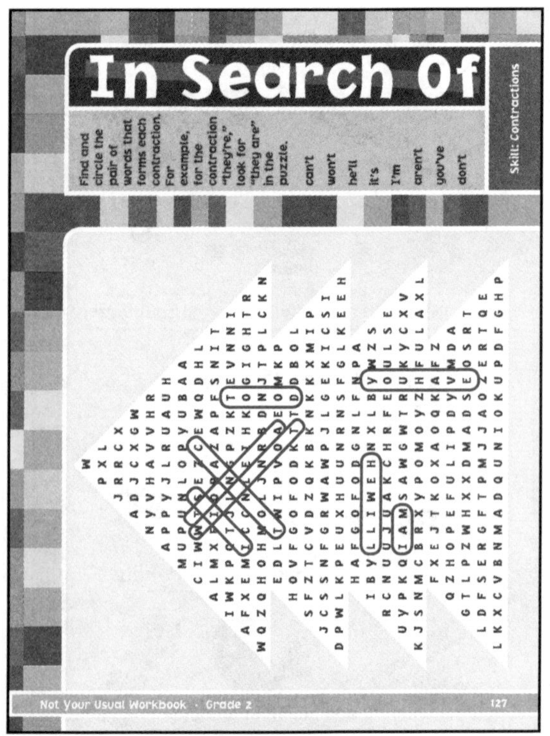

In Search Of

Skill: Contractions

Find and circle the pair of words that forms each contraction. For example, for the contraction "they're," look for "they are" in the puzzle.

can't
won't
he'll
it's
I'm
aren't
you've
don't

Page 127

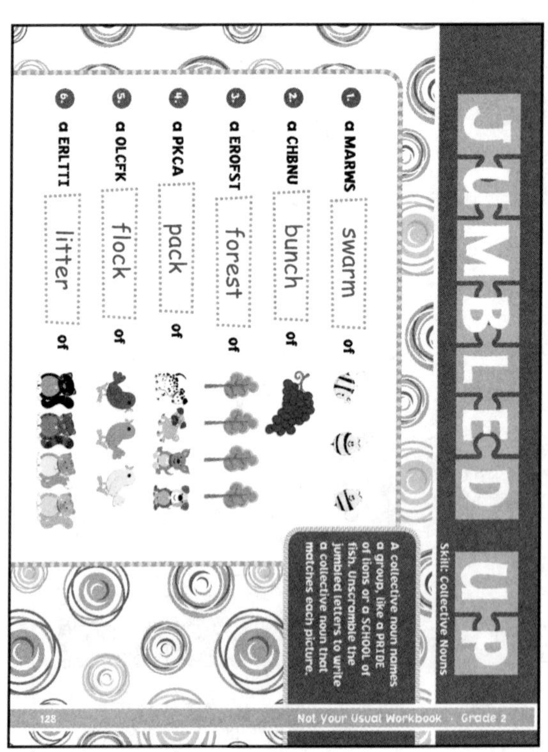

Jumbled Up

Skill: Collective Nouns

A collective noun names a group, like a PRIDE of lions or a SCHOOL of fish. Unscramble the jumbled letters to write a collective noun that matches each picture.

1. a MARWS swarm of
2. a CHBNU bunch of
3. a EROFST forest of
4. a PKCA pack of
5. a OLCFK flock of
6. a ERLTTI litter of

Page 128

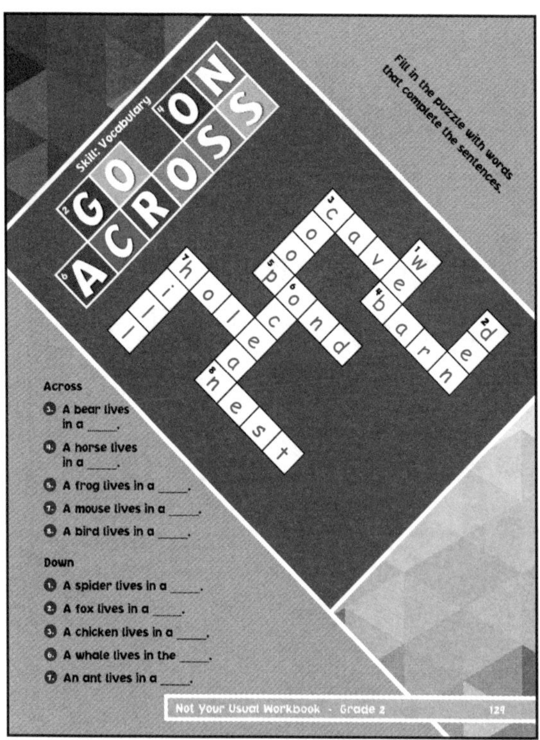

Page 129

Page 130

Page 131

Page 133

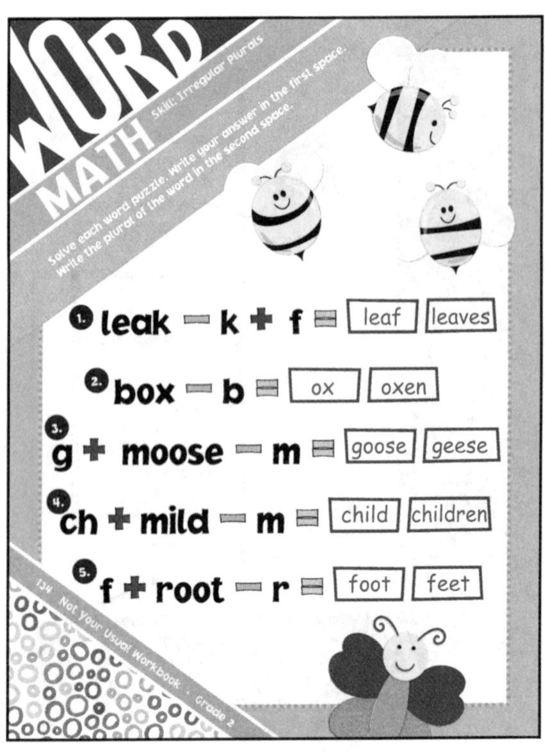

WORD MATH
Skill: Irregular Plurals
Solve each word puzzle. Write your answer in the first space. Write the plural of the word in the second space.
1. leak − k + f = leaf leaves
2. box − b = ox oxen
3. g + moose − m = goose geese
4. ch + mild − m = child children
5. f + root − r = foot feet
134 Not Your Usual Workbook · Grade 2

Page 134

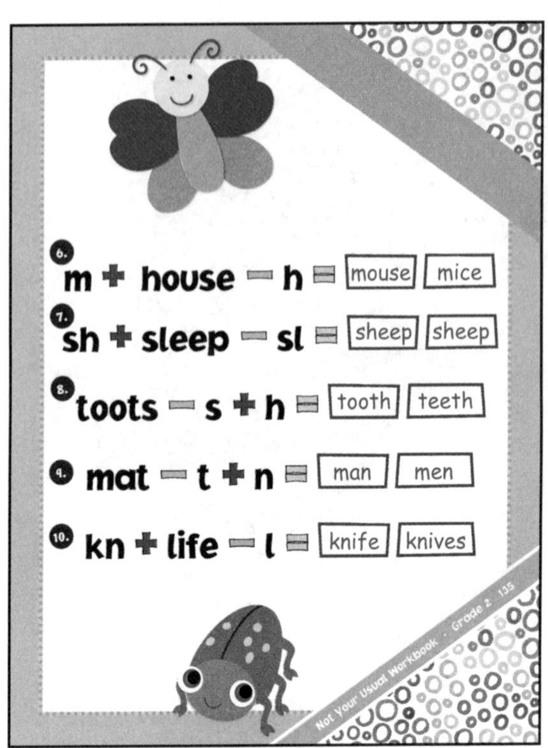

Page 135

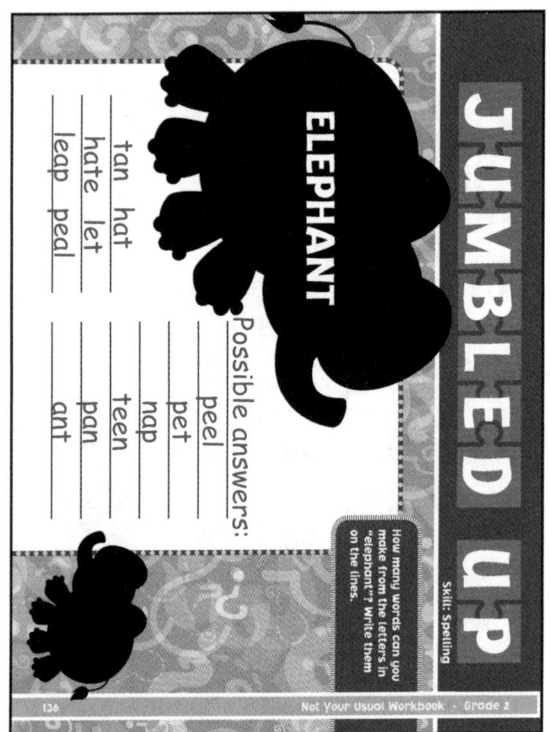

Page 136

Page 137

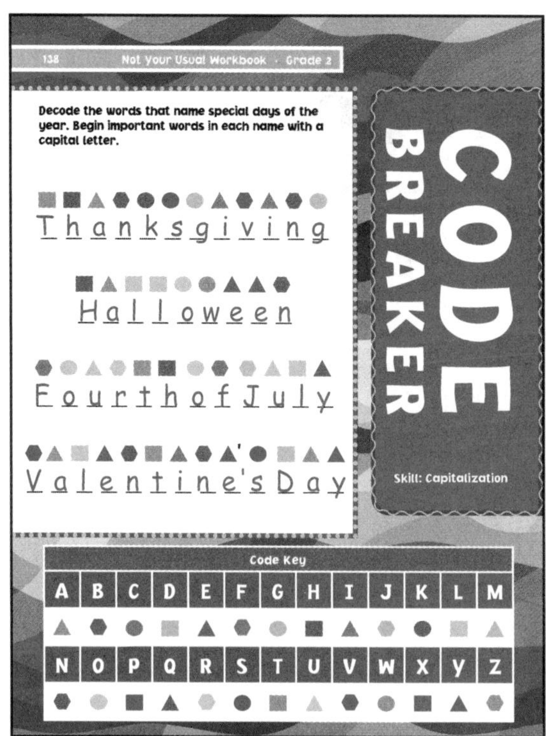

138 Not Your Usual Workbook · Grade 2

CODE BREAKER

Skill: Capitalization

Decode the words that name special days of the year. Begin important words in each name with a capital letter.

Thanksgiving

Halloween

Fourth of July

Valentine's Day

Code Key

A	B	C	D	E	F	G	H	I	J	K	L	M
N	O	P	Q	R	S	T	U	V	W	X	Y	Z

Page 138

Skill: Possessives

The world is a colorful place! Answer each question with a phrase that includes a possessive noun ending with an apostrophe (') and s. For example, you might write "the girl's hair."

Possible answers:

What is blue? the boy's shorts

What is red? the gift's bow

What is black? the dog's nose

What is orange? the duck's bill

What is green? the snowman's hat

What is purple? the lunch box's handle

Picture This!

Not Your Usual Workbook · Grade 2 139

Page 139

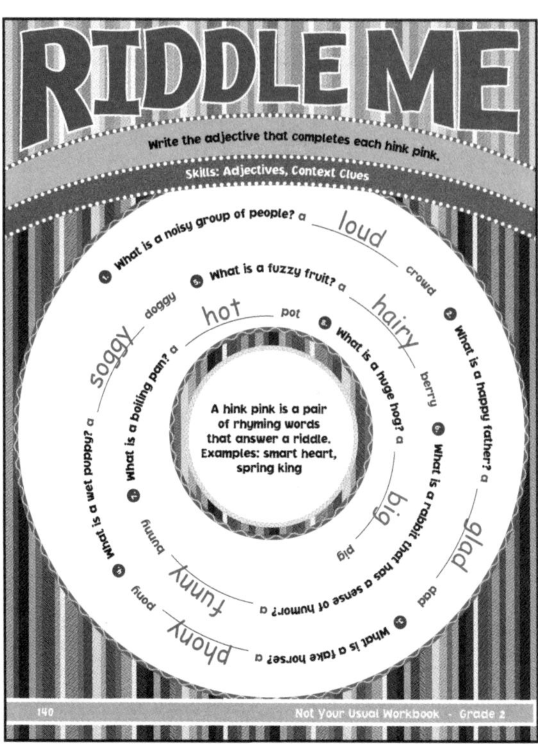

RIDDLE ME

Write the adjective that completes each hink pink.

Skills: Adjectives, Context Clues

What is a noisy group of people? a loud crowd

What is a fuzzy fruit? a hairy berry

What is a happy father? a glad dad

What is a huge hog? a big pig

What is a rabbit that has a sense of humor? a funny bunny

What is a boiling pan? a hot pot

What is a wet puppy? a soggy doggy

What is a fake horse? a phony pony

A hink pink is a pair of rhyming words that answer a riddle. Examples: smart heart, spring king

140 Not Your Usual Workbook · Grade 2

Page 140

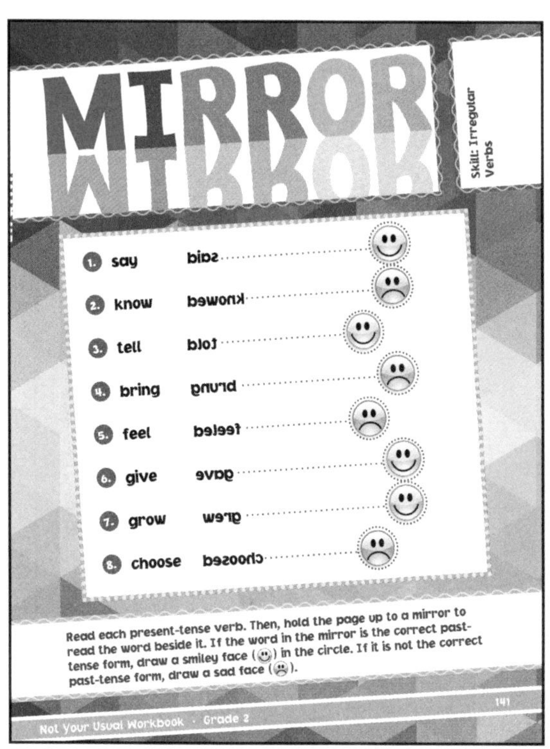

MIRROR

Skill: Irregular Verbs

1. say said
2. know knowed
3. tell told
4. bring brung
5. feel feeled
6. give gave
7. grow grew
8. choose choosed

Read each present-tense verb. Then, hold the page up to a mirror to read the word beside it. If the word in the mirror is the correct past-tense form, draw a smiley face (☺) in the circle. If it is not the correct past-tense form, draw a sad face (☹).

Not Your Usual Workbook · Grade 2 141

Page 141

Skill: Compound Sentences

Sentence Scramble

What a mess! These sentences got scrambled. Draw lines to match the sentence parts and make four compound sentences.

Page 142

Sudoku for you

Skill: Irregular Plurals

Write letters in the boxes so that each row and column has the letters to spell the plural of "ox." No letter should appear twice in the same row or column. Do not guess. Use logic!

O	**E**	X	N
N	X	O	E
X	N	E	**O**
E	O	**N**	X

Page 143

Skill: Spelling

Look at the scene. How many words can you think of to describe it? Try to write one word that begins with each letter of the alphabet. Read each word you wrote. Is it spelled correctly?

ALPHA-CHALLENGE

Page 144

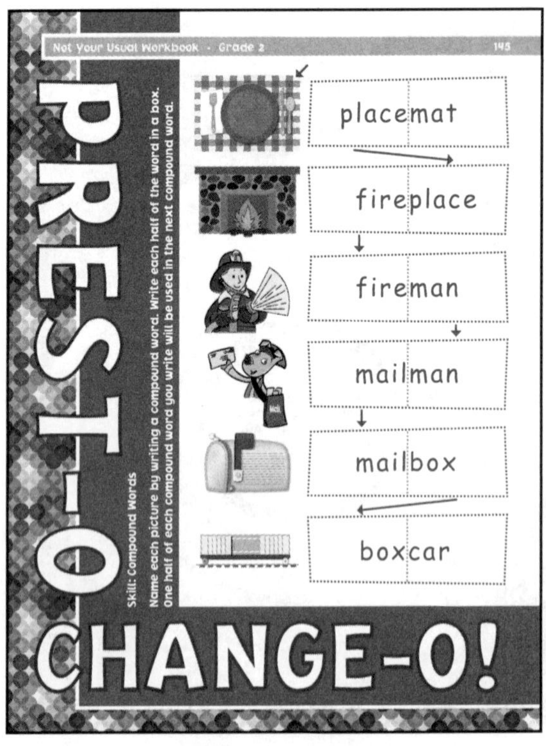

Skill: Compound Words

Name each picture by writing a compound word. Write each half of the word in a box. One half of each compound word you write will be used in the next compound word.

PREST-O CHANGE-O!

Page 145

Choose an animal from the word box. Write five sentences that give clues about the animal. Read your clues to a friend. Can he or she guess the animal?

1.
2.
3.
4.
5.

Sentences will vary.

Word Box

polar bear, kangaroo, elephant, penguin, dolphin, turtle

QUIZ WHIZ

Skill: Writing Sentences

146 Not Your Usual Workbook · Grade 2

Page 146

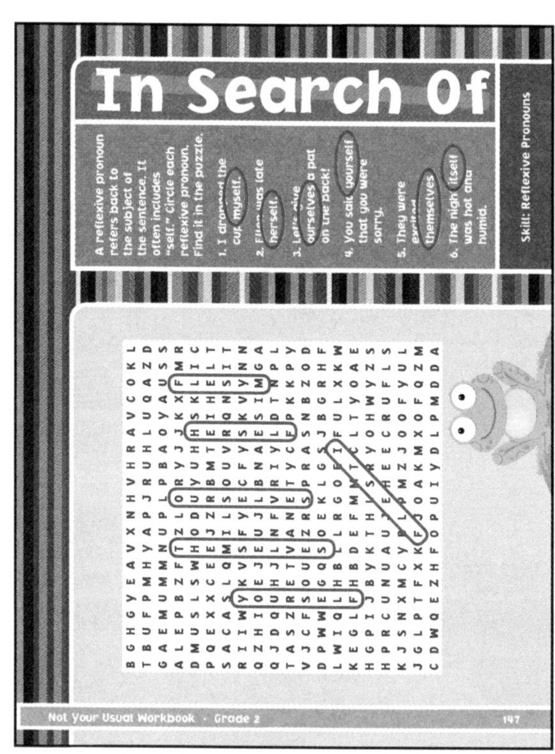
In Search Of

A reflexive pronoun refers back to the subject of the sentence. It often includes "self." Circle each reflexive pronoun. Find it in the puzzle.

1. I dropped the cup myself.
2. Ellen was late herself.
3. Let's give ourselves a pat on the back!
4. You said yourself that you were sorry.
5. They were ... themselves.
6. The night itself was hot and humid.

Skill: Reflexive Pronouns

Not Your Usual Workbook · Grade 2 147

Page 147

Skills: Prefixes, Suffixes, Word Roots

Write each word on the tree that shows its prefix or suffix.

unfair, cheerful, resell, reuse, unwise, useful, joyful, refill, uneven

un-: unfair, unwise, uneven

re-: resell, reuse, refill

-ful: cheerful, useful, joyful

Picture This!

148 Not Your Usual Workbook · Grade 2

Page 148

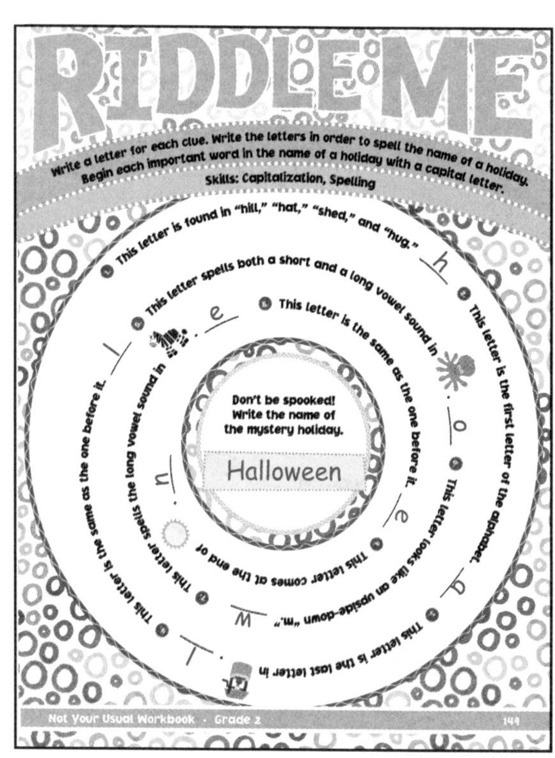
RIDDLE ME

Write a letter for each clue. Write the letters in order to spell the name of a holiday. Begin each important word in the name of a holiday with a capital letter.

Skills: Capitalization, Spelling

This letter is found in "hill," "hat," "shed," and "hug." h

This letter is the first letter of the alphabet. a

This letter is the last letter in ... l

This letter is the same as the one before it. l

This letter spells the long vowel sound in ... o

This letter looks like an upside-down "m." w

This letter spells both a short and a long vowel sound. e

This letter is the same as the one before it. e

This letter comes at the end of ... n

Don't be spooked! Write the name of the mystery holiday. Halloween

Not Your Usual Workbook · Grade 2 149

Page 149

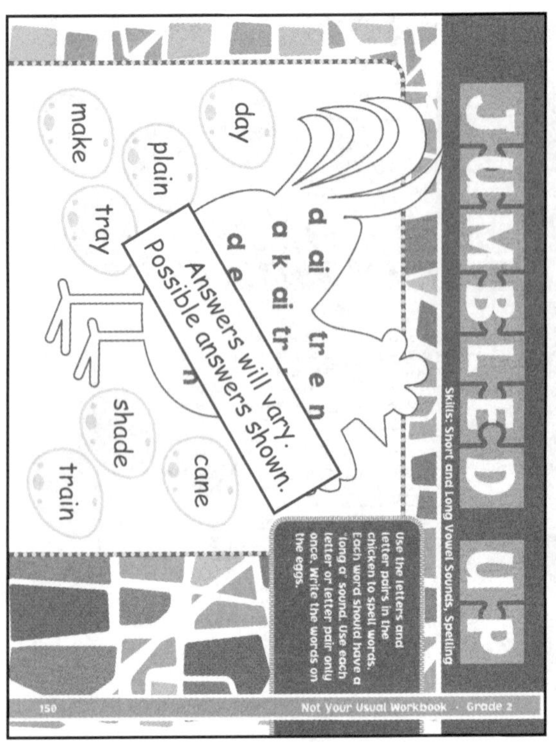
JUMBLED UP

Skills: Short and Long Vowel Sounds, Spelling

Use the letters and letter pairs in the chicken to spell words. Each word should have a 'long a' sound. Use each letter or letter pair only once. Write the words on the eggs.

Answers will vary. Possible answers shown.

day
plain
make
tray
shade
cane
train

150 Not Your Usual Workbook · Grade 2

Page 150

MAZE CRAZE

Skill: Adverbs

Help the alien find its spaceship. Follow the adverbs through the maze. Write a sentence on the lines that includes one of the adverbs you found.

Sentences will vary.

wild, calmly, desk, new, never, lot, soon, swim, gently, lazily, eat, on, kindly, slow, football, my, quickly, bear, pink, very, lamp, jump, push

Not Your Usual Workbook · Grade 2 151

Page 151

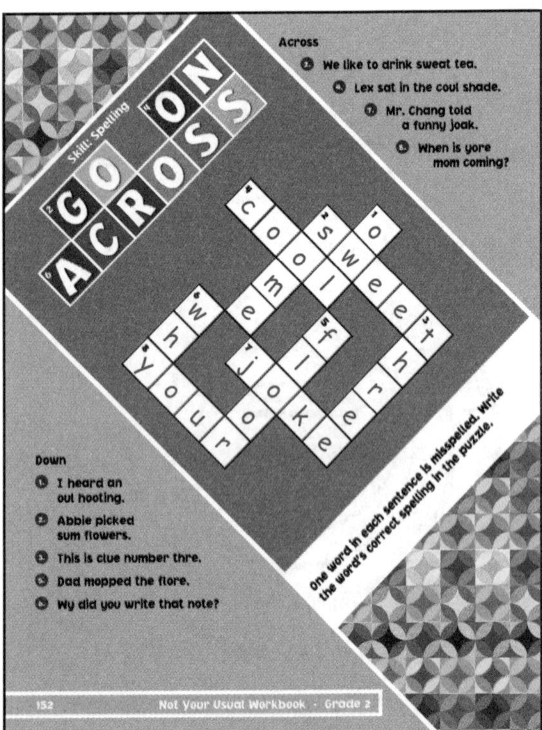
GO ACROSS ON

Skill: Spelling

Across

We like to drink sweat tea.

Lex sat in the coul shade.

Mr. Chang told a funny joak.

When is yore mom coming?

Down

I heard an oul hooting.

Abbie picked sum flowers.

This is clue number thre.

Dad mopped the flore.

Wy did you write that note?

One word in each sentence is misspelled. Write the word's correct spelling in the puzzle.

sweet, cool, joke, your, owl, some, three, floor, why

152 Not Your Usual Workbook · Grade 2

Page 152

MIRROR

Skill: Capitalization

1. grand canyon — Grand Canyon
2. omaha, nebraska — Omaha, Nebraska
3. amazon river — Amazon River
4. blue ridge mountains — Blue Ridge Mountains
5. great salt lake — Great Salt Lake
6. swiss alps — Swiss Alps
7. death valley — Death Valley
8. mississippi river — Mississippi River

Hold the page up to a mirror to read the names of specific places. Write them on the lines. Use a capital letter to begin each word.

Not Your Usual Workbook · Grade 2 153

Page 153

Skill: Contractions

Read the word on each baseball. On the baseball bats, write contractions made from the word. Some are done for you.

Possible answers:

not	wouldn't, won't, can't, didn't
will	you'll, he'll, they'll, I'll
is/are	you're, we're, she's, it's

Picture This!

154 Not Your Usual Workbook · Grade 2

Page 154

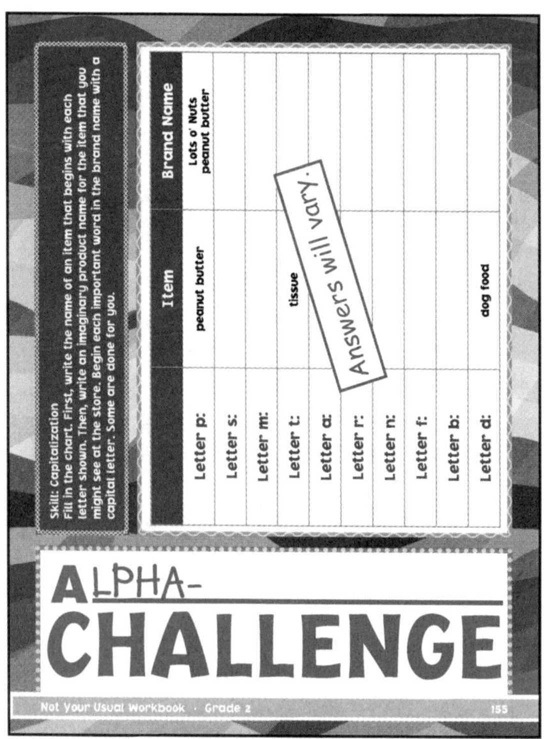

Skill: Capitalization

Fill in the chart. First, write the name of an item that begins with each letter shown. Then, write an imaginary product name for the item that you might see at the store. Begin each important word in the brand name with a capital letter. Some are done for you.

	Item	Brand Name
Letter p:	peanut butter	Lots o' Nuts peanut butter
Letter s:		
Letter m:		
Letter t:	tissue	
Letter a:		
Letter r:		
Letter n:		
Letter f:		
Letter b:		
Letter d:	dog food	

Answers will vary.

ALPHA-CHALLENGE

Not Your Usual Workbook · Grade 2 155

Page 155

156 Not Your Usual Workbook · Grade 2

CODE BREAKER

Skill: Possessives

Use the code to find the secret message. Write the sentence on the lines. Hint: You will need to add two apostrophes, two capital letters, and one period to write the sentence correctly.

8385 1964 95 97 29645 5048

Dad's bike is in Mike's shed.

Code Key									
a	b	d	e	h	i	k	m	n	s
3	1	8	4	0	9	6	2	7	5

Page 156

Frogs don't drink water,
but they absorb it through their skin.
Frogs prey on smaller animals,
and larger animals prey on frogs.
Skill: Compound Sentences
IN PIECES
Cut out the puzzle pieces. Match them to form four compound sentences.
Frogs can survive on land,
or frogs can survive in the water.
Some people think frogs are ugly,
yet they are symbols of good luck.
Not Your Usual Workbook · Grade 2
157

Page 157

Skill: Simple Sentences

Sentence Scramble

A simple sentence contains a subject and a verb. Draw a line to connect the words and form a simple sentence. Write it on the lines. Circle the noun or pronoun that the sentence is about. Underline the verb.

red | live | the | house | in | corner. | on | the | I

I live in the red house on the corner.

Not Your Usual Workbook · Grade 2 159

Page 159

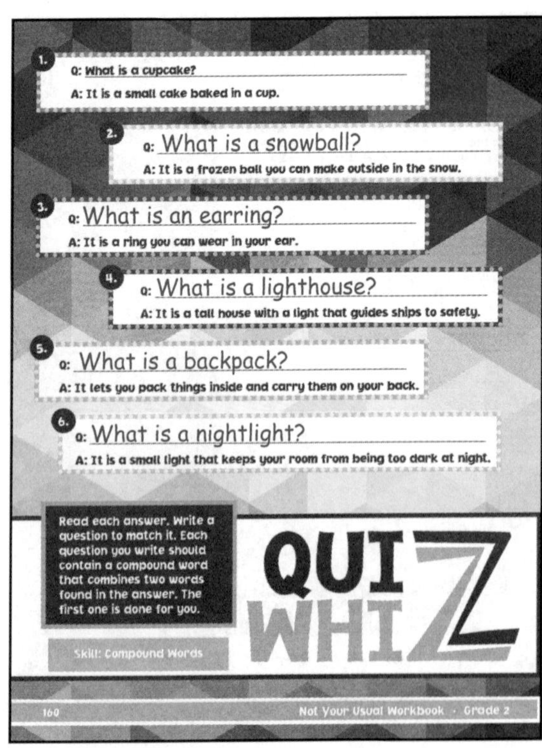

1. Q: What is a cupcake?
A: It is a small cake baked in a cup.
2. Q: What is a snowball?
A: It is a frozen ball you can make outside in the snow.
3. Q: What is an earring?
A: It is a ring you can wear in your ear.
4. Q: What is a lighthouse?
A: It is a tall house with a light that guides ships to safety.
5. Q: What is a backpack?
A: It lets you pack things inside and carry them on your back.
6. Q: What is a nightlight?
A: It is a small light that keeps your room from being too dark at night.
Read each answer. Write a question to match it. Each question you write should contain a compound word that combines two words found in the answer. The first one is done for you.
QUIZ WHIZ
Skill: Compound Words
160
Not Your Usual Workbook · Grade 2

Page 160

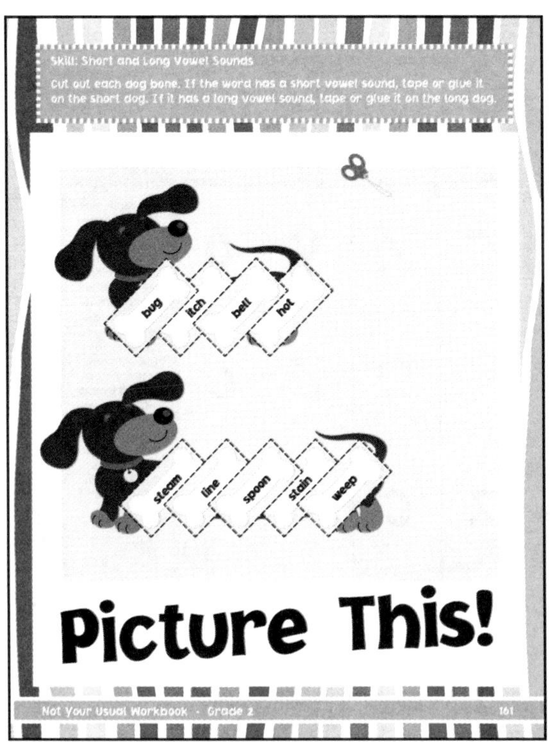

Skill: Short and Long Vowel Sounds

Cut out each dog bone. If the word has a short vowel sound, tape or glue it on the short dog. If it has a long vowel sound, tape or glue it on the long dog.

bug itch bell hot

steam line spoon stain weep

Picture This!

Not Your Usual Workbook · Grade 2 161

Page 161

In Search Of

Skill: Irregular Verbs

Solve the puzzle by finding and circling the past-tense form of each verb below. For example, if the word is "win," search for "won" in the puzzle.

say
feel
write
take
grow
drive
buy
wear

Not Your Usual Workbook · Grade 2 163

Page 163

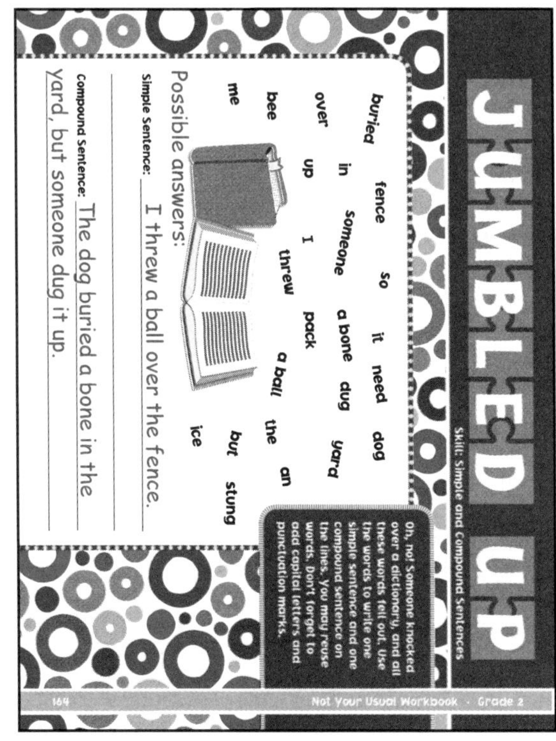

JUMBLED UP

Skill: Simple and Compound Sentences

Oh, no! Someone knocked over a dictionary, and all these words fell out. Use the words to write one simple sentence and one compound sentence on the lines. You may reuse words. Don't forget to add capital letters and punctuation marks.

buried fence so it need dog
over in Someone a bone dug yard
bee up I threw pack a ball the an
me but stung ice

Possible answers:

Simple Sentence: I threw a ball over the fence.

Compound Sentence: The dog buried a bone in the yard, but someone dug it up.

164 Not Your Usual Workbook · Grade 2

Page 164

Not Your Usual Workbook · Grade 2 165

PREST-O CHANGE-O!

Skills: Spelling, Vocabulary

Does it take magic to turn a cab into a bus? No, you just need to change one letter at a time! Write a word to match each clue. Each word should be the same as the word above it except for one changed letter.

Clue	Word
	c a b
a baby bear	c u b
to clean or pet something	r u b
it's under your feet	r u g
to bother	b u g
	b u s

Page 165

Not Your Usual Workbook · Grade 2 166

Sudoku for you

c	z	y	o
y	o	z	c
z	c	o	y
o	y	c	z

Skill: Vocabulary

Write letters in the boxes so that each row and column has the letters to spell a word you might use to describe these things: a blanket, a home, a bed, a chair, a room. No letter should appear twice in the same row or column. Do not guess. Use logic!

Page 166

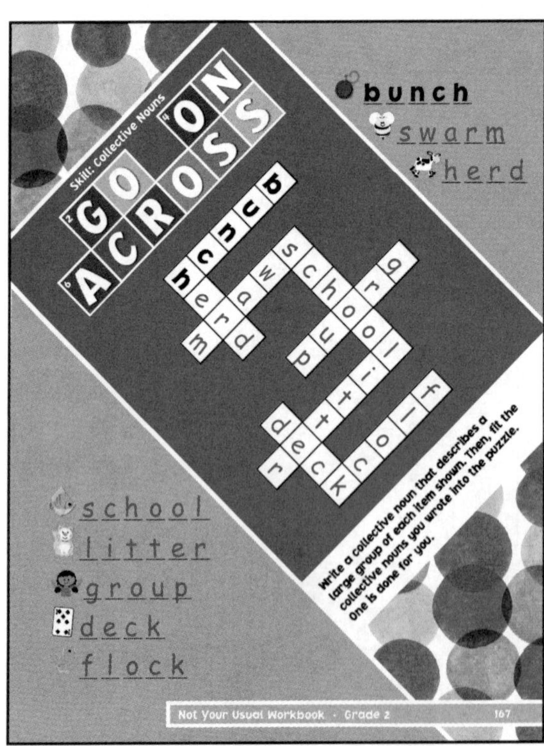

Skill: Collective Nouns

GO ON ACROSS

bunch

swarm

herd

school

litter

group

deck

flock

Write a collective noun that describes a large group of each item shown. Then, fit the collective nouns you wrote into the puzzle. One is done for you.

Not Your Usual Workbook · Grade 2 167

Page 167

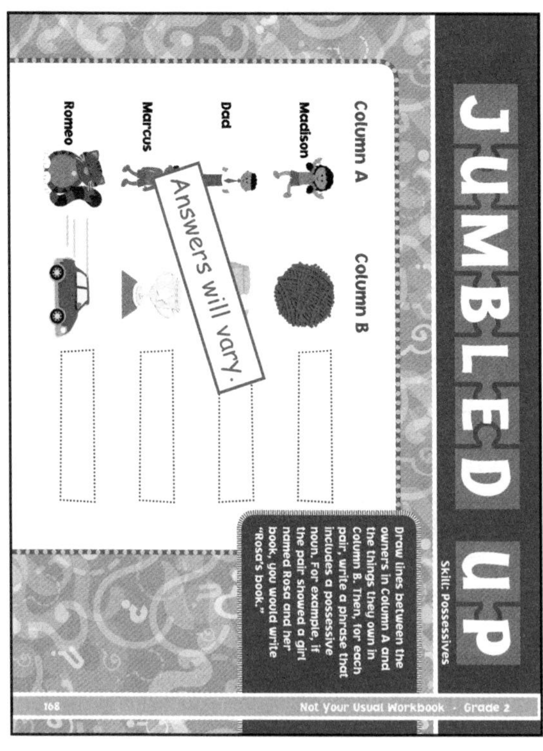

JUMBLED UP

Skill: Possessives

Draw lines between the owners in Column A and the things they own in Column B. Then, for each pair, write a phrase that includes a possessive noun. For example, if the pair showed a girl named Rosa and her book, you would write "Rosa's book."

Column A

Madison

Dad

Marcus

Romeo

Column B

Answers will vary.

168 Not Your Usual Workbook · Grade 2

Page 168

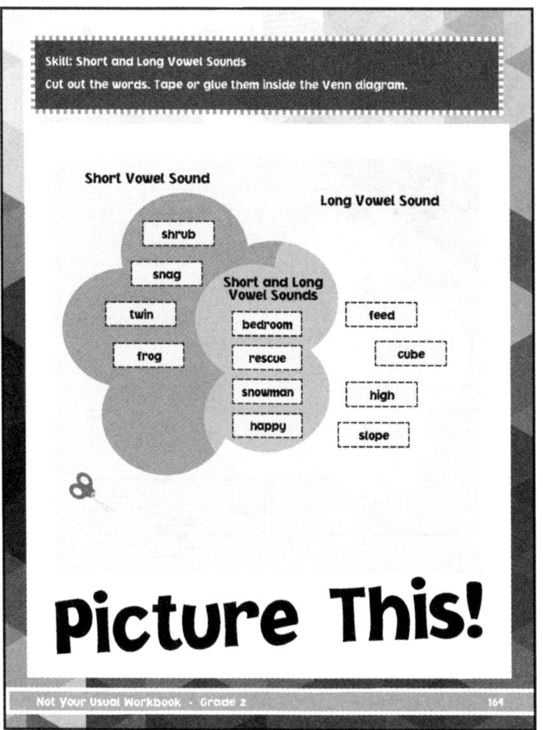

Skill: Short and Long Vowel Sounds

Cut out the words. Tape or glue them inside the Venn diagram.

Short Vowel Sound

shrub

snag

twin

frog

Short and Long Vowel Sounds

bedroom

rescue

snowman

happy

Long Vowel Sound

feed

cube

high

slope

Picture This!

Not Your Usual Workbook · Grade 2 169

Page 169

MAZE CRAZE

Skill: Spelling

Move from letter to letter to find words hidden in the puzzle. How many words can you find that have at least three letters? Write them on the lines.

S	O	D	F
H	T	A	C
U	M	R	E
P	I	Y	N

Possible answers:
hot, shot, put,
soda, fat, cat,
cart, near, year,
mare, care, face,
fad, sod, dot,
rat, mat, farm

Not Your Usual Workbook · Grade 2 171

Page 171

WORD MATH
Skill: Contractions
Solve each puzzle to find a pair of words. In the last blank, write the contraction for the words.
is
not
isn't
you
are
you're
they
have
they've
172 Not Your Usual Workbook · Grade 2

Page 172

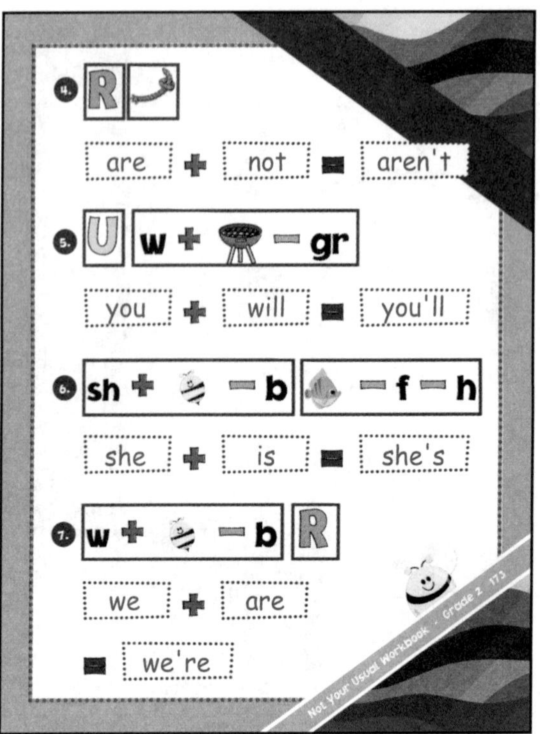

Page 173

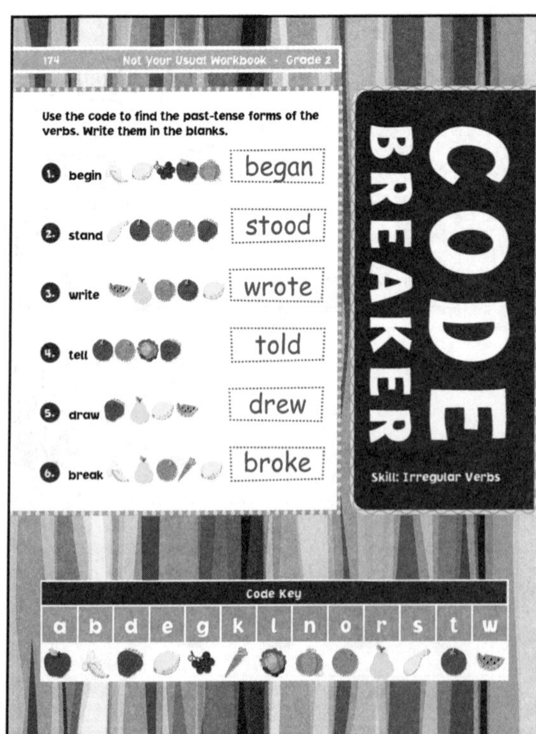

174 Not Your Usual Workbook · Grade 2
Use the code to find the past-tense forms of the verbs. Write them in the blanks.
begin
began
stand
stood
write
wrote
tell
told
draw
drew
break
broke
CODE BREAKER
Skill: Irregular Verbs
Code Key
a b d e g k l n o r s t w

Page 174

PREST-O CHANGE-O!

Skill: Long Vowel Sounds

How can you make food zoom? By changing one letter at a time! On each rung of the ladder, complete a word with a long vowel sound. Each word should be the same as the word above it except for one changed letter.

food
fool
pool
tool
toot
boot
boom
zoom

Page 175

Skills: Adjectives, Vocabulary

Read the adjective on each nest. On each egg, write a noun that the adjective could be used to describe.

warm

Answers will vary.

loud

colorful

Picture This!

Page 176

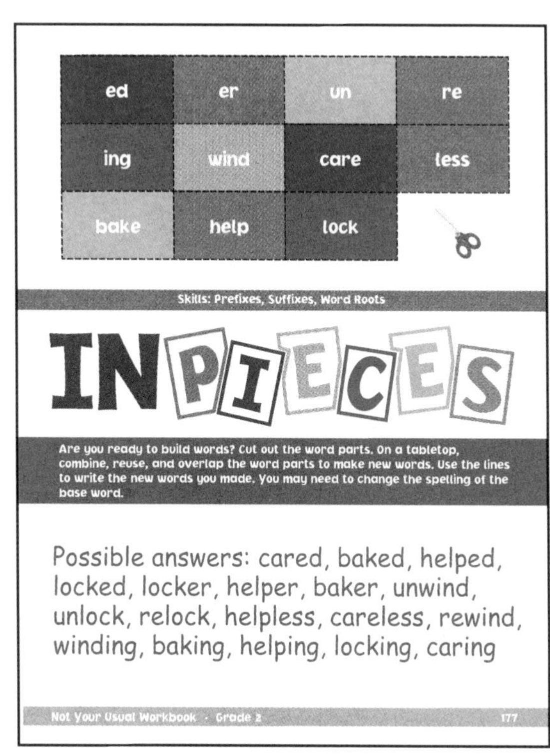

ed	er	un	re
ing	wind	care	less
bake	help	lock	

Skills: Prefixes, Suffixes, Word Roots

IN PIECES

Are you ready to build words? Cut out the word parts. On a tabletop, combine, reuse, and overlap the word parts to make new words. Use the lines to write the new words you made. You may need to change the spelling of the base word.

Possible answers: cared, baked, helped, locked, locker, helper, baker, unwind, unlock, relock, helpless, careless, rewind, winding, baking, helping, locking, caring

Page 177

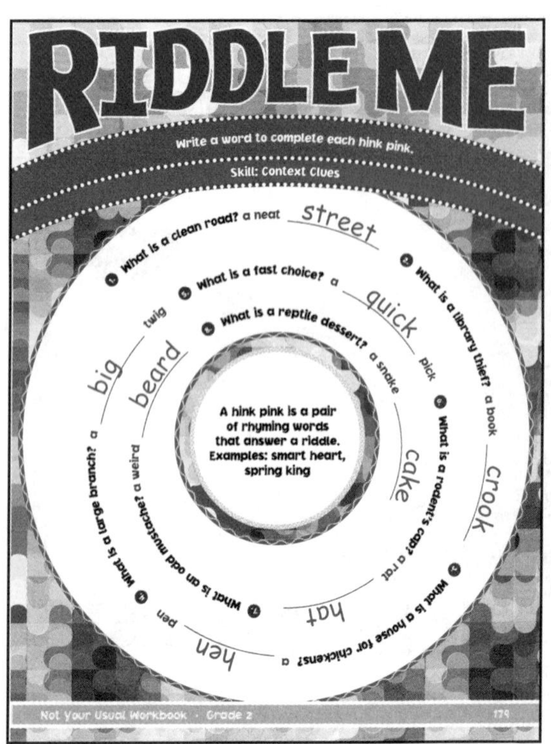

RIDDLE ME
Write a word to complete each hink pink.
Skill: Context Clues
What is a clean road? a neat street
What is a fast choice? a quick pick
What is a reptile dessert? a snake cake
What is a library thief? a book crook
What is a rodent's cap? a rat hat
What is a house for chickens? a hen pen
What is an odd mustache? a weird beard
What is a large branch? a big twig
A hink pink is a pair of rhyming words that answer a riddle. Examples: smart heart, spring king
Not Your Usual Workbook · Grade 2
179

Page 179

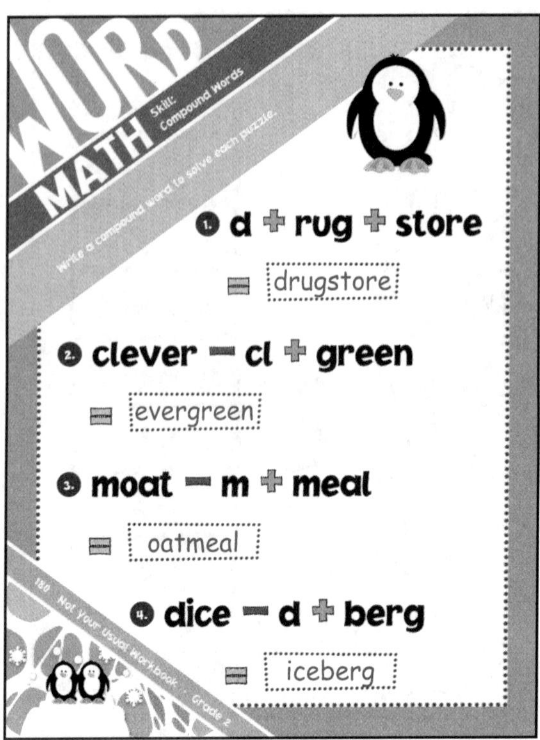

Page 180

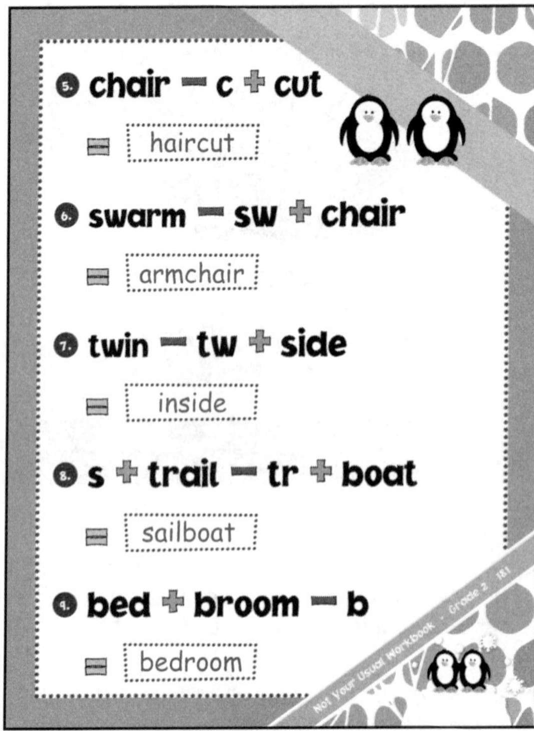

Page 181

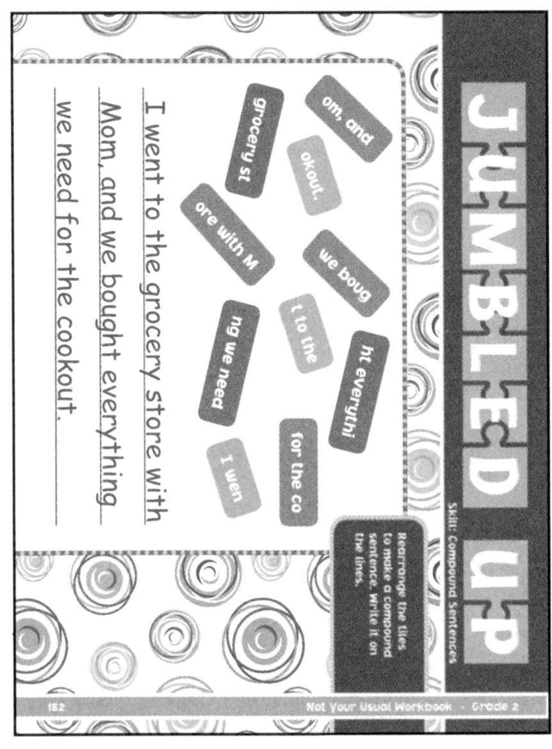

JUMBLED UP
Skill: Compound Sentences
Rearrange the tiles to make a compound sentence. Write it on the lines.
om, and
grocery st
okout.
ore with M
we boug
t to the
ht everythi
ng we need
for the co
I wen
I went to the grocery store with Mom, and we bought everything we need for the cookout.
182
Not Your Usual Workbook · Grade 2

Page 182

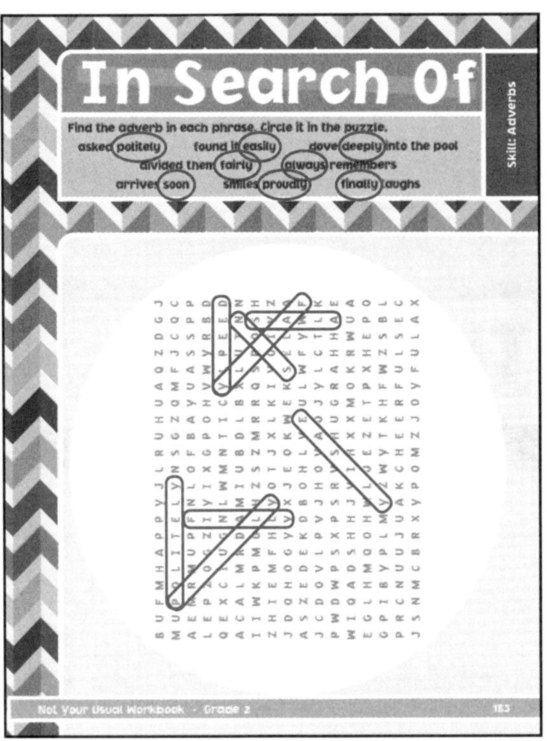

Page 183

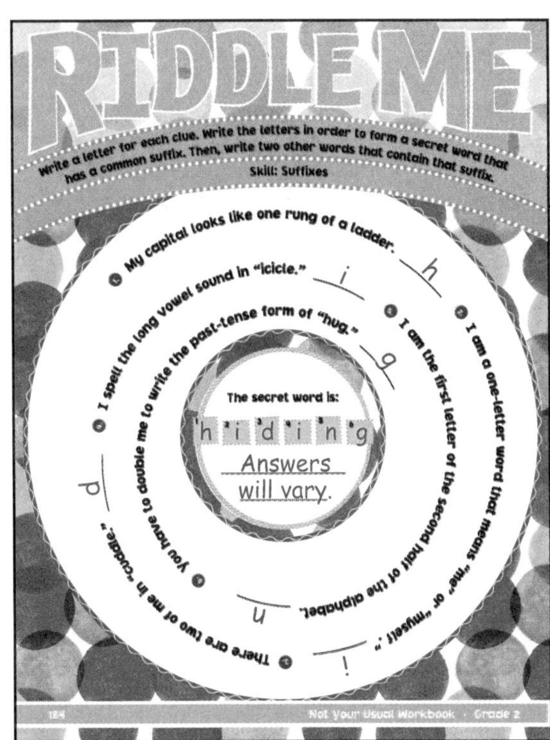

Page 184

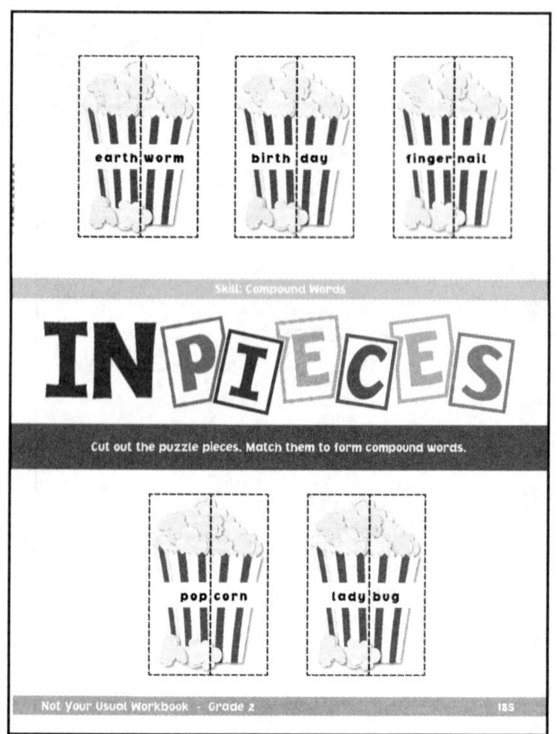
earth worm
birth day
finger nail

Skill: Compound Words

IN PIECES

Cut out the puzzle pieces. Match them to form compound words.

pop corn
lady bug

Not Your Usual Workbook · Grade 2 185

Page 185

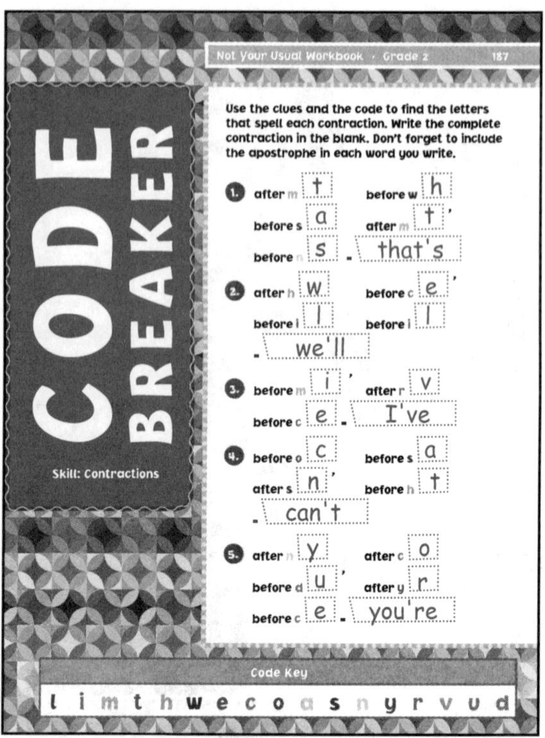
Not Your Usual Workbook · Grade 2 187

CODE BREAKER

Skill: Contractions

Use the clues and the code to find the letters that spell each contraction. Write the complete contraction in the blank. Don't forget to include the apostrophe in each word you write.

1. after m t before w h before s a after m t ' before n s = that's
2. after h w before c e ' before l l before l l = we'll
3. before m i ' after r v before c e = I've
4. before o c before s a after s n ' before h t = can't
5. after n y after c o before d u ' after y r before c e = you're

Code Key

l i m t h w e c o a s n y r v u d

Page 187

Skills: Vocabulary, Spelling

GO ACROSS ON

Read each clue. Write a word that has a similar meaning in the puzzle. Start from the outer squares and work in. The first letter of each answer is shown. Then, read clockwise around the center squares to find the secret word.

1. lots
2. finished
3. wish
4. touch
5. healthy
6. actual
7. trip
8. snug

The secret word is y e l l.

188 Not Your Usual Workbook · Grade 2

Page 188

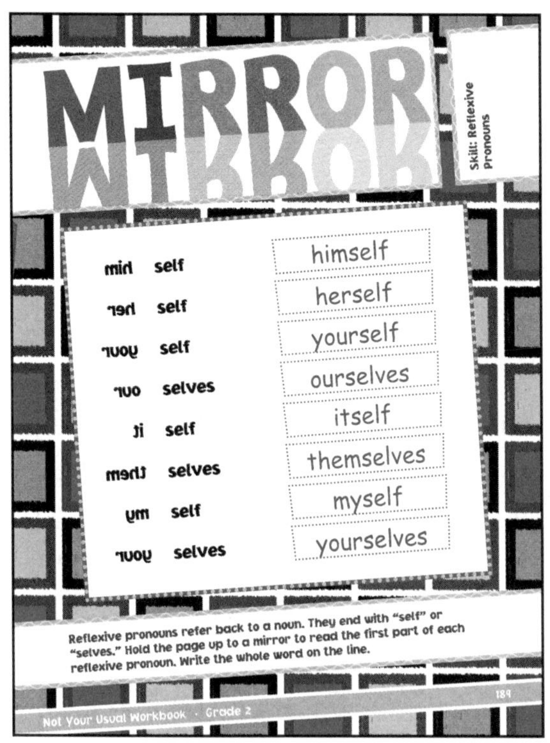

MIRROR

Skill: Reflexive Pronouns

him	self	himself
her	self	herself
your	self	yourself
our	selves	ourselves
it	self	itself
them	selves	themselves
my	self	myself
your	selves	yourselves

Reflexive pronouns refer back to a noun. They end with "self" or "selves." Hold the page up to a mirror to read the first part of each reflexive pronoun. Write the whole word on the line.

Not Your Usual Workbook · Grade 2 189

Page 189

MAZE CRAZE

Skills: Simple Sentences, Possessives

Follow the arrows through the maze to spell the words in a secret sentence. Write the sentence on the lines. To write the sentence correctly, you will need to add a capital letter, an apostrophe, and a period.

My dog's toy is a rubber bone.

190 Not Your Usual Workbook · Grade 2

Page 190

Not Your Usual Workbook · Grade 2 191

Sudoku for You

L	O	S	W
W	S	O	L
O	L	W	S
S	W	L	O

Skill: Central Message or Moral

Remember the story "The Tortoise and the Hare"? The moral of the story is:

"Slow and steady wins the race." Write letters in the boxes so that each row and column has the letters to spell the missing word. No letter should appear twice in the same row or column. Do not guess. Use logic!

Page 191

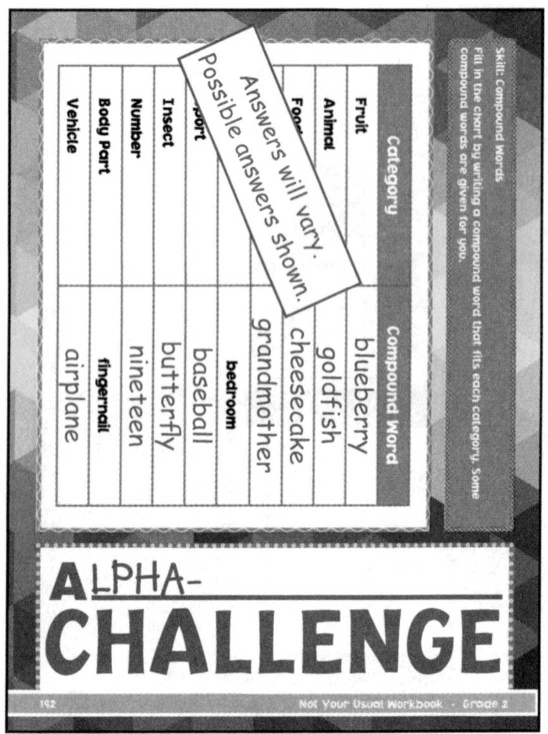

ALPHA-CHALLENGE
Skill: Compound Words
Fill in the chart by writing a compound word that fits each category. Some compound words are given for you.
Answers will vary. Possible answers shown.
Category
Compound Word
Fruit
blueberry
Animal
goldfish
cheesecake
grandmother
bedroom
baseball
Insect
butterfly
Number
nineteen
Body Part
fingernail
Vehicle
airplane

Page 192

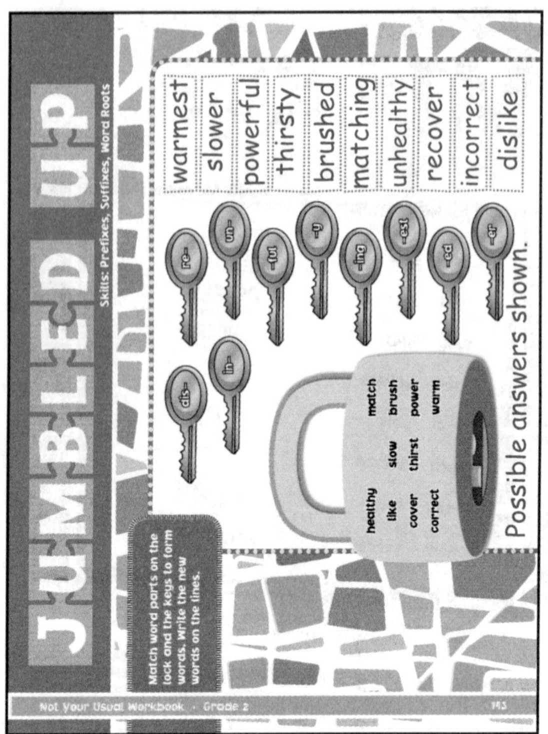

Page 193

Write a word to match each clue.
1. I have a long a sound, but there is no "a" in me!
eight
2. I have a short u sound spelled "u."
grub
3. My long e sound is spelled with two different vowels.
peach
4. I have a long a sound spelled "a-consonant-silent e."
space
5. I have a long i sound and end with a silent letter.
wife
6. I have a long o sound. I begin with a consonant blend.
float
7. My long e sound is spelled with a double letter.
sweep
8. If you added "e" to me, I would rhyme with "line."
pin
9. I end with a long a sound.
gray
Word Box
grub peach pin
wife eight float
space sweep gray
QUIZ WHIZ
Skills: Short and Long Vowel Sounds, Spelling

Page 194

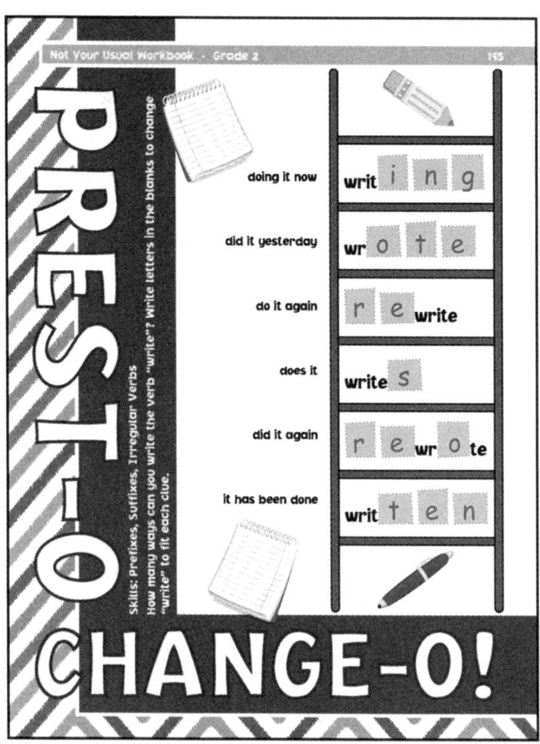

Not Your Usual Workbook · Grade 2
195
PREST-O CHANGE-O!
Skills: Prefixes, Suffixes, Irregular Verbs
How many ways can you write the verb "write"? Write letters in the blanks to change "write" to fit each clue.
doing it now
writ i n g
did it yesterday
wr o t e
do it again
r e write
does it
write s
did it again
r e wr o te
it has been done
writ t e n

Page 195

Skill: Word Roots
Read the base word in the center of each pinwheel. On the lines, write four words that use the base word. Hint: You may need to change the spelling of the base word before adding a prefix or suffix.
Possible answers shown.
move
moving
moved
remove
mover
help
helping
helper
helped
helpful
use
using
used
useful
reuse
like
dislike
liked
liking
likable
Picture This!
196
Not Your Usual Workbook · Grade 2

Page 196

Page 197

WORD MATH

Skills: Adjectives, Adverbs

Decode the words. Write them on the lines to complete the sentence. Then, find adjectives and adverbs in the sentence and write them in the blanks.

sh + tiny − t

sp + − b

− n + r

d + − br

− c + ly

scr + speech − sp + ed

h + − s

ch + − d + ful

b + − sh + ing

198 Not Your Usual Workbook · Grade 2

Page 198

The shiny red car sped far down the street and loudly screeched to a halt by the cheerful barking dog.

Adjectives	Adverbs
shiny	far
red	loudly
cheerful	
barking	

Not Your Usual Workbook · Grade 2 · 199

Page 199

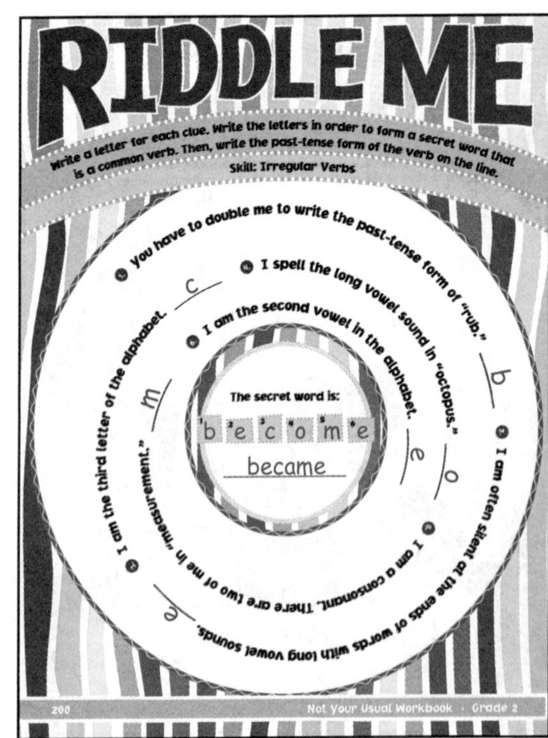
RIDDLE ME

Write a letter for each clue. Write the letters in order to form a secret word that is a common verb. Then, write the past-tense form of the verb on the line.

Skill: Irregular Verbs

You have to double me to write the past-tense form of "rub." b

I am often silent at the ends of words with long vowel sounds. e

I am the third letter of the alphabet. c

I spell the long vowel sound in "octopus." o

I am a consonant. There are two of me in "measurement." m

I am the second vowel in the alphabet. e

The secret word is: b e c o m e

became

200 Not Your Usual Workbook · Grade 2

Page 200

Page 201

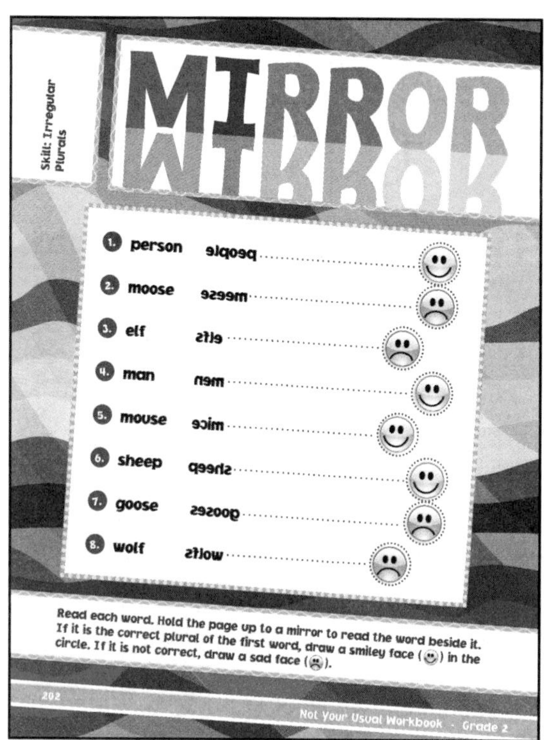

Page 202

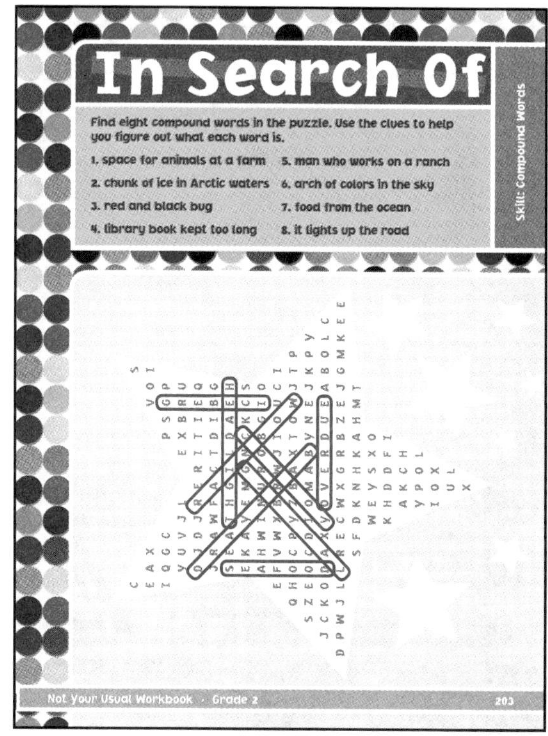

Page 203

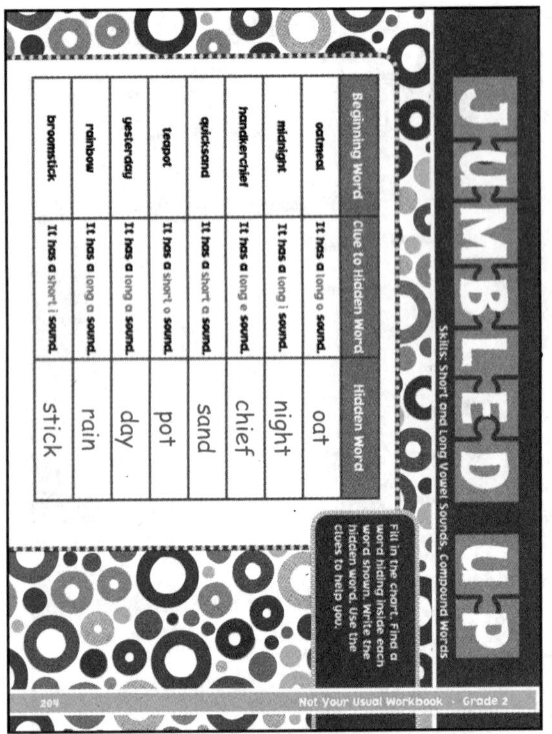

JUMBLED UP

Skills: Short and Long Vowel Sounds, Compound Words

Fill in the chart. Find a word hiding inside each word shown. Write the hidden word. Use the clues to help you.

Beginning Word	Clue to Hidden Word	Hidden Word
oatmeal	It has a long o sound.	oat
midnight	It has a long i sound.	night
handkerchief	It has a long e sound.	chief
quicksand	It has a short a sound.	sand
teapot	It has a short o sound.	pot
yesterday	It has a long a sound.	day
rainbow	It has a long a sound.	rain
broomstick	It has a short i sound.	stick

204 Not Your Usual Workbook · Grade 2

Page 204

Skill: Simple and Compound Sentences

Use the words in each box. Write simple sentences or compound sentences that contain the words. Use capital letters and punctuation marks correctly in each sentence you write.

bark meow when and dog cat

Compound Sentence:

space sky night planet

Simple Sentence:

Answers will vary.

sand play swim or crab shell

Compound Sentence:

Picture This!

Not Your Usual Workbook · Grade 2 205

Page 205

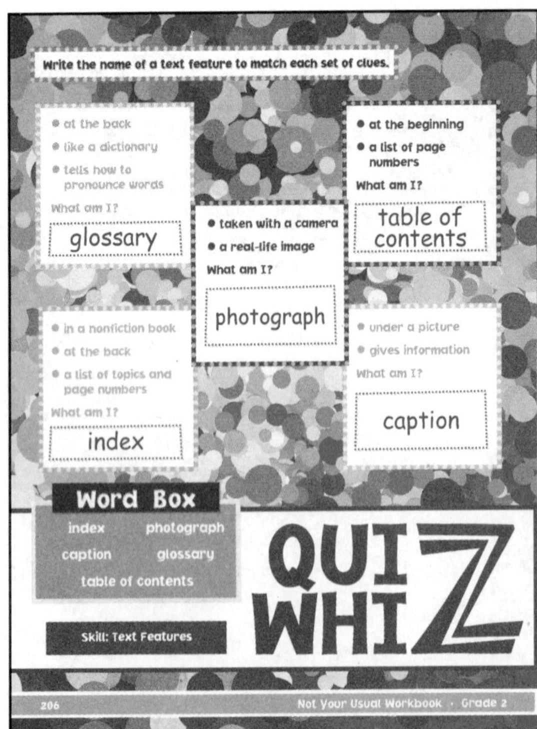

Write the name of a text feature to match each set of clues.

- at the back
- like a dictionary
- tells how to pronounce words

What am I? glossary

- at the beginning
- a list of page numbers

What am I? table of contents

- taken with a camera
- a real-life image

What am I? photograph

- in a nonfiction book
- at the back
- a list of topics and page numbers

What am I? index

- under a picture
- gives information

What am I? caption

Word Box

index photograph caption glossary table of contents

QUIZ WHIZ

Skill: Text Features

206 Not Your Usual Workbook · Grade 2

Page 206